PAUL J DAVIDSON

ASEAN

The Evolving Legal Framework for Economic Cooperation

TIMES ACADEMIC PRESS

© **2002 Times Media Private Limited**

First published 2002 by Times International Publishing
under the imprint **Times Academic Press**
Times Media (Academic Publishing)
Times Centre, 1 New Industrial Road, Singapore 536196
Fax: (65) 6 2889 254   E-mail: tap@tpl.com.sg
Online Book Store: http://www.timesacademic.com

Printed by B & JO Enterprise Pte Ltd, Singapore

National Library Board (Singapore) Cataloguing in Publication Data
Davidson, Paul J.
ASEAN : The Evolving Legal Framework for Economic Cooperation / Paul J. Davidson.
– Singapore : Times Academic Press, 2002.
p. cm.

ISBN : 981-210-185-3

1. ASEAN.   2. Foreign trade regulation – Asia, Southeastern.   3. Tariff –Law and legislation – Asia, Southeastern.   4. Investments, Foreign – Law and legislation – Asia, Southeastern.   5. Asia, Southeastern – Economic integration.

I. Title.

KNC742
343.59087 — dc21
SLS2002028743

CONTENTS

PREFACE

Economic cooperation is increasingly becoming dominated by rules-based international frameworks. A legal framework provides rules for relations among members of the community and a mechanism for settling disputes that arise among parties over the rules.

The member states of The Association of Southeast Asian Nations ("ASEAN") have been moving slowly towards developing a regional legal framework for economic cooperation among the member states of ASEAN. This book examines the various steps which have been taken towards economic cooperation in the region and, examines them in the context of the evolving legal framework for economic cooperation in ASEAN. Although politics and economics affect the development of a legal framework, this is not a book on politics or economics and does not provide a political or economic analysis. Rather, this book discusses the development of the legal framework as affected by economic and political developments.

The book reviews the development of agreements which form the rules for economic cooperation within the region including the rules which are evolving under the Framework Agreement on Enhancing ASEAN Economic Cooperation. As disputes will inevitably arise in any relationship, one of the elements of any legal system is to provide a means for settling these disputes. The book therefore examines the various mechanisms for dispute resolution available in intra-ASEAN economic relations and the role they play in the evolving legal framework for economic cooperation.

In international law, a hierarchy of legal frameworks exists, and regional frameworks must accord with broader, multilateral frameworks of which participants are also members. An examination is therefore made of how ASEAN fits within the existing multilateral international legal framework for trade and investment.

As well, the book also examines the role played in the emerging legal framework for economic cooperation by "Growth Triangles" (sub-regional economic cooperation) in ASEAN, and the movements towards broader economic cooperation in the larger region, namely, the proposals for an East Asian Economic Caucus ("EAEC") and for the Asian Pacific Economic Cooperation ("APEC") forum.

ACRONYMS

AEM	–	ASEAN Economic Ministers
AFTA	–	ASEAN Free Trade Area
AHGM	–	ASEAN Heads of Government Meeting
AIC	–	ASEAN Industrial Complementation
AICO	–	ASEAN Industrial Cooperation Scheme
AIJV	–	ASEAN Industrial Joint Venture
AIP	–	ASEAN Industrial Projects
AMM	–	Annual Ministerial Meetings
APEC	–	Asian Pacific Economic Cooperation
ASA	–	Association of Southeast Asia
ASC	–	ASEAN Standing Committee
ASEAN	–	Association of Southeast Asian Nations
BIT	–	Bilateral Investment Treaty
CEPT	–	Common Effective Preferential Tariff
COIME	–	Committee on Industry, Minerals and Energy
EAEC	–	East Asia Economic Caucus
FIPA	–	Foreign Investment Protection Agreement
GATT	–	General Agreement on Tarrifs and Trade
GPT	–	General Preferential Tariff
GSP	–	Generalised System of Preferences
ICSID	–	International Centre for the Settlement of Investment Disputes
JCC	–	Joint Cooperation Committee
JCM	–	Joint Consultative Meeting
JMM	–	Joint Ministerial Meeting
MFN	–	Most Favoured Nation
MIGA	–	Multilateral Investment Guarantee Agreement
NAFTA	–	North American Free Trade Area
PTA	–	Preferential Trading Arrangements
SCCAN	–	Special Co-ordinating Committee on ASEAN
SEOM	–	Senior Economic Officials Meeting
SOM	–	Senior Officials Meeting
TAPR	–	Paul J Davidson (ed), *Trading Arrangements in the Pacific Rim* (New York: Oceana Publications, 1995)
WTO	–	World Trade Organization

CHAPTER 1

INTRODUCTION

ASEAN

The Association of Southeast Asian Nations ("ASEAN") is perhaps the most dynamic region in the Asia Pacific, with annual economic growth in the region in the eighties and early nineties in the five to ten percent range. Although this economic growth has drastically decreased since mid-1998,[1] ASEAN continues to be an important region.

International trade and investment have been crucial to growth in this region, and have fuelled its economic development. International trade and investment in the region are increasingly becoming subject to international regulation by a rules-based system and, an international legal framework is evolving to regulate economic relations amongst trading partners.

ASEAN was established, inter alia, to promote economic cooperation in the region. Economic cooperation was not the sole, nor indeed a primary, reason for the establishment of ASEAN. In fact, in earlier periods, ASEAN was more concerned with other issues in the region. Although all these are important and have had an impact on the development of the legal framework within ASEAN, the following discussion will be primarily focussed on the evolving legal framework for economic cooperation in ASEAN.[2]

The members of ASEAN have been reluctant to be too "legalistic" in their relations with each other, preferring to conduct relationships the "ASEAN way", ie, by consensus (see discussion, *infra*, Chapter 2). However, with economic expansion in the region and closer economic cooperation among the members of ASEAN, they too have developed the need for more of a rules-based system to regulate their economic activity *inter se*. There has been the development of more of a "rules-based" framework generally to regulate international economic relations.[3] This book examines the evolution of ASEAN from a loosely-knit organization into more of a rules-based system. The member states of ASEAN have been moving slowly towards developing a legal framework for economic cooperation among the member states of ASEAN. Furthermore, one of the important economic groupings in the world today is the Asian Pacific Economic Cooperation ("APEC") forum of which ASEAN is an important element. The ASEAN way has had an impact on the form that economic cooperation within APEC has taken.

It is important, therefore, to have an appreciation of the legal framework for economic cooperation within ASEAN, and to examine the structure of this Association to determine its scope and operation, and how this grouping fits within the existing international legal framework for trade and investment.

Overview

This book will examine the evolving legal framework for economic cooperation in ASEAN. It will discuss the various steps which have been taken towards economic cooperation in the region, including the various agreements which form the basis for a wide range of cooperative activities in industrial development, trade and investment, and the documents leading to the ASEAN Free Trade Area ("AFTA").

The next part of this chapter presents a brief discussion of the idea of law and legal systems, particularly international law and frameworks for international economic law, which provides a background to the topic of legal frameworks for international economic cooperation. The following chapters then deal with the evolving legal framework within ASEAN.

In examining the legal framework for international economic relations within ASEAN, it is first necessary to examine the organizational structure of ASEAN and its international legal personality. Chapter Two provides an examination of the organizational structure of ASEAN which will give an understanding of how the

Association functions, and will provide an indication of the functions of the various components of the Association and how they interact. It will also provide an indication of how intra-ASEAN decisions are made and how ASEAN policies and law develop. An examination of the international legal personality of ASEAN demonstrates the extent to which the Association can be treated as a legal entity distinct from its underlying membership and its ability to enter into legal relationships with other states and regional organizations.

Chapter Three then examines early approaches to economic cooperation within the region. This includes a brief review of the following schemes for economic cooperation:

1. The Agreement on ASEAN Preferential Trading Arrangements ("PTA")
2. ASEAN Industrial Projects ("AIP")
3. ASEAN Industrial Complementation Scheme ("AIC")
4. The Basic Agreement on ASEAN Industrial Joint Ventures ("BAAIJV").

ASEAN has made remarkable strides in economic co-operation. Starting in the late 1980s and early 1990s, ASEAN leaders began to develop more ambitious means of economic co-operation. The most significant development in establishing a framework for economic cooperation in ASEAN is AFTA. ASEAN has expanded coverage of AFTA, expedited the liberalization process, and embarked on deeper regional economic integration accords since its establishment. ASEAN has also embarked on economic cooperation beyond the tariff reduction aspects of a free "trade area" and is developing a framework for economic cooperation through the "AFTA Plus" Scheme of the Framework Agreement on Enhancing ASEAN Economic Cooperation of which AFTA is a part. Cooperation is taking place, inter alia, in industry, services, investment and intellectual property. Chapter Four examines the legal framework of AFTA and the "AFTA Plus" Scheme of the Framework Agreement on Enhancing ASEAN Economic Cooperation.

Chapter Five examines the role of broader forms of economic cooperation in the region. Alongside the movement towards more economic cooperation within ASEAN, there are also movements towards broader economic cooperation in the larger region. The two main proposals are for an East Asian Economic Caucus ("EAEC") and for the Asian Pacific Economic Cooperation ("APEC") grouping. An examination of these proposals and how they affect the development of a legal framework for economic cooperation within ASEAN is set out in Chapter Five.

Because of the unsatisfactory rate of progress in ASEAN industrial and economic cooperation aimed at the integration of ASEAN as a whole, there has been some shift to focus on sub-regional economic cooperation. In sub-regional economic cooperation, the parties seek to create an environment that will facilitate the efficient flow of goods, services, investment and human resources within a more limited sphere. The economic "Growth Triangle" of Malaysia, Indonesia and Singapore is an interesting example of the development of sub-regional economic cooperation. Chapter Six examines the role played by this "Growth Triangle" in the emerging legal framework for economic cooperation.

As disputes will inevitably arise in any relations, one of the elements of any legal system is the provision of a means for settling these disputes. Chapter Seven, therefore, examines the various mechanisms for dispute resolution available in intra-ASEAN economic relations and the role they play in the evolving legal framework for economic cooperation.

Chapter Eight concludes the book with a discussion of how the above has affected the evolving legal framework for economic cooperation in ASEAN. It discusses how the implementation of "rules" and a "dispute settlement mechanism" has contributed to, and continues to contribute to, an evolving legal framework. Also, as one must bear in mind that aspects of an international legal framework for regulating trade and investment already exist (primarily the World Trade Organization/General Agreement on Tariffs and Trade ("WTO/GATT")), and that the ASEAN countries are participants to varying degrees in this framework which may put constraints on or may assist the future development of the legal framework for regional economic cooperation, it is necessary to examine how the emerging legal framework for economic cooperation in ASEAN accords with the existing international legal framework. Chapter Eight, therefore, examines the compatibility of the various schemes for economic cooperation within ASEAN with the existing international legal framework for economic cooperation.

The Legal Framework for Trade and Investment

Before looking at the evolving legal framework in ASEAN, it is necessary to first discuss the role of law, particularly international law, in providing a framework for international trade and investment.

1. The role of law in society

What is the purpose of laws and a legal system in a society? Essentially, a legal system performs two primary functions in society:

(i) Establishing Rules — A legal system provides rules for the orderly interchange/intercourse among members of society once people began to live together in society there developed a need for rules to govern their relationships with each other, whether these rules are called "laws" or something else.[4]

(ii) Dispute Settlement — A legal system and laws provide a mechanism for the settlement of disputes that arise among members of a society, concerning the rules established by that society. These mechanisms can take a number of forms, ranging from more formal to less formal methods of litigation, arbitration, mediation, conciliation, negotiation.

It should be noted that it is not necessary to have a "court" to have "law", or to have a "legal" system. It should also be noted that there is a difference between dispute settlement and enforcement of any settlement. While an Austinian view of law would require enforcement as an element of a legal system, others would question this requirement. "[It] is argued, people obey the law not because they are constrained to do so by force but because they consent or at least acquiesce in its operation and it is this consent rather than any threat of force which causes the legal system to work."[5] This is particularly relevant in international law.

> In the realm of international relations, however, there has developed in modern times a system of rules, admittedly not always clearly ascertained, which all civilized countries acknowledge to be binding upon them and which are not enforceable by coercion since there are no regular international forces empowered to perform the role of the policeman and bailiff in a system of national law. These rules are nevertheless treated as a system of international law....[6]

States "obey" international law, not primarily because of its enforceability, but because it is of mutual benefit for all participants in the legal system.

2. The idea of law

What is law? In order to appreciate, the role of international economic law it is necessary to have some appreciation of what law is. Law is that system of rules by which societies regulate conduct within the particular society.

There has been a general world trend to more of a rules-based system to regulate international economic activity.

> It would seem that the expanding number and the variety of international economic agreements, the new international economic organizations that are being established to realize their objectives and the legislative, executive and judicial organs which have been set up under them are the significant aspects of a system (systems?) of international economic regulation which is evolving in response to a desire for a rule-oriented economic society ... [7]

This can be seen in the development of the World Trade Organization ("WTO") with its unified dispute settlement mechanism and its Dispute Settlement Body ("DSB") including a standing Appellate Body to hear appeals on issues of law covered in the panel report and the legal interpretations developed by the panel.

3. *International law*

The *traditional definition* of international law is that body of law which is comprised for its greater part of the principles and rules of conduct which states feel themselves bound to observe, and therefore, do commonly observe in their relations *with each other*.[8]

In essence, international law is that body of rules without which it would be virtually impossible for states to have steady and frequent intercourse. It is in fact an expression of the necessity of their mutual relations. In the absence of some system of international law, the international society of states could not enjoy the benefits of trade and commerce, of exchange of ideas and of normal or routine communication.[9]

One of the primary sources of international law, and a source which is prevalent in international economic law, is treaties or agreements between or among members of international society. A state which is a party to a treaty or international agreement must necessarily act in accordance with its treaty obligations. Non-compliance with treaty obligations puts the erring state at the risk not only of legal sanctions (where sanctions are provided in case of breach), but of isolation from other members of the community of nations.

In talking of "international" law it is necessary to elucidate what is meant by the term "international". At its most basic level, international refers to relations between two or more states thus international law may involve those rules which regulate the conduct of only two states *inter se* — however the term international law is generally used to denote more general principles of law which are binding on the world community at large.

There are very few rules, however, which can claim universal application and when one uses the term "international law" one must be clear as to the international community to which the particular rules apply. For example, one must be aware of the distinction between regional international law and international law of a more universal application. In the area of international economic law there are "universal" rules of law which have been developed within the WTO (although even the WTO cannot claim complete universality as some economies are still outside the WTO), as well as "regional" rules of law, eg, the European Community laws or the North American FTA laws which only apply to member economies.

International Economic Law

International economic activity is subject to regulation by the rules of international law. As John H. Jackson, a leading authority on international economic law, has stated:

> ... international trade relations in the world today ... is a very complex mix of economic and governmental policies, political constraints, and above all an intricate set of constraints imposed by a variety of "rules" or legal norms.[10]

In order to be better prepared to engage in international economic relations it is necessary to have an understanding of this international legal framework which establishes the parameters within which international trade in goods and services and foreign investment is conducted. Such a framework is necessary in order to promote increased order and predictability in international transactions.

Economic activity involving states or nationals of different states is subject to regulation by both rules of private international law and rules of public international law. Private international law is concerned with how economic transactions are regulated under various systems of domestic law and the attempts that have been made to achieve some uniformity in these domestic laws, eg, the law regarding the international sale of goods. Public international law is concerned with setting the international legal framework within which the domestic rules are developed and with the establishment of interstate relations which affect trade and investment.

This study is concerned primarily with the role of public international law in establishing the framework for international economic relations. Specifically, it is concerned with the development of the legal framework for economic cooperation among the member states of ASEAN.

It is arguable that, in theory, each state is free to regulate, as it pleases, economic transactions which take place with it or within its boundaries. However in practice, international economic relations are governed by an international legal framework which comprises both multilateral agreements and bilateral agreements, as well as agreements on a regional basis. In addition, there has developed, and is developing, customary international law which also forms part of the legal framework which regulates international economic activity.

In order to attract foreign investment a state must "provide a legal framework to guarantee foreign investors legal rights and commercial entitlements. In general, the more distance there is between the social, political and economic systems of the host country and those of the investing country, the more need for a highly developed legal framework."[11] This framework must accord with the rules of any international legal framework of which the country is a member. The rules of international law may provide the only predictability or stability to a potential investment or trade development situation.

In considering the establishment and development of international economic relations, governments are constrained in their policy choices by sets of rules, procedures and principles that may limit their options. International economic law forms the international legal framework which establishes the parameters within which international trade in goods and services and foreign investment is conducted. Such a framework is necessary in order to promote increased order and predictability in international transactions. This framework may be at the multilateral, plurilateral or bilateral level. However, any rules developed at a "lower" level must accord with obligations entered into at a "higher" level. The accompanying diagram illustrates (page 14) this overlapping system of international legal frameworks. Countries which are members of "smaller" frameworks would be bound and constrained by their obligations under the "larger" framework, eg, any regional rules would have to accord with obligations under the WTO for nations which are members of both the regional grouping and the WTO. It should be noted that there may exist a number of different legal frameworks governing different aspects of countries relations, of which countries may be members at the same time as long as their obligations under one regime do not conflict with their obligations under another regime. Frameworks may overlap with, or be independent of other

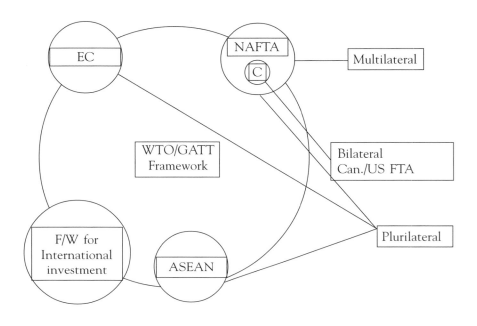

Graphic Example of Relationship among different International
Legal Frameworks

frameworks. For example, the WTO/GATT framework sets out rules
governing aspects of international trade, but has not yet been involved
to a great degree with investment issues.

Much of international economic law is to be found in the GATT/
WTO framework which has evolved to become the main framework for
regulating international economic transactions. The GATT/WTO
framework is gradually becoming a more legalistic as opposed to
diplomatic regime. A legal regime emphasizes the adjudication of
disputes based on detailed rules, procedures and precedents; a
commercial diplomacy regime relies on the negotiation of unique
solutions to individual problems based on general principles applied to
the circumstances at hand.[12]

The cornerstone of the GATT is Article I paragraph 1 which lays down the general rule that the trade of each contracting party is to be treated no less favourably than that of any other country. Basically it requires countries not to discriminate in their trade regulation among countries that are also members of the GATT, ie, contracting parties agree to conduct their commercial relations with each other on the general basis of equality of treatment or non-discrimination.

However, this general principle is subject to a number of exceptions, the one of most relevance for purposes of this study, being Article XXIV which allows for the creation of regional groupings.

Regional Trading Arrangements

Regional trade arrangements are addressed in the GATT and WTO rules. In the 1996 Singapore WTO Ministerial Declaration, Ministers reaffirmed the primacy of the multilateral trading system and renewed their commitment to ensure that regional trade arrangements are complementary to it and consistent with its rules. The main thrust of these rules appears to be to protect the MFN principle. The provisions in the GATT rules that govern regional arrangements are contained primarily in Article XXIV:[13]

1. The establishment of a free trade area is acceptable under GATT so long as its purpose is to facilitate trade within the region and not to raise barriers to trade with outside economies. (Article XXIV: 4)
2. Duties and other restrictive regulations of commerce shall not be higher or more restrictive than the corresponding duties and other regulations of commerce existing in the same constituent territories prior to the formation of the free trade area. (Article XXIV: 5b)
3. Duties and other restrictive regulations of commerce shall be eliminated on substantially all trade between the constituent territories in respect of products originating in such territories. (Article XXIV: 8b)
4. Entry into a free trade area shall be promptly notified to the WTO. (Article XXIV: 7a)

Regional agreements among less developed economies are accorded special treatment, through the so-called Enabling Clause:[14]

1. A mutual reduction or elimination of tariffs and non-tariff measures may be permitted notwithstanding the provisions of Article I of the GATT.
2. Members shall not raise barriers to, or create undue difficulties for, the trade of any other contracting parties.
3. The arrangement shall not constitute an impediment to the reduction or elimination of tariff and non-tariff barriers on an MFN basis.
4. Members shall notify the arrangement to the WTO.
5. The contracting parties shall afford adequate opportunity for prompt consultation.

The following chapters examine the development of the regional legal framework for international economic relations that is evolving among the members of ASEAN and examines how this evolving legal framework accords with the existing multilateral legal framework.

Endnotes

1   1998: -7.16 (-13.13 to 5.23); 1999: 3.42 (.85 to 10.92); 2000: 5.41 (2.97 to 9.89) [source: ASEAN website].
2   For a general discussion of ASEAN, see, inter alia, Sandhu, KS, et al (eds), *The ASEAN Reader* (Singapore: ISEAS, 1992).
3   See *infra* and, see generally: Jackson, John H, *The World Trading System Law and Policy of International Economic Relations*, 2nd ed (Cambridge/London: The MIT Press, 1997); and Michael J Trebilcock and Robert Howse, *The Regulation of International Trade*, 2nd ed (London and New York: Routledge, 1999).
4   See, eg, discussion in Harris, Phil, *An Introduction to Law*, 2nd ed (London: Weidenfeld and Nicolson,1984), on what distinguishes laws from other rules.
5   Lloyd, Dennis, *The Idea of Law* (Middlesex: Penguin Books Ltd, 1964), p 37.
6   *Ibid*, p 38. The question is often asked, Is international law "law"?. Since there is no supreme sovereign in international law and there is no legislative body, no compulsory judicial tribunal and no international police force or other enforcing body, it is argued by some that international law lacks the characteristics of a legal system and cannot be regarded as law. A full discussion of theories of international law is beyond the scope of this book. For further discussion, see, *inter alia*, DAmato,

Anthony, Is International Law Really Law, chapter 1 in *International Law: Process and Prospect*, 2nd ed (New York: Transnational Publisher's Inc, 1995); Kindred, Hugh M, et al, *International Law Chiefly as Interpreted and Applied in Canada*, 6th ed (Toronto: Emond Montgomery, 2000); Malanczuk, Peter, *Akehurst's Modern Introduction to International Law*, 8th ed (New York: Routledge, 2001).

7 Kohona, Palitha TB, *The Regulation of International Economic Relations Through Law*, (Dordrecht: Martinus Nijhoff Publishers, 1985), ch 2, The regulation of international economic relations through multilateral agreements and international organizations, pp.20-42, at 38.

8 Starke, JG, *Introduction to International Law*, 10th ed (London: Butterworths, 1989), p 3.

9 See, *ibid*, pp 14 -15.

10 John H Jackson, *The World Trading System Law and Policy of International Economic Relations* (Cambridge/ London: The MIT Press, 1989), p 299. As with any legal system, the development of a legal framework to regulate international economic relations raises many complex questions which involve economic, political or social, as well as legal, issues. In fact, when dealing with the regulation of international trade and investment, one cannot separate out political and economic or social issues from the legal issues or vice versa. International economic law does not develop in a vacuum but is predicated on and reflects the underlying economic, political, and social considerations.

11 Jing-dong Yuan and Lorraine Eden, Export Processing Zones in Asia: A Comparative Study (1992) XXXII *Asian Survey*, p 1045.

12 Michael Hart, *A North American Free Trade Agreement The Strategic Implications for Canada* (Ottawa: Centre for Trade Policy and Law and the Institute for Research on Public Policy, 1990), p 15: 'From the beginning, of course, GATT contained elements of both, with some members prepared to build on the legal dimension while others preferred the diplomatic approach'.

13 The following is from APEC Secretariat, Economic Committee, *The Impact of Subregionalism in Apec* (Singapore: APEC Secretariat, 1997), pp 6&7.

14 Differential and More Favourable Treatment Reciprocity and Fuller Participation of Developing Countries, Decision of 28 November, 1979 (L/4903). See discussion, *infra*, chapter 8.

CHAPTER 2

ORGANIZATIONAL STRUCTURE AND LEGAL PERSONALITY

Origins of ASEAN

Although there were prior attempts at regional organization, the first real regional association in Southeast Asia was the Association of Southeast Asia ("ASA"). The ASA was established in 1961 among Malaya, the Philippines and Thailand with the objective of furthering economic and cultural progress through mutual cooperation and assistance among its members.[1] Although it made progress in some areas,[2] its effectiveness was limited by the exclusion of Indonesia and the opposition which arose by Indonesia and the Philippines to the proposal to include Singapore, Sarawak and North Borneo as part of Malaysia. As an attempt at settlement of this confrontation, a proposal for a closer association among Malaysia, the Philippines and Indonesia was made, to be known as MAPHILINDO.[3] Although MAPHILINDO was formally approved, it never became fully operational. In 1965 a new government was installed in Indonesia which was desirous of membership in a regional organization. Discussions then led to the formation of ASEAN on 8 August 1967.[4]

ASEAN is a regional organization. The original membership comprised Indonesia, Malaysia, the Philippines, Singapore and Thailand. Brunei Darussalam became the sixth member in January 1984 and Vietnam became its seventh member in July 1995. At an informal summit held in Jakarta on 30 November 1997,[5] it was agreed that Cambodia, Laos and Myanmar would join ASEAN together leading to the realisation of an ASEAN comprising all ten Southeast Asian countries. Although the members of ASEAN were anxious to have an association comprising all ten Southeast Asian countries, because of political difficulties in Cambodia, it became impossible to admit Cambodia at the time, and Laos and Myanmar became the eight and ninth members in July 1997.[6] Cambodia was finally admitted as the tenth member on the 30 April, 1999.[7]

The aims, principles and purposes of ASEAN, as stated in the Bangkok Declaration, include the acceleration of economic growth, social progress and cultural development in the region through joint endeavours; the promotion of active collaboration and mutual assistance on matters of common interest; the provision of assistance for the greater utilization of industries and the expansion of trade; and, the maintenance of close and beneficial cooperation with existing international and regional organizations with similar aims and purposes, and the exploration of all avenues for even closer cooperation among themselves.[8]

Initial Organization of ASEAN

At the time ASEAN was formed, the individual member states (Indonesia, Malaysia, the Philippines, Singapore and Thailand) were hesitant to accord it strong powers over the members, preferring to maintain a high level of individual sovereignty. This feeling of the member states can be seen in an earlier statement of Ruslan Abdulgani, then Deputy First Minister of Indonesia,

> We fought to win the right to express and to develop our national identities. Must we now merge all this into a common denominator in our continuing struggle? I think we must not be so unrealistic ...Our solidarity must not be allowed to mitigate against the fullest possible development of the national characteristics of each of our countries.[9]

This desire was reflected in the 1967 *Bangkok Declaration* which established ASEAN with a structure which was organizationally loose and which avoided the trappings of a strong regional organization.

Under the system which was established, the supreme decision-making authority resided with the five states' Foreign Ministers at the Annual Ministerial Meetings. The Foreign Ministers of the five ASEAN nations met once a year to set the policy for cooperation and also to make final decisions on proposals presented by the Standing Committee. This meeting was held in the capitals of the member countries, organized on an alphabetical rotational basis. Special or additional meetings were held as required or when necessary.[10]

Below the Ministerial Meetings was the ASEAN Standing Committee ("ASC") comprised of the Ambassadors of the ASEAN countries accredited to the host country.[11] This Committee was set up to carry out the day to day work of the Association in between the Ministerial Meetings and to follow up the projects agreed upon at the Annual Ministerial Meetings. The ASC was established to handle routine matters to ensure continuity and to make decisions which could not await the Ministerial Meetings and to submit for the consideration of the Foreign Ministers all reports and recommendations of the various ASEAN committees. This Committee was organized in the country where the Annual Meeting was held and was under the chairmanship of that host nation's Foreign Minister.

Responsible to the Standing Committee was the group of Ad-Hoc and Permanent Committees comprised of senior national government officials which focussed on specific regional issues. Initially, in 1968, the Standing Committee set up five Ad-Hoc Committees which soon became Permanent Committees, and by 1976 the number of Permanent Committees had expanded to 11 concerned with the following areas:

1. Food and Agriculture;
2. Shipping;
3. Communication, Air Traffic, Services, Meteorology;
4. Commerce and Industry;
5. Civil Air Transportation;
6. Land Transportation and telecommunications;
7. Finance;
8. Tourism;
9. Science and Technology;
10. Mass Media; and
11. Socio-Cultural Activities

These committees provided regular forums for specialists on specific issues and held their offices in the member countries for three years by rotation. In addition to these Permanent Committees, there were a number of Ad-Hoc Committees established for specific purposes, eg the Special Co-ordinating Committee on ASEAN ("SCCAN") which was established to deal with cooperation and negotiation with outside economic groups.

Lastly, came the National Secretariats, one representing each signatory state and each representing the individual concerns of that state. Each Secretariat was responsible to coordinate all ASEAN Matters in its respective country so that ASEAN's activities would be pursued as agreed. The secretariats also met on a formal basis to negotiate and prepare the agenda for the Standing Committee and ultimately the Ministerial Meeting and thus were, arguably, the most influential bodies within the structure. Each National Secretariat was located within the Foreign Ministry and had the position of Secretary-General at its head.

Development of the ASEAN Organizational Structure

While this decentralized structure ensured strict state control, it created insurmountable obstacles for ASEAN as an organization. For example, the overlapping bureaucratic structure caused delay; issues were often considered by a number of committees and sub-committees and were then submitted to the Standing Committee and then to the Ministerial Meeting. As a result, many suggestions were never considered nor realized.[12] The Ambassadors of the member countries who comprised the Standing Committee had only a one year tenure. Thus, there were no "Aseanocrats" to coordinate activities. Also, as the National Secretariats were departments in the Ministry of Foreign Affairs of each country; these officials often lacked the total view of the association.[13] In addition, although economic cooperation was a goal of the association, there was no high level body directly in charge of making decisions and executing economic policies.

The initial reform of ASEAN's structure took place after the first summit meeting of the heads of government on 24-25 February

1976 at Denpasar, Bali, in Indonesia.[14] The Bali Conference saw the member states sign their first treaty, The Treaty of Amity and Cooperation in Southeast Asia[15], accept the ASEAN Concord[16], promote agreements on Preferential Trading Arrangements ("PTA") and the ASEAN Industrial Projects ("AIP"), and produce plans for ASEAN Industrial Complementation ("AIC"). In addition, they signed the Agreement on the Establishment of the ASEAN Secretariat.[17]

As regards the latter, the member states agreed to establish an ASEAN Secretariat with its headquarters in Jakarta and undertook to review the ASEAN organizational structure on a regular basis. The Secretariat was to fill the need for a central administrative organ to promote greater efficiency in the coordination of the ASEAN organs and more effective implementation of ASEAN projects and activities.

The Bali Summit also introduced a number of innovations to ASEAN's organizational structure. The Declaration of ASEAN Concord contained explicit statements concerning the reform of ASEAN's structure. Meetings of the Heads of Government of the member states were to take place as and when necessary; this body, the so-called 'summit meetings' became the supreme organ of ASEAN. It was also provided that Ministerial Meetings on economic matters were to take place regularly or as deemed necessary to consider matters related to economic cooperation. As a result, the ASEAN Economic Ministerial Meetings became an organ having full and independent power to make decisions on economic matters.[18]

The Economic Ministers agreed on a decentralised structure with five permanent economic committees through which the ASEAN Economic Ministers directed economic cooperation within ASEAN. Each ASEAN member country was responsible for hosting one committee, ie, designating the chair, providing the secretariat, convening and hosting meetings, etc. The five committees and their host countries were as follows:

1.   Committee on Trade and Tourism (COTT) — Singapore;
2.   Committee on Industry Minerals and Energy (COIME) — the Philippines;

3.   Committee on Food, Agriculture and Forestry (COFAF) — Indonesia;
4.   Committee on Finance and Banking (COFAB) — Thailand;
5.   Committee on Transportation and Communications (COTAC) — Malaysia.

Each of these committees was supported or serviced by a host of sub-committees, expert groups, working groups and other subsidiaries. The primary tasks of these five committees were threefold: (i) to review the proposed basic guidelines covering economic cooperation in their particular area and submit them to the ASEAN Economic Ministers Meeting for deliberation; (ii) to review proposed projects with the aid of an interim technical secretariat in the host country and selected groups of experts; and (iii) to submit project proposals and recommend action to the ASEAN Economic Ministers. Committees were responsible to and received directions from the Economic Ministers.

Over the years further proposals were made to further strengthen and revamp the structure and mechanism of ASEAN. For example, recommendations were made by the Group of Fourteen on ASEAN Economic Cooperation and Integration at its meeting in June 1987 for strengthening the ASEAN institutions.[19] It was proposed that "ASEAN institutions should be suitably structured and endowed with resources, expertise and systems to ensure that co-operation is not hampered by deficiencies in these areas".[20]

Another study was conducted by a 'Panel of Eminent Persons' established by the 23rd ASEAN Ministerial Meeting held in Jakarta on 24-25 July 1990. This Panel was mandated "to study and make the necessary recommendations on strengthening and revamping the structure and mechanism of ASEAN, in particular the ASEAN Secretariat." In their report[21] they noted:

> ASEAN's institutional structure, however, has not evolved in line with the rapidly changing environment. Apart from minor modifications, it has remained basically the same since the 1976 ASEAN Heads of Government Meeting in Bali, Indonesia (the *Bali Summit*).[22]

A number of the recommendations included in their report were subsequently turned into decisions by the ASEAN Heads of Government at their 4th ASEAN Summit held in Singapore on 27-28 January 1992.[23] Paragraph 8 of the Singapore Declaration[24] provides:

RESTRUCTURING OF ASEAN INSTITUTIONS

8.   To strengthen ASEAN we have agreed that:
— ASEAN Heads of Government shall meet formally every three years with informal meetings in between;
— The ASEAN organizational structure, especially the ASEAN Secretariat, shall be streamlined and strengthened with more resources;
— The Secretary-General of the ASEAN Secretariat shall be redesignated as the Secretary-General of ASEAN with an enlarged mandate to initiate, coordinate and implement ASEAN activities;
— The Secretary-General of ASEAN shall be appointed on merit and accorded ministerial status;
— The professional staff of the ASEAN Secretariat be appointed on the principle of open recruitment and based on a quota system to ensure representation of all ASEAN countries in the Secretariat;
— The five present ASEAN Economic Committees be dissolved and the Senior Economic Officials Meeting (SEOM) be tasked to handle all aspects of ASEAN economic cooperation; and
— A ministerial-level Council be established to supervise, coordinate and review the implementation of the Agreement on the Common Effective Preferential Tariff (CEPT) Scheme for the ASEAN Free Trade Area (AFTA).

A further review of ASEAN's overall organizational structure in order to further improve its efficiency and effectiveness, taking into account the expansion of ASEAN activities, the enlargement of ASEAN membership, and the regional situation was recommended by the members at the 6th ASEAN Summit.[25]

ASEAN's Present Organizational Structure

ASEAN's present organizational structure is as follows.

1. The ASEAN Heads of Government Meeting ("AHGM")

The supreme decision making authority is the ASEAN Heads of Government Meeting ("AHGM") — the "ASEAN Summits". The first such meeting took place in Bali, Indonesia, from 23-25 February 1976. At this meeting the aims and purposes embodied in the Bangkok Declaration were reaffirmed and the Declaration of ASEAN Concord and the Treaty of Amity and Cooperation in Southeast Asia, as well as the Agreement on the Establishment of the ASEAN Secretariat were signed. The second summit meeting was held in Kuala Lumpur, Malaysia from 4-5 August 1977, to commemorate the Tenth Anniversary of ASEAN and to assess the progress in the implementation of the decisions taken at Bali. The third summit was held ten years later, from 14-16 December 1987 in Manila, the Philippines. This summit coincided with the 20th Anniversary of ASEAN and focussed on economic cooperation. At this meeting the heads of state endorsed a number of new steps towards economic cooperation. The fourth summit was held in Singapore from 27-28 January 1992. This meeting marked the 25th Anniversary of ASEAN and focussed on economic cooperation in the region including the formation of an ASEAN Free Trade Area ("AFTA").

Up to the Singapore meeting in 1992, the heads of state had been following the practice of meeting as and when necessary to give directions to ASEAN; there was no institutionalisation of the meetings. However, the Fourth ASEAN Summit decided that the ASEAN Heads of Government would meet formally every three years and informally at least once in between to lay down directions and initiatives for ASEAN activities. In 1995, the Fifth ASEAN Summit in Bangkok decided to hold annual Informal Summits. At the fifth summit, the Heads of State and Government of ASEAN also agreed, inter alia, to adopt an Agenda for Greater Economic Integration which included accelerating the progress towards the actualization of AFTA before the target date of 2003.[26] They also agreed to adopt a General Dispute Settlement

Mechanism ("DSM") to apply to all disputes arising from ASEAN economic agreements.[27]

The sixth meeting of the ASEAN Heads of State was held in Hanoi on 15 December 1998. The heads of government adopted the "Hanoi Plan of Action",[28] and for the first time committed the Association to a broad middle term plan specifying an array of activities aimed at the achievement of its development goals for the year 2020. The pacing of the activities within the Hanoi Action Plan is meant to address the Asian financial and economic crisis and to prevent its recurrence and the Hanoi Plan of Action firms up the ASEAN answer to the crisis which is to step up economic integration of the ASEAN countries into a single market and investment area where goods and services, as well as investment capital, are allowed free and easy flow.

The most recent ASEAN Summit was held in Brunei Darussalam on 5-6 November 2001. This was the first working summit since the Leaders decided in Singapore in 2000 to devote more time to important matters of substance and reduce ceremonial proceedings.[29] The Leaders discussed the immediate concerns of addressing a severe world economic slowdown while contributing to international efforts to combat terrorism, and at the same time agreed on the need to identify new priorities and respond decisively to longer term challenges facing Southeast Asia. They also discussed pushing the frontiers of economic cooperation beyond existing commitments for free-trade and investment areas, and agreed to go beyond AFTA and the ASEAN Investment Area (see *infra*) by deepening market liberalization for both trade and investment. They specifically agreed to speed up negotiations on liberalising intra-ASEAN trade in services, and agreed to implement an *ASEAN Integration System of Preferences* for newer members by the beginning of January 2002. This will allow Cambodia, Laos, Myanmar and Vietnam to gain tariff-free access to the more developed ASEAN markets earlier than the agreed target date of 2010 for all members.

Four Informal Summits have been held: in Jakarta in December 1996; in Kuala Lumpur in December 1997; in Manila in November 1999; and in Singapore in November 2000.

2. Ministerial-Level Meetings

Below the AHGM are the Ministerial-level Meetings. No group of Ministers is supreme over others nor are any Ministers subordinate to any other.[30] This arrangement is reflected in the fact that each group is responsible only to the Heads of Government and transmits its reports of meetings to the ASEAN Secretariat which in turn transmits these reports to the ASEAN Foreign Ministers for purposes of coordination.

(i) The Annual Ministerial Meeting ("AMM")

The AMM or the annual meeting of the Foreign Ministers remains the most important organ for coordinating all policies of the different ASEAN working units. The AMM is responsible for the formulation of policy guidelines and reviews all decisions and hands down the approved policies and programmes to the Standing Committee or other bodies concerned for their guidance and implementation.

The AMM meets annually in each of the member countries on a rotational basis, in alphabetical order, and special meetings of the Foreign Ministers may be held whenever necessary. At the 1977 Kuala Lumpur Summit, the ASEAN Heads of Government agreed that the AMM could include other relevant Ministers as and when necessary.

(ii) The ASEAN Economic Ministers ("AEM")

One of the most important of the ministerial-level meetings is the AEM which was established in 1976 and given the independence to oversee economic cooperation. Usually, the AEM meet every six months or as deemed necessary. Up until the Singapore Summit in 1992, the AEM operated through five economic committees (see above); however these were dissolved and the Senior Economic Officials Meeting ("SEOM") is now tasked to handle all aspects of ASEAN economic cooperation. This is in line with the "streamlining" of the ASEAN organizational structure. The AFTA Council was established by the Fourth Summit to supervise, coordinate, and review the implementation of the CEPT Scheme for AFTA (see Chapter 4).

(iii) Sectoral Economic Ministers Meeting

Ministers for specific sectors of economic cooperation meet as and when necessary to give guidance on ASEAN cooperation. There are meetings of Ministers on Energy, Ministers on Agriculture and Forestry, Ministers on Tourism, and Ministers on Transport. The sectoral Economic Ministers report to the AEM. The ASEAN Finance Ministers have also agreed to meet regularly.

(iv) Other Non-Economic ASEAN Ministerial Meetings

Meetings of Ministers in other fields of ASEAN cooperation, such as Health, Environment, Labour, Rural Development, Poverty Alleviation, Social Welfare, Education, Science and Technology, Information, Justice/Law and Transnational Crimes, are held regularly. While there is coordination between meetings of other Ministers and the Annual Ministerial Meeting, each meeting of Ministers may report directly to the Heads of Government.

3. The ASEAN Standing Committee ("ASC")

This body carries on ASEAN's activities in-between the Annual Ministerial Meetings and has existed since the inception of ASEAN. As described above, this committee is organised in the country where the Annual Meeting is to be held and is under the chairmanship of that host nation's Foreign Minister. It is comprised of the Ambassadors of the other ASEAN countries accredited to the host country and was set up to carry out the day to day work of the Association and to follow up the projects agreed upon at the Annual Ministerial Meetings. As an advisory body to the Permanent Committees, the ASC reviews the work of Committees with a view to implementing policy guidelines set by the AMM. The ASC meets three to five times a year and is the principal organ which enables ASEAN activities, including primary decision-making, to function without interruption. All reports and recommendations of the various ASEAN committees are submitted to the ASC for submission to the Ministerial meetings. In 1976, the Secretary-General of the newly created ASEAN Secretariat became a member of this committee.

4. *The ASEAN Secretariat*

As discussed above, the ASEAN Secretariat was established in 1976 during the Bali Summit to act as a central administrative organ for the Association and to provide for greater efficiency in the coordination of ASEAN organs and for more effective implementation of ASEAN projects and activities. Pursuant to the agreement establishing the Secretariat, it is to serve as the central organ to coordinate cooperation of the member states and to function as a coordinating organ between different committees set up within the framework of ASEAN, and also between governments and different organs.

In 1993, the Protocol amending the Agreement on the Establishment of the ASEAN Secretariat was signed at the 25th AMM in Manila and provided the Secretariat with a new structure and vested it with an expanded set of functions and responsibilities to initiate, advise, coordinate and implement ASEAN activities. This was another indication of a movement to a more structured institutional approach to cooperation.[31]

In accordance with the Protocol, the Secretary-General[32] was redesignated as the Secretary-General of ASEAN and appointed on merit for a renewable five-year term. The Secretary-General was given an enlarged mandate to initiate, advise, coordinate and implement ASEAN activities, and also accorded ministerial status.[33] New terms and conditions for attracting high-calibre professional staff through open recruitment were also provided.

The ASEAN Secretariat is headed by the Secretary-General and has four Bureaus. The AFTA Bureau, in addition to handling the implementation and monitoring of AFTA, also handles other related issues such as the elimination of non-tariff barriers, the harmonising of tariff nomenclature, the issue of standards and conformance and customs valuation and procedures. The Bureau of Economic Cooperation handles such matters as agriculture, banking, energy, finance, food, intellectual property, investment, services, and transportation. The Bureau is also responsible for issues related to industrial cooperation and, generally, non AFTA issues. The Bureau of Functional Cooperation has been actively engaged in drawing up and coordinating the implementation of the Action Plans for Science and

Technology, Environment, Culture and Information, Social Development and Drug Abuse Control. The Bureau for ASEAN Cooperation and Dialogue Relations provides advisory services to the various ASEAN bodies on the project appraisal system adopted by the ASEAN Standing Committee. Under this system, project appraisal, implementation, monitoring and evaluation procedures have been set up. The Bureau assists in programme/project development and in prioritizing project proposals competing for external and internal resources for funding support.

At a Special Meeting of the ASEAN Foreign Ministers in Kuala Lumpur in May 1997, the Ministers agreed to the creation of an additional post of Deputy Secretary-General at the ASEAN Secretariat. One Deputy Secretary-General assists the Secretary-General on AFTA and Economic Cooperation while the other assists in Functional Cooperation, ASEAN Cooperation and Dialogue Relations and Administration, Finance and Personnel. The Deputy Secretaries-General are appointed based on nominations by the governments of ASEAN member countries.

At the Sixth ASEAN Summit in 1998[34], the Heads of State and Government mandated the review of the overall organizational structure of ASEAN in order to further improve efficiency and effectiveness. The ASEAN Standing Committee upheld the basic mandate of the Secretary-General of ASEAN as set out in the 1992 Protocol, and agreed that the ASEAN Secretariat should function as a coordinating Secretariat to help facilitate effective decision-making within and amongst ASEAN bodies. It was agreed that the Secretariat would put more emphasis on substantive matters, while its tasks on servicing the various meetings would be precisely defined.

The Secretariat is located in Jakarta.

The Secretariat also serves as the focal point of communication between foreign governments and organizations and the Association.

5. The Secretary-General of ASEAN

The Secretary-General is appointed on merit by the ASEAN Heads of Government with the recommendation of the AMM and is accorded ministerial status with the mandate to initiate, advise, coordinate and implement ASEAN activities. The Protocol Amending the Agreement on the Establishment of the ASEAN Secretariat which was signed in Manila on 22 July 1992, provides that the Secretary-General is responsible to the Heads of Government Meeting and to all Meetings of ASEAN Ministers when they are in session and to the chairman of the ASC.

6. ASEAN National Secretariats

In each member country the day-to-day work is coordinated by an ASEAN National Secretariat headed by a Director-General[35]. As noted above, each Secretariat is responsible for the coordination of all ASEAN matters in its respective country so that ASEAN's activities will be pursued as agreed. The Secretariats also meet on a formal basis to negotiate and prepare the agenda for the Standing Committee and ultimately the Ministerial Meeting and thus are, arguably, the most influential bodies within the structure. National Secretariats are located within the respective Foreign Ministries.

7. Other organs

In addition to the above organs, there are also a number of other bodies within the institutional structure of ASEAN.

(i) The Joint Ministerial Meeting ("JMM")

The Joint Ministerial Meeting was established by the 1987 Manila Summit and comprises the ASEAN Foreign Ministers and Economic Ministers under the joint chairmanship of the AMM and AEM chairmen. A joint meeting can be initiated either by the Foreign Ministers or the Economic Ministers. It meets as and when necessary to facilitate the cross-sectoral coordination of and consultation on ASEAN activities. It usually meets prior to the Summit.

(ii) Senior Officials Meeting ("SOM")

The Senior Officials Meeting are meetings of Foreign Ministry Officials (usually at Permanent Secretary or equivalent levels) which are held to discuss political matters. At the Third Summit in 1987, it was agreed that these meetings would be formally part of the ASEAN machinery.

(iii) Senior Economic Officials Meeting ("SEOM")

Senior Economic Officials Meetings were originally held to prepare for AEM meetings. As with the SOM, they were given formal status at the Third ASEAN Summit. They now also meet outside AEM meetings to help coordinate and implement ASEAN economic activities. As noted above, at the Fourth Summit in Singapore in 1992, the SEOM was tasked to handle all aspects of ASEAN economic coordination.

(iv) Joint Consultative Meeting ("JCM")

This mechanism was also introduced at the Third Summit to facilitate the intersectoral coordination of ASEAN activities at officials level. The Joint Consultative Meeting comprises SOM, SEOM and ASEAN Director-Generals, as well as the Secretary-General of ASEAN. The Secretary-General reports the results of the Meeting directly to the AMM and AEM.

(v) Other Senior Officials Meetings

In addition to the above, other Senior Officials Meetings are regularly held on environment ("ASOEN"), on drugs ("ASOD"), and on civil service matters — the ASEAN Conference on Civil Service Matters ("ACCSM"). This latter body has also been institutionalized as part of the ASEAN machinery.

(vi) ASEAN Committees in Third Countries

ASEAN has external relations with a number of third countries and international organizations. In order to facilitate these relationships, committees have been set up to conduct consultative meetings with host governments supplementary to formal meetings between ASEAN and the governments. Presently, there are 15 ASEAN Committees in third countries, namely: Beijing, Bonn, Brussels, Canberra, Geneva, Islamabad, London, Moscow, New Delhi, Ottawa, Paris, Seoul, Tokyo, Washington and Wellington. The Chairmen of the ASEAN Committees in Third Countries submit progress reports to the ASC on the activities of the Committees and seek guidance as needed from the ASC.

(vii) Other Committees

ASEAN is not a separate legal entity and, as such, does not have its own international relations, and is not a member of, eg, the WTO. However, to support the conduct of ASEAN's external relations, ASEAN has established a number of committees composed of heads of diplomatic missions. For example, the ASEAN Geneva Committee was set up to coordinate the member countries' position on matters involving trade and tariff negotiations in Geneva.

Other dialogue committees have been established in the capitals of countries with which ASEAN maintains formal dialogues.

Reasons for the Loose Structure

Although there has been some strengthening of the institutional organisation of ASEAN, the Association still maintains a relatively loose institutional structure. A number of reasons have been put forward as to why ASEAN established this flexible, loose structure. These include the following:[36]

1. ASEAN is an instrument of cooperation, not integration.
2. Formal structures would be costly and the states have no resources to maintain them.
3. Structures and laws or treaties would have prematurely imposed obligations upon members which were just beginning to relate to one another and to learn to cooperate.
4. The architects of ASEAN believed that the easier way to work together would be through the use of what they discovered to be common ways of doing things such as friendly consultations, mutual restraint, self-restraint, mutual help and neighbourly relations. All of these together with their common desire to promote peace, progress and security in the region would produce a social community, not a legal community.

These reasons remain valid with respect to ASEAN's current institutional structure. However, the primary reason for the loose structure remains the lack of supra-national objectives.

> This dictates that the primary responsibility for the viability of ASEAN is vested in each and every member country rather than in some supra-national ASEAN body or bodies. ... The result of such a non-supranational and equal national responsibility approach to an institutional organization is, whether by design or default, a highly decentralized organizational structure.[37]

Although this structure has served ASEAN well up to now, it is probable that as ASEAN develops and matures, there will be a need for more formal structures and the officials will have to depend more on them and less on the present ways. This can be seen in the evolution of the organizational structure described above. As ASEAN has evolved and enlarged, there has been a movement toward more of an institutional framework and, as ASEAN develops even more, and more emphasis is put on economic cooperation, ASEAN will have to develop even more of a formal organizational structure. This was recognised at the Sixth Summit Meeting in Hanoi on 16 December 1998. At that meeting the ASEAN Heads of State agreed on the Hanoi Plan of Action which provides, inter alia:

X.   IMPROVE ASEAN'S STRUCTURES AND MECHANISMS

   10.1 Review ASEAN's overall organizational structure in order to further improve its efficiency and effectiveness, taking into account the expansion of ASEAN activities, the enlargement of ASEAN membership, and the regional situation.

   10.2 Review and streamline ASEAN external relations mechanisms with its Dialogue Partners, regional organizations and other economic groupings.

   10.3 Review the role, functions and capacity of the ASEAN Secretariat to meet the increasing demands of ASEAN and to support the implementation of the Hanoi Plan of Action.[38]

The ASEAN Eminent Persons Group ("EPG") on Vision 2020 has made several recommendations regarding the restructuring of ASEAN's institutions and has stated that:

> ASEAN needs to develop new institutions and practices in order to stay cohesive and relevant in the 21st century. Its international esteem and influence will only rise, if it can be seen, as stated in V2020, to be "a concert of Southeast Asian nations", that is, ten nations acting in concert, with common intentions and resolve.
>
> ... The ASEAN Secretariat will no doubt continue to play an increasing role, for which it must be provided with adequate resources to do so effectively. [39]

This evolution of the organizational structure corresponds to the evolution of more of a rules-based organization with a more legalistic dispute settlement mechanism (see discussion, *infra*, chapter 7). This can be compared with developments at the broader international level. As the international economic framework has developed into more of a rules-based legal framework, it has evolved from the more diplomatic methods of the GATT to the more legalistic approach of the WTO, with corresponding organizational developments.[40] Initially, the GATT eschewed any organizational structure, referring only to the "CONTRACTING PARTIES".[41] This reflected the reluctance of some participants to have any reference to an organization. This can be compared with the administrative organization of the WTO, which evolved as the organization to administer the GATT and other economic agreements.

Legal Personality

There is no doubt that the individual member states of the Association of Southeast Asian Nations are recognized as sovereign states with full treaty making powers. The more problematic question is as to the

ORGANIZATIONAL STRUCTURE OF ASEAN

ASEAN HEADS OF GOVERNMENT MEETING

ASEAN ECONOMIC MINISTERS	ASEAN MINISTERIAL MEETING	OTHER MINISTERIAL MEETINGS
	Joint Ministerial Meetings	
Senior Economic Officals Meetings	Senior Officials Meeting	Other Senior Officials Meetings
	Joint Consultative Meeting	ASEAN Committees in Third countries

ASEAN STANDING
COMMITTEE MEETING

ASEAN SECRETARIAT
(Secretary-General)

ASEAN NATIONAL
SECRETARIATS

international legal status of the Association as an entity distinct from the member states.[42]

> It is not and was not meant to be a supranational entity acting independently of its members. It has no regional parliament or council of ministers with law-making powers, no power of enforcement, no judicial system.[43]

ASEAN is not a sovereign body but is a regional grouping of sovereign states. However, this does not mean that ASEAN cannot have an international legal personality in and of itself. Although states are the principal subjects of the international legal system, international law does recognize the claim of other candidates for international legal personality.[44] In order to be recognized as an international legal person, a candidate must be accepted as such by the existing international community, ie, it must be shown that the practice of states demonstrates their willingness to permit the candidate to exercise certain functions under, and be entitled to certain rights accorded by, international law. Recognition does not necessitate recognition of full legal capacity which a state might obtain upon recognition, but may entail recognition of legal personality for a more limited purpose.

Since ASEAN is an international governmental organization, set up by the agreement of its member states, its legal personality depends to a large degree upon its constituent instruments. Whereas a sovereign state *prima facie* possesses the totality of international rights and duties recognized by international law, the rights and duties of an international organization such as ASEAN depend on its purposes and functions as specified or implied in its constituent documents.[45] It is therefore necessary to look at the constituent documents of ASEAN to determine its international legal personality; however, an international organization's legal personality is not determined solely by its constituent documents. It is also necessary to look at the rights and duties which have developed in practice through the organization's dealings with the world community.[46]

Looking firstly at its constituent documents, it was the Bangkok Declaration signed in Bangkok in August 1967 which gave birth to ASEAN. There is some debate as to the legal status of this document.

'Although some people consider this declaration as a mere statement of intent for cooperation, there are others who see in it an international treaty with legally binding commitments between the signatories.'[47] Practice has shown the latter view to be more accurate.

"Treaty" is defined by the Vienna Convention on the Law of Treaties 1969 as "an international agreement concluded between States in written form and governed by international law, whether embodied in a single instrument or in two or more related instruments and whatever its particular designation...."[48] This definition would imply that what is meant is some form of international agreement that is intended to create binding legal relations among the parties to the agreement. If there is no "agreement ... governed by international law", ie, a legally binding agreement, there is no "treaty". The difference in views as to the status to be accorded the Bangkok Declaration reflects differing views as to whether or not it was intended to create legal relations among the signatories. Although lacking in detail, the Bangkok Declaration goes beyond "a mere statement of intent for cooperation", to enumerate the aims and purposes of the Association and to establish a machinery to carry out the aims set forth in the Declaration.[49] The intent to be bound by the terms of the Declaration has been borne out by the parties' subsequent conduct in conducting their relations in accordance with the terms of the Declaration and while perhaps not a strong treaty, one can argue that it is a treaty nonetheless.[50] The parties have further developed, and continue to develop, the institutional structure for cooperation established by the ASEAN Declaration, and have entered into a number of agreements in furtherance of its objectives.

Regardless of the legal characteristics of the Bangkok Declaration, as was seen in the discussion above, at the time the ASEAN was formed, the individual member states were hesitant to accord it strong powers over the members, preferring to maintain a high level of individual sovereignty. This desire was reflected in the 1967 Bangkok Declaration which established ASEAN with a structure which was organizationally loose and avoided the trappings of a strong regional organization.

Quite unlike other regional organizations, ASEAN has *deliberately* chosen not to adopt a formal "character". A standard charter generally would have contained provisions on machinery and institutions with defined duties, powers and functions provid[ing] for the legal capacity of the organization; mandate the creation of a secretariat empowered to act on behalf of the Association in its concourse with other international entities; prescribed an amendatory procedure and perhaps even specify the lifetime of the organization. That all these are not part of ASEAN initial development was surely not a result of incompetence.[51]

However, while this decentralized structure ensured strict state control, it created numerous obstacles for ASEAN as an organization and in 1976 at Bali there was a restructuring of the Association.

The Treaty of Amity and Cooperation in Southeast Asia[52], which was signed at Bali, was important from the perspective of the development of an ASEAN personality in that it outlined an intent to create a number of rights and obligations which were, for the first time, clearly legally enforceable. Chapter III of the treaty (Arts.4-12) sets out a number of provisions dealing with cooperation. Article 4 provides that,

> The High Contracting Parties shall promote active cooperation in the economic, social, technical, scientific and administrative fields as well as in matters of common ideals and aspiration of international peace and stability in the region and all other matters of common interest.

The following articles expand on this obligation to cooperate. In the area of economic cooperation, Article 7 provides that "they *shall* intensify economic cooperation" and that "for this purpose, they *shall* adopt appropriate regional strategies for economic development and mutual assistance." (emphasis added)

The Treaty also deals with settlement of disputes. Chapter IV of the treaty outlines an important set of procedures for the pacific settlement of disputes which includes the establishment of a High

Council. Intra-regional disputes are to be resolved through negotiation, adjudication and the active participation of members of the High Council.[53]

> Although its dispute-settlement mechanism has not been resorted to by the signatories, it is available for them to use and provides a legal framework governing relations among states in the region, mandating cooperation and the peaceful settlement of regional disputes. It thus supplements the more traditionally ASEAN way of quiet and informal diplomacy.[54]

The Declaration of ASEAN Concord, among other things, outlined the main features of an evolving ASEAN external policy.[55] This included the provision that,

> Member states shall vigorously develop an awareness of regional identity and exert all efforts to create a strong ASEAN community ...

The Declaration of ASEAN Concord took the legally enforceable obligations of member states further and adopted a programme of action as a framework for ASEAN cooperation. For example, it emphasized cooperation on commodities, industrial cooperation and cooperation in trade, and perhaps most importantly outlined general objectives regarding the improvement of ASEAN machinery. As regards the latter, the member states signed the Agreement on the Establishment of the ASEAN Secretariat. This Agreement "may be considered as an initial step in formalizing the legal personality of ASEAN as a corporate entity governed by its own constitution and by-laws".[56]

As discussed above, this structure has been further altered. However, any proposals for change to the structure have always been,

> sensitive to the fact that Asean is an inter-governmental regional organisation without a supranational objective. In drawing up the proposals...due attention [has always been] given to the need to leave decision-making firmly in the hands of Governments and to the need for achieving consensus in policy formulation.[57]

Thus, looking at its current organizational structure, although there has been an improvement in the structure, it can be seen that ASEAN remains an inter-governmental regional organization without a supranational objective. The member countries still maintain ASEAN as a forum for consultation and cooperation only, with each member retaining its individual identity. Unlike the European Community, ASEAN as an entity in its present form does not have any legal controls over the regional economy.

> [This] emphasis on the sovereignty of each country results in the limitation of power and authority of outside organizations such as the ASEAN Secretariat, and in the lack of determination by the member countries to wholly support ASEAN activities.[58]

However, all of this does not mean that ASEAN as an organization has not developed any international legal personality distinct from the international legal personality of its member states. More and more, other countries have shown and are showing an interest in dealing with ASEAN as a collectivity.

ASEAN's commitment to develop its external relations was enunciated at the First Meeting of the ASEAN Heads of Government in 1976 which "expressed ASEAN's readiness to develop fruitful relations and mutually beneficial cooperation with other countries in the region".[59] The Second Summit in 1977 also reiterated that economic cooperation with third countries or groups of countries be further intensified and expanded.[60]

ASEAN has developed "dialogue" relations to further pursue external relations with other countries. ASEAN's dialogue relations have promoted trade and investment, facilitated the transfer of technology and know-how, and improved access of ASEAN products into the markets of its dialogue partners. They have also served as an avenue for ASEAN to engage in dialogue on regional and global issues with some of the most important countries of the world and to secure development and technical assistance. As economic cooperation has become the most important area of cooperation of ASEAN's relations with its Dialogue Partners, ASEAN's cooperation with its Dialogue Partners has extended to industrial development, transfer of technology, energy, communications, transport and tourism.

The first group of countries with which ASEAN formally established full dialogue relations (in 1976) were Australia, Japan and New Zealand, the major trading partners of ASEAN.[61] ASEAN established dialogue relations with the United States (US) in 1977, the European Union (EU) in 1980, Canada in 1981, the Republic of Korea in 1991, India in 1995, and China and Russia in 1996. Pakistan established Sectoral Dialogue relations with ASEAN in 1997.

Both the European Community and Canada have entered into economic cooperation agreements with ASEAN to formalize these dialogues. Although these agreements are technically with the member states of ASEAN rather than with ASEAN as a separate entity, it is in these dealings and in an examination of ASEAN's external relations with foreign states that the development of a separate international legal personality can be seen. Indeed, it could be said that the development of ASEAN's international personality is a result of its international linkages.[62] The capacity to enter into relations with other international entities has been viewed as the most important element of legal personality as it is the essence of legal personality that the entity must be able to enter into relations with other members of the community. This element stresses the importance of recognition as an element of legal personality — until recognition has been given by other members of the legal community, the new entity cannot participate in the international system even if it is willing and capable of doing so.

Linkages include the system of ad-hoc committees and joint consultative groups which ASEAN has established to deal with its expanding network of international contacts. These committees perform a number of functions including maintaining continuity of contacts and formal links with the countries and international organizations with which the ASEAN conducts dialogues. Of particular interest is the ASEAN Geneva Committee which was set up to coordinate the member countries' position on matters involving trade and tariff negotiations in Geneva.

Apart from Dialogue relations with its existing Dialogue partners, the Fourth ASEAN Summit of 1992 agreed that, as a part of an increasingly interdependent world, ASEAN should engage in consultative relationships with interested non-dialogue countries and international organizations.[63] This was again emphasized at the Fifth ASEAN Summit when the ASEAN Heads of Government called for ASEAN to "remain outward looking and deepen its external relations with its partners in a globally interdependent world".[64]

A relatively recent development in ASEAN's external relations has been the development of the "ASEAN+3". The ASEAN+3 grouping brings together the ten Southeast Asian member states of ASEAN with the three powerful Northeast Asian states of China, Japan, and South Korea to discuss how Japan, China, and the Republic of Korea should cooperate with ASEAN. There has been discussion of how ASEAN+3 might evolve into an "East Asian Summit", in which member countries will participate as an individual member of East Asia, in order to advance cooperation in the East Asia region.[65]

Indications of the ASEAN member countries' view towards the development of an ASEAN identity can be garnered, inter alia, from the G-14's Report,[66] particularly in Part B, "Managing *ASEAN'S* External Economic Relations" (emphasis added). Recommendations in this Part include the following:

> *ASEAN* should ensure concerted and effective participation in the Uruguay Round of GATT. *Its* participation should be guided...[67]

and

> *ASEAN* should intensify bilateral dialogue relations with *its* major trading partners. Specifically, *it* should seek...[68] (emphasis added)

Of note is the statement of the ASEAN Heads of Government at the Manila Summit in 1987:

> The Heads of Government agreed that ASEAN has grown into a viable and dynamic organization fostering the spirit of regional cooperation and solidarity and strengthening national and regional resilience. *They noted that ASEAN has also*

developed a distinct identity and has become an effective vehicle
for joint approaches to regional and international issues....[69]
(emphasis added)

Most recently, the Foreign Ministers of the ASEAN Member
Countries have stated that, "development cooperation activities in the
dialogue process *should involve ASEAN as one regional entity*".[70]
(emphasis added)

Thus, both ASEAN itself and members of the world community
with which it deals recognise some independent legal personality known
as ASEAN, even if this personality at the present time is only very
limited.[71] As was pointed out at the beginning of this section,
recognition of an international legal personality does not necessitate
recognition of full legal capacity which a state might obtain upon
recognition, but may entail recognition of legal personality for a more
limited purpose.

An interesting development in the recognition of ASEAN as a
separate entity was the signing of the Memorandum of
Understanding between the Government of the Kingdom of
Thailand, ASEAN and the Government of Canada Regarding the
ASEAN Grain Post-Harvest Programme in Bangkok on 8 July
1988.[72] This agreement was signed by *ASEAN* as a party. The
member countries had agreed that the Government of the Kingdom
of Thailand would act as its representative for the purposes of the
MOU and Thailand signed both in its own capacity and as the
representative of ASEAN. This procedure has been followed in
subsequent MOUs.[73]

Also, although ASEAN has an informal structure without
supranational law-making powers, it would not be true to say that
decisions from ASEAN do not have binding effect in any circumstances.

> In practice, it is accepted that the decision of the
> chairman of the ASEAN Standing Committee which proposes
> the groundwork for the annual Ministerial meetings binds the
> members of the committee, even though there is no explicit
> judicial basis for this. Moreover the "consensus" model of
> ASEAN Ministerial meetings implies that once a decision has

been made, the member countries undertake to abide by them, irrespective of the lack of a supra-national court to enforce such decision.[74]

The ASEAN Way — Decision-Making in ASEAN

In order to better understand how the legal framework is developing within ASEAN and some of the factors which may limit the development and structure of the legal framework, it is necessary to have some appreciation of the decision-making process within ASEAN.

> Seemingly, the way of making regional decisions dealing
> with co-operation among the member States adopted by ASEAN
> reflects its attitude of rejecting being a supra-national body like
> the European Communities.[75]

The structural organization discussed above results from, and is compounded by, the manner of decision-making which exists in the ASEAN region. The underlying approach to decision-making in ASEAN is the consensus approach embodied in the Malay terms *musyawarah* and *mufakat*. As the former Prime Minister of Singapore, Lee Kuan Yew has commented:

> We have made progress in an ASEAN manner, not through
> rules and regulations, but through *Musyawarah* and consensus.[76]

Musyawarah, the process of decision-making through discussion and consultation, and *mufakat*, the unanimous decision that is arrived at, are associated with the traditional approach to decision-making in the region and have played a role in village politics for centuries and, culturally, can be identified as part of the regional social system.[77] The concept involves processes including intensive informal and discreet discussions behind the scenes to work out a general consensus which then acts as the starting point around which the unanimous decision is finally accepted in more formal meetings. The ASEAN way relies to a large extent on the personal approach in contrast to the Western way of dependence on structures and their functions.[78]

This "consensus" approach has become the "ASEAN Way" and is reflected in the processes and structures of ASEAN.[79] The likely positions of member countries are felt out in advance in order to avoid any confrontational issues at formal meetings and only issues with some degree of acceptability will be presented at the regional level. However, while ensuring an element of cohesion, this process is cumbersome.

Even once a consensus has been arrived at, not everyone is obliged to participate in it because ASEAN allows bilateral and other arrangements for cooperation.

> If a member is not ready to participate, his participation in the consensus does not oblige him to act on it. All that is needed is his agreement in principle. Some exceptions to this are the cultural projects ... and the ASEAN positions in relation to international issues.[80]

In certain cases, ASEAN provides for a membership-minus-x principle, by which it is meant that agreement on the matter will be arrived at by a consensus but implementation need only involve those which are able at the time. The others may join in the implementation when they are able to do so. A reaffirmation of this principle is in the 1992 Framework Agreement on Enhancing ASEAN Economic Cooperation:

> All Member States shall participate in intra-ASEAN economic arrangements. However, in the implementation of these economic arrangements, two or more Member States may proceed first if other Member States are not ready to implement these arrangements.[81]

Towards a More Legalistic Approach?

As ASEAN develops and matures, there may be a need for more institutionalization of its work and the dependence on cultural and traditional ways may recede.[82] HE Rodolfo C Severino, Jr, ASEAN Secretary-General, has pointed out that 'the financial crisis had convinced East Asian countries that they must move away from a "relationship-based" way of doing business and creating wealth to one that was more "rules-based" and market-driven.'[83] We have seen in looking at the development of ASEAN that there has been a slow movement towards more structure in the institutions and organization of ASEAN as an entity, although the emergence of a strong ASEAN identity has been constrained by a preoccupation with consensus and the mistrust of a strong ASEAN identity with powers parallelling the member states in some areas.[84]

The members of ASEAN have adopted a Protocol on Dispute Settlement Mechanism[85] providing for a more formalised dispute settlement mechanism in the area of ASEAN economic cooperation. This is in keeping with the move towards the development of more of a legal framework to regulate economic activity *inter se*, and in keeping with the general trend internationally to 'legalism' in regulating international economic relations.

Also, as noted above, the members of ASEAN have also recently adopted Rules of Procedure of the High Council set up by the Treaty of Amity and Cooperation. Although the treaty which was entered into on 24 February, 1976, mentioned a High Council to settle disputes through regional processes, the mechanism has not been resorted to. The adoption of the Rules of Procedure, however, reflects a further step in the "judicialization" of ASEAN.

Proposals have been made to create more of a legal framework for ASEAN, including a restructuring of the ASEAN decision-making process. For example, the Philippines initiated a proposal for an ASEAN Treaty of Economic Cooperation which would entail a legal framework binding ASEAN into a form of legal entity.[86] Also, in *A Time for Initiative — Proposals for Consideration of the Fourth ASEAN Summit* (ASEAN Institutes of Strategic and International Studies, 4 June 1991), it was recommended that 'the Fourth Summit should discuss and decide upon the adoption of a legal framework for expanding economic cooperation in the form of a Treaty' (at p 8). This proposal received serious consideration by the AMM and AEM. However, it was decided in the end to enter into a framework agreement which was considered to be a "less legally binding" document.[87] However, even though this agreement may not be as "legally binding" a document as the proposed ASEAN Treaty of Economic Cooperation, it "has raised the level of intra-ASEAN cooperation and commitment closer to Treaty Arrangements".[88]

Despite the lack of a "proper" legal regime in ASEAN at the regional level and the significant differences in the economic laws of the member states, a legal framework for economic cooperation within the region and between the region and other countries has nevertheless developed. This framework will be explored in the following chapters.

Endnotes

1   Bangkok Declaration (Association of Southeast Asia), done at Bangkok, 31 July 31 1961. Reproduced in Hass, *Basic Documents of Asian Regional Organisation* (N.Y.: Oceana, 1974), Vol IV, 1259.

2   Inter alia, visa requirements were modified, agreement was reached on freer exchange of information on primary commodities, and a common fund was created to carry out joint projects.

3   Manila Accord, 1963, adopted in Manila on 11 June 1963; Manila Declaration, 1963, adopted in Manila on 4 August 1963; Joint Statement, Summit Conference, 1963, adopted in Manila, 5 August 1963; reproduced in Hass, *Basic Documents of Asian Regional Organisation* (N.Y.: Oceana, 1974), Vol IV at 1261, 1264, and 1265 respectively.

4   The ASEAN Declaration (Bangkok Declaration), Bangkok, 8 August 1967, reproduced in: Paul J Davidson (ed), *Trading Arrangements in the Pacific Rim* (New York: Oceana Publications, 1995) (hereafter, *TAPR*), Document I.B. 2 (see Appendix 1). For a more detailed discussion on the ASA and MAPHILINDO and the factors which inspired the member countries to form ASEAN, see Vinita Sukrasep, *ASEAN in International Relations* (Bangkok: Institute of Security and International Studies, 1989), pp 3-18.

5   Joint Press Statement, The First Informal Meeting of the Heads of Government of ASEAN, Jakarta, 30 November 1996, *TAPR*, Document I.B.5.f.

6   Declaration on the Admission of The Lao People's Democratic Republic into the Association of Southeast Asian Nations, Subang Jaya, Malaysia, 23 July 1997, *TAPR*, Document I.B.3.a; Declaration on the Admission of The Union of Myanmar into the Association of Southeast Asian Nations, Subang Jaya, Malaysia, 23 July 1997, TAPR, Document I.B.3.b.

7   Declaration on the Admission of the Kingdom of Cambodia into the Association of Southeast Asian Nations, *TAPR*, Document I.B.3.g.

8   The ASEAN Declaration (Bangkok Declaration), 2nd para.

9   As quoted in Soemardjan Selo, 'Introduction' to RP Anand and PV-Quisumbing (eds), *ASEAN Identity, Development and Culture* (Manila: UP Law Center and East West Center Culture Learning Institute, 1981), at xiii.

10 The Bangkok Declaration states that Special Meetings of Foreign Ministers may be convened as required (para 3(a)).

11 These ambassadors served for a one year period.

12 Vinit Sukrasep, *ASEAN in International Relations* (Bangkok: Institute of Security and International Studies, 1989), p 22.

13 *Ibid.*

14 *TAPR*, Document I.B.5.a.

15 *TAPR*, Document I.B.3; see Appendix 2.

16 *Ibid.*

17 *TAPR*, Document I.B.6.

18 See, Amado Castro, 'Economic Cooperation and the Development of an ASEAN Culture', in RP Anand and PV-Quisumbing (eds), *ASEAN Identity, Development and Culture* (Manila: UP Law Center and East West Center Culture Learning Institute, 1981), at 229: 'the first meeting of ASEAN Economic and Planning Ministers [which took place in Jakarta on 26-27 November 1975] ... made a number of recommendations regarding economic cooperation. Since the meeting was convened largely in preparation for the first meeting of the ASEAN Heads of Government, [their] recommendations ... formed much of the substance of the Declaration of ASEAN Concord signed at Bali in February 1976.'

19 *ASEAN, The Way Forward, The Report of the Group of Fourteen on ASEAN Economic Cooperation and Integration* (Kuala Lumpur: Institute of Strategic and International Studies (ISIS) Malaysia, 1987).

20 *Ibid*, at 71.

21 Tan Sri Ghazali Shafie, et al, 'Strengthening the Structure and Mechanism of ASEAN, with Special Reference to the ASEAN Secretariat', Report prepared for the Asean Standing Committee, July 1991 (unpublished). See also, Chng Meng Kng, 'ASEAN's Institutional Structure and Economic Co-operation' (1990) 6 *ASEAN Economic Bulletin*, pp 268-282, for an evaluation of ASEAN's institutional structure and its evolution in the wider framework of ASEAN's objectives as a regional organization with a view to understanding the limits and possibilities of institutional change.

22 Tan Sri Ghazali Shafie, *ibid*, p 6.

23 For a discussion of the report and comments on the institutional decisions of the Singapore summit as well as further comments on institutional requirements of ASEAN, see Jacques Pelkmans, 'Institutional requirements of ASEAN with special reference to AFTA', in Pearl Imada and Seiji Naya (eds), *AFTA the Way Ahead* (Singapore: ISEAS, 1992), pp 99-133. Jacques Pelkmans was a member of the panel which prepared the report.

24 *TAPR*, Document I.B.8.

25 Hanoi Plan of Action, 16 December 1998, Art X, 'Improve ASEAN's Structures And Mechanisms', *TAPR*, Document I.B.5.j; see Appendix 3.

26 For further discussion on AFTA, see Chapter Four, *infra*.

27 See Chapter Seven, *infra*, for a discussion of dispute settlement in ASEAN.

28 Hanoi Plan of Action, 16 December 1998, *TAPR*, Document I.B.5.j; see Appendix 3.

29 At the 4th Informal Summit, ASEAN Leaders agreed to meet in an annual summit without the distinction of its being either an informal or formal summit.

30 Amado A Castro, 'Economic Cooperation and the Development of an ASEAN Culture', in RP Anand and PV-Quisumbing (eds), *ASEAN Identity, Development and Culture* (Manila: UP Law Center and East West Center Culture Learning Institute, 1981), at 230-231.

31 'Not coincidentally [with the signing of the formal binding agreement on the Common Effective Preferential Tariff Scheme for the ASEAN Free Trade Area in 1992], also in 1992, ASEAN decided to enlarge and professionalize the Secretariat and empower it to take initiatives and undertake a more active role, particularly in the implementation of ASEAN economic arrangements and in the management of ASEAN cooperation in the social and cultural, as well as economic, areas.' (Severino, Rodolfo C, Secretary-General of ASEAN, Asia Policy Lecture: 'What ASEAN is and what it stands for', The Research Institute for Asia and the Pacific, University of Sydney, Australia, 22 October 1998).

32 For an elaboration of the functions and powers of the Secretary-General, see the Agreement on the Establishment of the ASEAN Secretariat, Bali, 24 February 1976, Art 3, *TAPR*, Document I.B.6.

33 See, 'Secretariat restructuring completed', *ASEAN Update*, September 1993, at 4.

34 TAPR Documents I.B.5.i and I.B.5.j.

35 Following the creation of the ASEAN Secretariat with a Secretary-General at its head, the heads of of the National Secretariats were redesignated as Director-Generals to avoid confusion and the National Secretaries became known as Office of the Directors-General in the respective ASEAN countries.

36 See, Estrella Solidum, 'An ASEAN Perspective on the Decision-Making Process in the European Community, in Purificacion V Quisumbing and Benjamin B Domingo (eds), *EEC and ASEAN: Two Regional Community Experiences*, (Manila: Foreign Service Institute and UP Law Center, 1983), p 129.

37 Chng Meng Kng, 'ASEAN's Institutional Structure and Economic Co-operation', (1990) 6 *ASEAN Economic Bulletin*, 268 at 272.

38 Hanoi Plan of Action, *TAPR* Document I.B.5.j; Appendix 3.

39 Report of the ASEAN Eminent Persons Group (EPG) on Vision 2020 (Singapore: ASEAN Secretariat, November, 2000).

40 Reich, Arie, 'From Diplomacy to Law: The Juridicization of International Trade Relations' (1996/97) 17 *Northwestern Journal of International Law & Business*, pp 775-849.

41 This was the term used to indicate the Contracting Parties acting in concert. 'Thus multilateral decisions under GATT are to be taken by the "CONTRACTING PARTIES acting jointly" and not by any "organization" body.' (Jackson, John H, *The World Trading System – Law and Policy of International Economic Relations*, 2nd ed (Cambridge/London: The MIT Press, 1997), pp 37-38.

42 For a discussion of some of the major constraints in bringing about the existence of a well-defined legal order in ASEAN, see, Purification Valera Quisumbing, 'An ASEAN Perspective on the Legal and Institutional Aspects of the Community Emerging Legal Framework of ASEAN', in Purificacion V Quisumbing and Benjamin B Domingo (eds), *EEC and ASEAN: Two Regional Community Experiences* (Manila: Foreign Service Institute and UP Law Center, 1983), pp 69-88 at 70-79.

43 Severino, Rodolfo C, Secretary-General of ASEAN, Asia Policy Lecture: 'What ASEAN is and what it stands for', The Research Institute for Asia and the Pacific, University of Sydney, Australia, 22 October 1998.

44 JG Starke, 'The ASEAN Association as an entity of international law', (1983) 57 Aust LJ, 56 at 56: 'Consistently with their obligations under the United Nations Charter and under general international law, States are free to form themselves into groupings or associations, with permanent or quasi-permanent machinery, thereby creating a kind of unincorporated entity recognised by the international community, with some inevitable impact on international law.'

45 *Advisory Opinion on Reparation for Injuries Suffered in the Service of the United Nations* (1949) ICJ 174 at 180.

46 *Ibid.*

47 Soemardjan Selo, in the 'Introduction' to RP Anand and PV-Quisumbing (eds) *ASEAN Identity, Development and Culture* (Manila: UP Law Center and East West Center Culture Learning Institute, 1981), at x.

48 1155 UNTS 331; (1989) 8 ILM 679, Art.2(1)(a).

49 The ASEAN Declaration, 2nd and 3rd parts.

50 For a contrary opinion, see, Vitit Muntarbhorn, 'ASEAN and the Treaty-Making Process', *ASEAN Economic Cooperation for the 1990s*, A Report Prepared for the ASEAN Standing Committee (Philippines: Philippine Institute for Development Studies and ASEAN Secretariat, 1992), pp 106-117 at 110: 'On a balance of probabilities, [that the Bangkok Declaration is an international treaty] is unlikely.'

51 Purificacion Valera Quisumbing, 'An ASEAN Perspective on the Legal and Institutional Aspects of the Community Emerging Legal Framework of ASEAN', in Purificacion V Quisumbing and Benjamin B Domingo (eds) *EEC and ASEAN: Two Regional Community Experiences* (Manila: Foreign Service Institute and UP Law Center, 1983), pp 69-88 at 76.

52 Appendix 2.

53 Articles 13-17.

54 Severino, Rodolfo C, Secretary-General of ASEAN, Asia Policy Lecture: 'What ASEAN is and what it stands for', The Research Institute for Asia and the Pacific, University of Sydney, Australia, 22 October 1998. At their meeting held on 23 of July 2001 in Hanoi, the High Contracting Parties adopted Rules of Procedure of the High Council (*TAPR*, Document I.B.3.j. See Chapter 7, *infra*, for a further discussion.

55 For a more detailed treatment of the development of ASEAN's external relations, see, Agerico O Lacanlale, 'Community Formation in ASEAN's External Relations', in RP Anand and PV-Quisumbing (eds), *ASEAN Identity, Development and Culture* (Manila: UP Law Center and East West Center Culture Learning Institute, 1981), pp 378-409.

56 Ingles, Jose D, 'Problems and Progress in Regional Integration: The Case of ASEAN', in RP Amand and PV-Quisumbing (eds), *ASEAN Identity, Development and Culture* (Manila: UP Law Center and East-West Center Culture Learning Institute, 1981), p 217 at 224.

57 *ASEAN, The Way Forward, The Report of the Group of Fourteen on ASEAN Economic Cooperation and Integration* (Kuala Lumpur: Institute of Strategic and International Studies (ISIS) Malaysia, 1987), p 71.

58 Vinita Sukrapsep, *ASEAN in International Relations* (Bangkok: ISIS, 1989), p 50.

59 Joint Press Communique, Meeting of the ASEAN Heads of Government, Bali, 23-24 February 1976, para 4, *TAPR*, Document I.B.5.a.

60 Joint Press Communique, Meeting of the ASEAN Heads of Government, Kuala Lumpur, 1977, paras 30-38, *TAPR*, Document I.B.5.b.

61 ASEAN also entered into a dialogue relationship with the United Nations Development Programme ("UNDP"), a recognised international organization, in 1976. ASEAN-UNDP's long-standing relations began almost from the inception of ASEAN in 1967. However, it was in the early 1970s that the relationship assumed a more tangible form, when UNDP sponsored a massive study to assist ASEAN with its first economic cooperation initiatives. This initiative provided the basis for ASEAN's subsequent cooperation in industrial development, agriculture and forestry, transport, finance, monetary and insurance services. (See *infra*, Chapter 3)

62 'It is perhaps this ability to present a unified front in international forums, as well as in its external dialogues, that ASEAN has been increasingly recognized as a viable and a cohesive entity rather than as an organization to be dismissed as one of the many futile experiments at regional community formation.': Agerico O Lacanlale, 'Community Formation in ASEAN's External Relations', in RP Anand and PV-Quisumbing (eds), *ASEAN Identity, Development and Culture* (Manila: UP Law Center and East West Center Culture Learning Institute, 1981), pp 378-409 at 399.

63 Singapore Declaration of 1992, Singapore, 28 January 1992, para 6, *TAPR*, Document I.B.8.

64 Bangkok Summit Declaration of 1995, Bangkok, 15 December 1995, para 11, *TAPR*, Document I.B.5.e.

65 ASEAN+3 Summit Meeting, Singapore, 24 November 2000 (*TAPR*, Document I.B.9.m).

66 *ASEAN, The Way Forward, The Report of the Group of Fourteen on ASEAN Economic Cooperation and Integration* (Kuala Lumpur: Institute of Strategic and International Studies (ISIS) Malaysia, 1987).

67 *Ibid*, p.62.

68 *Ibid*, p.65.

69 Joint Press Statement, Meeting of the ASEAN Heads of Government, Manila, 14-15 December 1987, para 6, *TAPR*, Document I.B.5.c.

70 Joint Communique of the 34th ASEAN Ministerial Meeting, Hanoi, 23-24 July 2001, *TAPR*, Document I.B.4.a (34).

71 See also, Vitit Muntarbhorn, 'ASEAN and the Treaty-Making Process', *ASEAN Economic Cooperation for the 1990s*, A Report Prepared for the ASEAN Standing Committee (Philippines: Philippine Institute for Development Studies and ASEAN Secretariat, 1992), pp 106-117 at 111-113, for a discussion of international legal personality of ASEAN.

72 *ASEAN Documents Series 1988-1989* (Jakarta: ASEAN Secretariat, 1989), pp 41-44.

73 For example, The Memorandum of Understanding with the European Union on Economic Cooperation in Standards, Quality, and Conformity Assessment, 4 January 1999. The MOU was signed by the Secretary-General of ASEAN on behalf of the Member countries.

74 Vitit Muntarbhorn, *The Challenge of Law – Legal Cooperation Among Developing Countries* (Bangkok: ISIS, 1987), p 17. See below for a discussion of the 'consensus' model.

75 Teuku Mohammad Radhie, 'Regional Cooperation in Law and Development Study in the ASEAN Region, in Teuku Mohammad Radhie & Nobuyuki Yasuda, *Law and Development Study in ASEAN Countries* (Tokyo: Institute of Developing Economies, 1991), p 43.

76 Opening Address by HE Lee Kuan Yew, (then) Prime Minister of Singapore, in *15th ASEAN Ministerial Meeting and Post-Ministerial Meeting with the Dialogue Countries, Singapore, 14-18 June 1982* (Jakarta: ASEAN Secretariat, 1982), p 9.

77 For a more detailed discussion of the consensus model, see, Pushpa Thambipillai and J Saravanamuttu, *ASEAN Negotiations – Two Insights* (Singapore: ISEAS, 1985), especially at pp 10-13.

78 Estrella D Solidum, "The Role of Certain Sectors in Shaping and Articulating the ASEAN Way', in RP Anand and PV-Quisumbing (eds), *ASEAN Identity, Development and Culture* (Manila: UP Law Center and East West Center Culture Learning Institute, 1981), pp 130-148 at 138; see also, Estrella Solidum, 'An ASEAN Perspective on the Decision-Making Process in the European Community, in Purificacion V Quisumbing and Benjamin B Domingo (eds), *EEC and ASEAN: Two Regional Community Experiences* (Manila: Foreign Service Institute and UP Law Center, 1983), pp 127-131.

79 'The "ASEAN Way" is one of consensus; the regional organization was only able to move forward when all countries were ready.' (Naya, Seiji and Michael G Plummer, 'Economic Co-operation after 30 Years of ASEAN', (1997) 14 *ASEAN Economic Bulletin*, pp 117 at 119)

80 *Supra*, note 78, 'The Role of Certain Sectors ...' at 139.

81 Art 1, para 3. This can also be seen in the Bangkok Summit Declaration of 1995 (para 8) where the Heads of State and Government, in speaking of ASEAN economic cooperation, stated: 'All ASEAN economic cooperation decisions shall

be made by flexible consensus so that Member Countries wishing to embark on any cooperation scheme may do so while the others can join at a later date'.

82 'I thus envision ASEAN as evolving into a more rules-based association': 'The ASEAN Way and the Rule of Law', article by Rodolfo C Severino, Secretary-General of ASEAN, at the International Law Conference on ASEAN Legal Systems and Regional Integration, Kuala Lumpur, 3 September 2001. (http://www.aseansec.org/newdata/asean_way.htm)

83 Rodolfo C. Severino, Jr., ASEAN Secretary-general, 'Reforms and Integration in East Asia Could Strengthen Regional Stability', 14 August 1999, http://www.aseansec.org/golek.html.

84 Vitit Muntarbhorn, 'ASEAN and the Treaty-Making Process', in *ASEAN Economic Cooperation for the 1990s*, A Report prepared for the ASEAN Standing Committee (Philippines: Philippine Institute for Development Studies and ASEAN Secretariat, 1992), 106 at 116.

85 Protocol on Dispute Settlement Mechanism, 20 November 1996, *TAPR*, Document I.B.7.o.

86 See discussion in *ASEAN Economic Cooperation for the 1990s*, A Report Prepared for the ASEAN Standing Committee (Philippines: Philippine Institute for Development Studies and the ASEAN Secretariat, 1992), especially at 25-30 ('An ASEAN Framework Agreement: Foundation for the Future') and 113-117 ('Instruments for Integration').

87 See discussion of the Framework Agreement on Enhancing ASEAN Economic Cooperation, *infra*, Chapter 4.

88 Closing Statement by HE Mrs Corazon C Aquino, President of the Republic of the Philippines, at the Fourth ASEAN Summit, Singapore, 28 January 1992, *in Meeting of the ASEAN Heads of Government, Singapore, 27-28 January 1992* (Jakarta: ASEAN Secretariat, 1992), at 35.

CHAPTER 3

EARLY ECONOMIC COOPERATION IN ASEAN

...regional trade relationships have become more important...closer economic cooperation among ASEAN member countries is imperative.[1]

Introduction

Although a multilateral legal framework for regulating trade and investment where all parties are governed by the same rules may be the ideal, the reality is that, because of political and economic factors, such a system is very difficult to obtain. Rather, while multilateral rules have developed to regulate certain aspects of international trade and investment, they are not the sole elements of the international legal framework. Much of the international regulation of trade and investment is also determined by the international legal framework which has evolved at the regional level among different groupings of countries which have developed regional rules of international law to govern their relations *inter se*. This is particularly so in the realm of international economic relations where various regional groupings have been formed to promote economic cooperation among the members of the group. However, such regional rules must not be in conflict with the broader international legal obligations which the members may have at the multilateral level, and the multilateral rules must therefore be kept in mind in constructing the regional system.

The obligations under the WTO form the basis for the international legal framework governing trade between ASEAN and its trading partners as well as among members of ASEAN.[2] Any legal framework for economic cooperation at the regional level will have to accord with obligations under the WTO, eg, the provisions of GATT, insofar as it deals with aspects which come within the GATT framework (trade in goods), and within the GATS (as regards trade in services).

Perhaps the most fundamental obligation under GATT, is the MFN clause of Article I which sets out the principle of non-discrimination in trade.[3] GATT members are obliged to give unconditional MFN treatment to the trade of all contracting parties, ie, they are obliged to apply tariffs and other trade barriers equally to imports from all other contracting parties. A strict application of this rule would prohibit regional economic cooperation in trade as by its very nature such economic cooperation entails preferential trade provisions.

However, the MFN obligation is subject to a number of exceptions under GATT itself, most notably for the purposes of regional economic cooperation, that of Article XXIV providing for customs unions and free trade areas, and, in the case of developing countries, that of the Tokyo Round Agreement on Differential and More Favourable Treatment of Developing Countries.[4]

What Legal Framework for ASEAN Economic Cooperation?

Much has been written about the appropriate model which ASEAN should follow in moving toward closer economic cooperation among its members. Many of these writings have dealt with the lessons to be drawn from the European Community[5]. In the early years of ASEAN, the European Community was often held out as an example worth emulating and, in fact, in 1980 the ASEAN Chambers of Commerce and Industry recommended the framing of a formal treaty of economic cooperation along the lines of the Treaties of Rome and Paris in order to provide the parameters and to serve as guideposts for the public and private sectors for bringing about ASEAN cooperation.[6]

However, the EC model has not been followed and, given the differences in the two regions and the objectives of cooperation in each, this should not be surprising. As former Singapore Senior Minister S Rajaratnam has pointed out, "the European Community was never made by ASEAN's architects the model for ASEAN regionalism ... ASEAN's objective has never been and is unlikely to ever be, the political and economic integration of the six [now ten] member nations."[7] Rather, ASEAN is an instrument of cooperation, not integration and one must consider what is the appropriate framework within which this can take place in ASEAN.

In the short to medium run, the European Community is unlikely to be an appropriate model.[8] The European Community is based on a customs union which requires a common commercial policy toward trading partners outside the region. Furthermore, the European Community has chosen to go far beyond a customs union to achieve a high degree of integration of the member economies. These measures require the acceptance of certain limitations on national sovereignty in relation to international commercial matters which ASEAN member states are at present unlikely to be willing to accept.

Economic cooperation in ASEAN has been slow to develop because of the dominance of national interest. However, a legal framework for regional economic cooperation is evolving and this development has received increased impetus from the recent moves toward the creation of an ASEAN free trade area (AFTA) (see *infra*, Chapter 4). In establishing a framework for this new level of economic cooperation within ASEAN, the difference between a free trade area and a customs union must be kept in mind. In a free trade area the members are free to set their own external trade policy, whereas in a customs union the members have to agree on a common external trade policy. Because of the economic differences in the membership of ASEAN, a free trade area is a more appropriate form of cooperation than a customs union.

The following discussion reviews early attempts at establishing a framework for economic cooperation at the regional level in ASEAN. These agreements form some of the early "rules" of the evolving legal framework in ASEAN.

Regional Economic Cooperation in ASEAN[9]

Industrial cooperation has been an important cornerstone of ASEAN economic cooperation and various industrial cooperation initiatives have been pursued with the aim of enhancing the industrial competitiveness of the region. Industrial cooperation schemes based on the principles of resource pooling and market sharing have been introduced to facilitate effective exploitation of economies of scale.

The First Steps to Economic Cooperation – The Declaration of ASEAN Concord (1976) and Subsequent Agreements:

In 1970-72 a United Nations Study Team was organized to make recommendations regarding economic cooperation in ASEAN. The Study Team's report appeared in mid-1973 and served as a blueprint for much of ASEAN economic cooperation.[10] The report recommended three separate but interrelated techniques of cooperation for industrial development: selective trade liberalisation, a system of complementarity agreements, and a system of "package deal" agreements. At the Seventh ASEAN Ministerial Meeting held at Jakarta, Indonesia, 7-9 May 1974, it was agreed that "the three techniques...might be useful techniques for ASEAN cooperation."[11]

The first substantive steps toward economic cooperation in ASEAN were then taken with the signing of the Declaration of ASEAN Concord in 1976 at the First ASEAN Summit in Bali. This Agreement set the ground rules for ASEAN cooperation in trade and industry. This was followed by a number of agreements which formed the basis for a wide range of cooperative activities in industrial development and trade. Although these were strictly regional agreements, they established a legal framework within which rules for carrying on business in the region could be enacted. These agreements thus had implications for foreign companies wishing to trade with or invest in the region and therefore formed part of the international legal framework for trade and investment with and in ASEAN.

These agreements have been dealt with in detail elsewhere[12] and I will only comment on them briefly as regards their role in the evolving legal framework for economic cooperation in the region. To a large degree, these schemes have been replaced as a result of actions taken under the Framework Agreement on Enhancing ASEAN Economic Cooperation.[13]

1. Agreement on ASEAN Preferential Trading Arrangements

The Bali Summit in 1976 set out a programme of action for cooperation in a number of fields including economic cooperation. Specifically, in the area of cooperation in trade, the Declaration of ASEAN Concord provided, inter alia, that "Member states shall progress towards the establishment of preferential trading arrangements...."[14] Pursuant to this provision, the ASEAN member states entered into an Agreement on ASEAN Preferential Trading Arrangements ("PTA") on 24 February 1977.[15] This Agreement provides that the member states of the ASEAN are to extend trade preferences to each other in accordance with the provisions of the Agreement and the rules, regulations and decisions agreed within its framework.[16]

Under Section 2 Article 3 of the PTA Agreement, provisions on preferential trading are specified as follows:

1.   long-term quantity contracts;
2.   purchase finance support at preferential interest rates;
3.   preference in procurement by government entities;
4.   extension of tariff preferences;
5.   liberalisation of non-tariff measures on a preferential basis; and
6.   other measures.

Among these methods, ASEAN put emphasis on tariff preferences among member countries. Under the Agreement,[17] an effective ASEAN margin of tariff preference was accorded on a product-by-product basis and where tariff preferences were negotiated on a multilateral or bilateral basis, the concessions so agreed were extended to all parties on an ASEAN most-favoured-nation basis, except where special treatment was accorded to products of ASEAN industrial projects (see below). Preferences were negotiated on a voluntary, product-by-product basis until April 1980. After that time, tariff preferences were complemented by across-the-board tariff reductions for imports of certain values.[18] The adoption of across-the-board tariff cuts was accompanied by the introduction of exclusion lists of "sensitive items" to protect certain industries. At the beginning, the margin of preference was as low as 10%. Then it was increased to 20-25% in 1981, and later on, to 40% or more.

The object of the PTA was to create a larger market for the goods coming within its provisions by creating an area of preferential trade for certain goods. This was of potential significance for Third country-ASEAN business arrangements as an incentive for foreign investment in the region in order to gain access to this enlarged market. The preferential arrangements under the PTA were first offered on 1 January 1978 with a list of 71 commodities and the arrangements were expanded from time to time.

At the Manila Summit in 1987, the states parties to the PTA adopted The Protocol on Improvements on Extension of Tariff Preferences Under the ASEAN Preferential Trading Arrangement[19] to expand the PTA's coverage through a reduction of the items in the exclusion list of each contracting state and an increase in the Margin of Preference ("MOP").

In order to receive preferential treatment, products had to satisfy the Rules of Origin under the Agreement on ASEAN PTA. These Rules of Origin were to ensure that the benefits of any preference given by one member state to another accrued to products that were wholly or to a substantial extent made up of material, parts and labour originating in the ASEAN member countries.

The 1977 Agreement provided that products which were manufactured in an ASEAN country incorporating imported materials, parts or components, including those of undetermined origin, were considered as originating in that country if the total value of the material, parts, or components imported from non-ASEAN countries or of undetermined origin did not exceed 50%[20] of the FOB value of the products manufactured and the final process of manufacture was performed within the territory of that ASEAN country. The 1987 Protocol on Improvements to the PTA provided that the ASEAN content requirement in the rules of origin be reduced from 50% to 35% on a case-by-case basis for a period of five years.[21] In a further "Protocol to Amend the Agreement on ASEAN Preferential Trading Agreements",[22] it was agreed that the Rules of Origin for the ASEAN PTA should be substituted with the Rules of

Origin for the Common Effective Preferential Tariff (see discussion *infra*, Chapter 4).[23]

At the Manila Summit, the parties also adopted the Memorandum of Understanding on Standstill and Rollback of Non-Tariff Barriers Among ASEAN Countries[24] to further effect the provisions of the ASEAN PTA. Under the Memorandum, the parties were obliged not to introduce new or additional non-tariff measures which would hamper the flow of intra-ASEAN trade and at the same time to take steps to eliminate these same non-tariff measures.

The PTA Scheme was not very successful in promoting intra-ASEAN trade because of some basic structural problems arising from the lack of complementarity of ASEAN economies.[25] Although the number of items eligible for preferential treatment under the PTA continued to grow, many of the products eligible for these preferences were unimportant in intra-ASEAN trade. Also, most significant products were excluded on the "exclusion lists" due to their "sensitive" nature.[26] "Regional interests were only accorded priority if they coincided with or promoted national interests."[27]

These failings were addressed to some extent by the Manila Summit which sought to reduce the exclusion lists and broaden the margin of preferences, as well as tackle the problem of non-tariff barriers. Further, at the 23rd Meeting of the AEM at Kuala Lumpur from 7-8 October 1991, it was agreed to further deepen the MOP of existing PTA items; to further reduce the items in the exclusions lists; and, for all member countries to reduce the ASEAN content requirement to 40% for the first five years, at the end of which time this would be reviewed with a view to raising it back to the original 50%.[28]

The PTA has now been phased into the Common Effective Preferential Tariff ("CEPT")under the ASEAN Free Trade Area. The 7th ASEAN Free Trade Area Council in Brunei Darussalam in September 1995 agreed that products in the PTA would be phased into the CEPT Scheme effective 1 January 1996.[29]

2. ASEAN Industrial Projects ("AIP")

One of the suggestions of the UN Study Group was the so-called package deal concept. Under this arrangement, a large industrial plant

serving the entire region's needs for a particular product was to be set up
in one country only. To ensure acceptability of such an arrangement,
each country would have one large industrial project producing a
different product for the regional market.

The Declaration of ASEAN Concord issued after the Summit
Meeting in Bali in 1976 provided that,

> Member states shall cooperate to establish large-scale
> ASEAN industrial plants, particularly to meet regional
> requirements of essential commodities.[30]

This agreement to cooperate led to the Basic Agreement on ASEAN
Industrial Projects on 6 March 1980.[31]

However, due to difficulties in agreeing on the allocation of
projects, this scheme also was not very successful. Five such projects
were approved by the ASEAN Economic Ministers: two ammonia urea
plants (Indonesia and Malaysia), phosphate fertilizer (Philippines),
diesel engines (Singapore) and soda ash (Thailand). The ammonia urea
projects of Indonesia and Malaysia were established by Supplementary
Agreements in 1980[32] and a Thai potash mining project, which replaced
the soda ash project, was finally established by a Supplementary
Agreement in 1991[33]. However, the phosphate fertilizer project of the
Philippines was cancelled and a copper fabrication plant proposed as a
replacement. Also, because of difficulties with getting the other member
countries, particularly Indonesia, to agree on limiting their diesel engine
industries, Singapore withdrew this proposal.

3. ASEAN Industrial Complementation ("AIC")

In addition to the above schemes involving the government sector, early
proposals for economic cooperation also comprised two schemes of
private sector cooperation — the ASEAN Industrial Complementation
("AIC") Scheme and the ASEAN Industrial Joint Venture ("AIJV")
Scheme. The moving force behind these schemes was the ASEAN
Chambers of Commerce and Industry ("ASEAN-CCI").[34]

When the AIP Scheme ran into difficulties, the focus of
cooperation turned toward industrial complementation in the form

of the AIC. This scheme was governed by the Basic Agreement on ASEAN Industrial Complementation entered into on 18 June 1981 in Manila.[35] These projects consisted of organized trade exchanges of specified or manufactured products as agreed among the member states and required the participation of at least four member states unless otherwise approved. Cooperation took the form of coordination of investment projects so that ASEAN companies would not compete with each other. The objective of the AIC was to divide different stages of production of vertically integrated industries among different ASEAN countries in order to take advantage of economies of scale.

AIC products were industrial products manufactured in an ASEAN member country and allocated to that particular country as its participation in the AIC package. Such products were entitled to the privileges provided for in the Agreement, including exclusivity privileges for a limited period of time and preferences in accordance with the Agreement on ASEAN Preferential Trading Arrangements.

The AIC Scheme was designed to encourage the private sector's contribution to economic cooperation by giving it the initiative to identify and formulate the AIC package. Again progress was very slow in the area of industrial complementation due to national interests and the difficulty in finding projects in which all member states could participate. AIC Schemes were attempted in the automotive sector, but one of the major difficulties was that differences in brands and types of products among the ASEAN countries made cooperation difficult.

This led to the development of the Brand-to-Brand Complementation ("BBC") Scheme for the automotive industry.[36] The BBC Scheme was an offshoot of the AIC concerned with the production and exchange of automotive parts and components to facilitate horizontal specialization in the production of these products in the region. The Scheme encouraged automotive brand owners to exploit economies of scale of production through rationalization and specialization of automotive production units by allowing exchange of approved automotive parts and components for specific automotive brand models. These automotive parts and components were granted 50% Margin of Preference ("MOP") by the participating importing countries as well as local content accreditation.[37] The aim of this scheme was to allow the private sector to determine the division of production within the same brand. Nominations for a BBC Scheme were made by the brand owner and were to be submitted to COIME[38] with specifications of brand, vehicle type, model, sub-groups, components or parts and proposed participating countries.[39]

Again, this scheme met with limited success, with Singapore, Brunei and Indonesia choosing not to join the BBC Scheme.[40]

4. Basic Agreement on ASEAN Industrial Joint Ventures ("AIJV")[41]

The ASEAN Industrial Joint Venture ("AIJV") was approved by the ASEAN foreign ministers on 7 November 1983.[42] Because of the problems with the AIP and the AIC Schemes, the AIJV was designed to give more flexibility to industrial cooperation. The AIJV Scheme provided a framework for encouraging the private sectors of the ASEAN member countries to join together in industrial ventures and take advantage of the economies of scale of production made possible by the presence of a large regional market. Advantages offered to AIJV partners included access to an enlarged market through preferential market access to participating countries and, in certain circumstances, a monopoly position in the market for limited periods of time in order to establish a market presence.

An AIJV did not require the participation of all (or most) member states but only required private investors from at least two ASEAN member states and allowed for participation by a non-ASEAN partner. Under the Agreement establishing the AIJV Scheme, the equity participation from each participating ASEAN country was set to be a minimum of 5% and the total ASEAN equity ownership to be a minimum of 51%[43] (the other 49% could be held by a non-ASEAN partner).

Again, as with the PTA, the advantage of an AIJV was an enlarged market. Not only did the manufacturer have access to the domestic market where the investment was located but it also had a preferential access to the market of the other ASEAN JV partner(s). As well as preferences being given by the member country(ies) of the other AIJV partner(s), preferences could also be offered by the other non-AIJV ASEAN members.

Under the AIJV Scheme, approved AIJV entity and products enjoyed exclusive AIJV privileges for a period of 4 years from the date of its commercial production. After the exclusivity period, any other company in the participating countries, manufacturing the same products as an AIJV product, upon application and issuance of a certificate of entitlement, could also enjoy the same AIJV privilege. Importation of an approved AIJV product enjoyed a 90% MOP from the prevailing MFN rate and local content accreditation where applicable.

The AIJV Scheme was essentially a private sector initiative which was brought into effect by the *Basic Agreement on ASEAN Industrial Joint Ventures* ("BAAIJV"), initially adopted on 7 November 1983. This original agreement was amended by Supplementary Agreements dated 7 November 1983 and 16 June 1987, and replaced by a revised BAAIJV, signed at the Third ASEAN Summit Meeting in Manila on 15 December 1987. The revised BAAIJV made a number of improvements to the scheme to render it more flexible, easier to implement and more attractive to investors.

At their meeting in October 1992, the ASEAN Economic Ministers initialled the Second Protocol to Amend the Revised BAAIJV. The Protocol provides for the adoption of a Common Effective Preferential Tariff ("CEPT") on AIJV products; the removal of the exclusivity privilege; the relaxation of the minimum 5% equity requirement; and the extension of the waiver period of the multilateralization provision of the PTA.[44]

The objective of the governments of the ASEAN member states in establishing the AIJV Scheme was to provide a format within which the ASEAN governments and the private sector through the ASEAN Chambers of Commerce and Industry ("ASEAN-CCI") could collaborate to identify opportunities, formulate programmes and design projects for pursuing industrial joint ventures on the basis of mutual and equitable benefits for the member countries and increased industrial production for the region as a whole. The premise of the AIJV Scheme was that consolidation of markets among ASEAN countries, even if only two countries were involved, could support meaningful industrial joint ventures which could strengthen and broaden the base of the industrial sector of their respective economies by more efficient utilization of their industries and expansion of trade in the region.

The AIJV Scheme was administered by the ASEAN Committee on Industry, Minerals and Energy ("COIME") until this committee was dissolved by the Singapore Declaration of 1992. COIME was one of the five permanent economic committees within the ASEAN through which the ASEAN Economic Ministers directed economic cooperation within ASEAN.

As with the above schemes, the AIJV Scheme had only a very limited success.

At the 27th Meeting of the ASEAN Economic Ministers on 7-8 September 1995, the Ministers agreed that until a new ASEAN industrial cooperation scheme was adopted and implemented, all new applications for the AIJV and BBC Schemes could be processed and approved under the existing schemes. All approved projects would continue to enjoy the rightful privileges.[45] Approved AIJV entities and products will continue to enjoy AIJV privileges until 31 December 2002.

The existing AIJV and BBC Schemes will be phased out with the introduction of the new industrial cooperation schemes.

Progress towards economic cooperation through these agreements was relatively modest.[46] This had much to do with the nature of ASEAN itself and of the member states which comprise ASEAN. As discussed above, at the time ASEAN was formed, the individual member states were hesitant to accord it strong powers over the members, preferring to maintain a high level of individual sovereignty. This attitude still continues to a large degree today. However, the Members of ASEAN have been entering into closer economic relations and this has led to the evolution of more agreements to govern this relationship.

The purpose of examining these schemes is not so much to provide the details of these schemes (they are of limited importance now with the implementation of AFTA), as it is to illustrate the complexities of economic cooperation and the need for detailed rules to govern the economic relations of parties. An examination of the schemes and the agreements to implement them illustrates the necessity of the development of a legal framework to regulate the conduct of their economic activity.[47] The Agreements set out rules which form part of the evolving legal framework in ASEAN. As economic cooperation among the parties evolves, so does the legal framework. Law is not static, but dynamic, and the framework evolves to take into account developments in the economic, social and political arenas. The following chapter examines how this framework is evolving in ASEAN with the implementation of the Framework Agreement on Enhancing ASEAN Economic Cooperation.

Endnotes

1   *ASEAN Economic Cooperation for the 1990s — A Report Prepared for the ASEAN Standing Committee* (Philippines: Philippine Institute for Development Studies and the ASEAN Secretariat, 1992), at 7.

2   As noted above (Chapter 2), the Members of ASEAN set up the ASEAN Geneva Committee to coordinate the member countries' position on matters involving trade and tariff negotiations in Geneva.

3   The MFN ideal is also embodied in many other treaties, however, the following discussion will be restricted to MFN within GATT.

4   The 'enabling clause'. See discussion, *infra*, Chapter 8. 'The "enabling clause" is presumed to continue in the WTO, although its status may not be entirely clear.' (John H Jackson, *The World Trading System — Law and Policy of International Economic Relations*, 2nd ed (Cambridge: The MIT Press, 1997), p 164.)

5   See, eg, Hans Christoph Rieger, 'The Treaty of Rome and its Relevance for ASEAN' (1991) 8 *ASEAN Economic Bulletin*, pp 160-172, and references cited there.

6   *Ibid*, pp 160-161.

7   Straits Times, Singapore, 14 January 1989.

8   '...ASEAN will never be like the EU': Rodolofo C Severino, 'Will ASEAN be Like the EU?', remarks at the European Policy Center, Brussels, 23 March 2001 (http://www.aseansec.org/secgen/sg_eu.htm).

9   See, *inter alia*, Hans Christoph Rieger and Tan Loong-Hoo, 'Background Paper – Colloquium on ASEAN Economic Co-operation: The Tasks Ahead', in *ASEAN – The Tasks Ahead* (Singapore: ISEAS, 1987), pp 35-80, especially at 38-55); and Alan Broinowski, ed, *ASEAN into the 1990s* (New York: St. Martin's Press, 1990) especially at pp 58-82: Srikanta Chatterjee, 'ASEAN Economic Co-operation in the 1980s and 1990s'.

10   *Economic Cooperation for ASEAN*, Report of a United Nations Study Team on ASEAN Economic Cooperation (United Nations, 1973).

11 Joint Communique of the Seventh ASEAN Ministerial Meeting, Jakarta, Indonesia, 7-9 May 1974, para 10, *TAPR*, Document I.B.4.a(7).

12 See, eg, Sopiee, Noordin, et al (eds), *ASEAN at the Crossroads* (Malaysia: Institute of Strategic and International Studies, 1987).

13 See *infra*, Chapter 4.

14 Part B, para 3(ii).

15 Agreement on ASEAN Preferential Trading Arrangements, Manila, 24 February 1977 (in force, 1 January 1978), *TAPR*, Document I.B.7.a, as amended by the Protocol on Improvements on Extension of Tariff Preferences Under the ASEAN Preferential Trading Arrangement, Manila, 15 December 1987, *TAPR*, Document I.B.7.g.

16 Article 1(1).

17 Article 8.

18 Initially, items with an annual import value of less than US$50,000 in 1978 trade statistics qualified for tariff reductions of 20% across-the-board. Later, the cut-off ceiling was raised to US$500,000 in May 1991 and to US$1 million in January 1992. In November 1992 the ceiling was further raised to US$10 million (Suthiphand Chirathivat, 'ASEAN Economic Integration with the World through AFTA', Chapter 2, in Tan, Joseph (ed), *AFTA in the Changing International Economy* (Singapore: ISEAS, 1996), footnote 3).

19 Manila, 15 December 1987, *TAPR*, Document I.B.7.g.

20 40% in the case of Indonesia except that on certain categories of manufactured products to be agreed on from time to time, the requirement of 50% of non-ASEAN content could apply.

21 From 60% to 42% in the case of Indonesia. [To be reviewed with a view to reverting to original levels after this period.]

22 Bangkok, 15 December 1995, *TAPR*, Document I.B.7.k.

23 This corresponded with the phase in of the PTAs into the CEPT.

24 Manila, 15 December 1987, *TAPR*, Document I.B.7.i.

25 See, Gerald Tan, 'ASEAN Preferential Trading Arrangements — An Overview' (1987), in KS Sandhu, et al (eds), *The ASEAN Reader* (Singapore: ISEAS, 1992), pp 237-241 at 240; and see, United Nations Conference on Trade and Development, 'Regional, Subregional, and Interregional Economic Cooperation and Integration Among Developing Countries: Exchange of Experiences Among Groupings of Developing Countries — An Evaluation of the ASEAN Experience', UNCTAD/ECDC/331, 25 September 1992, especially at 3: 'The ASEAN trade liberalization programme is more instructive on account of its shortcomings. The absence of complementarities among the ASEAN economies with similar commodity endowments was the basic drawback in the ASEAN region.'

26 See, Florin A Alburo, 'The ASEAN Summit and ASEAN Economic Co-operation', in Seiji Naya and Akira Takayama (eds), *Essays in Honour of Professor Shinichi Ichimura* (Singapore: ISEAS, and Honolulu: Resource Systems Institute, East-West Center, 1990), pp 299-306 at 302.

27 Meyanathan, Sahathavan and Haron, Ismail, 'ASEAN trade cooperation: A survey of the issues', in Sopiee, Noordin, et al (eds) *ASEAN at the Crossroads* (Malaysia: Institute of Strategic and International Studies, 1987) at 27.

28 Joint Press Statement, The Twenty-Third Meeting of the ASEAN Economic Ministers, Kuala Lumpur, Malaysia, 7-8 October 1991, para 23, *TAPR*, Document I.B.4.b(23).

29 Joint Press Statement, The Seventh AFTA Council Meeting, Brunei Darussalam, 6 September 1995, para 11, *TAPR*, Document I.B.8 (aa). The ASEAN Free Trade Area and the CEPT are discussed in Chapter 4, *infra*.

30 Part B.2.(i).

31 *TAPR*, Document I.B.7.d.

32 Supplementary Agreement to the Basic Agreement on ASEAN Industrial Project ASEAN Urea Project (Indonesia), Kuala Lumpur, 6 March 1980, and ditto (Malaysia): *ASEAN Documents Series 1967-1988* (3rd ed), (Jakarta: ASEAN Secretariat, 1988), pp 265-267 (Indonesia) and 268-270 (Malaysia).

33 Supplementary Agreement to the Basic Agreement on ASEAN Industrial Projects — ASEAN Potash Mining Projects (Thailand), Thailand, 20 July 1991: *ASEAN Documents Series 1991-1992* (Jakarta: ASEAN Secretariat, 1992) pp 42-44.

34 The role of the private sector in leading economic development and in furthering economic cooperation is increasing and becoming more important. An example within ASEAN is the role the private sector has played in the development of the Growth Triangle concept. This is very much a development which has been led by the private sector (see discussion in Chapter 4). The role of the private sector will be increasing even more in the future.

35 *TAPR*, Document I.B.7(e).

36 Memorandum of Understanding Brand-to-Brand Complementation on the Automotive Industry Under the Basic Agreement on ASEAN Industrial Complementation (BAAIC), Pattaya, Thailand, 18 October 1988, *TAPR*, Document I.B.7(j).

37 *Ibid*, section 9.

38 Now the Senior Economic Officials Meeting ("SEOM") which replaced COIME as of the Singapore Declaration of 1992.

39 Memorandum on BBC, Section 7, para (a).

40 Pangestu, Mari, Hadi Soesastro and Mubariq Ahmad, 'A New Look at Intra-ASEAN Economic Co-operation', (1992) 8 *ASEAN Economic Bulletin*, 333 at 338. However, the Memorandum of Understanding on the BBC scheme was amended to enable Indonesia to participate. See, 'Ministers accelerate implementation of AFTA', *ASEAN Update*, October 1994, pp 1-3 at 3.

41 For a more detailed treatment of this topic, see, Paul J Davidson, 'ASEAN Industrial Joint Ventures' (Ottawa: ASEAN Canada Business Council, 1989).

42 Basic Agreement on ASEAN Industrial Joint Ventures, Jakarta, 7 November 1983: *ASEAN Documents Series 1967-1988* (3rd ed), pp 274-278.

43 This requirement was liberalised for companies applying for AIJV status up to 31 December 1996. For companies applying before that time the minimum ASEAN

equity ownership was reduced to 40%: Revised Basic Agreement on ASEAN Industrial Joint Ventures, 1987, Article 1(5), as amended by the Protocol to Amend the Revised Basic Agreement on ASEAN Industrial Joint Ventures, 1 January 1991, *TAPR*, Document I.B.7.f(2) and the Protocol to amend the BAAIJV Agreement, initialled at the 26th AEM Meeting (Joint Press Statement, 26th Meeting of the ASEAN Economic Ministers, Chiangmai, Thailand, 22-23 September 1994, *TAPR*, Document I.B.4.b(26)).

The 1994 Protocol also lowered the local content requirement from 50% to 40% to align the rules of origin of the AIJV scheme to that of the CEPT scheme.

The 1994 Protocol further provided that the minimum ASEAN equity will not apply to an entity in any of the following cases:

a) where the participating countries in a proposed AIJV product agree to a higher equity participation by non-ASEAN investors;

b) where more than 50% of the product produced by such entity will be exported to non-ASEAN markets;

c) where the product is already being produced by an entity in a participating country prior to its inclusion in the final list; or

d) where an entity has already been approved by a participating country to produce that product prior to the inclusion of the product in the final list.

44 Joint Press Statement of the 24th Meeting of the ASEAN Economic Ministers, The Philippines, 22-23 October 1992, para 10, *TAPR*, Document I.B.4.b(24).

45 Joint Press Statement of the 27th Meeting of the ASEAN Economic Ministers, Brunei Darussalam, 7-8 September 1995, para 14, *TAPR*, Document I.B.4.b (27). See discussion of ASEAN Industrial Cooperation (AICO) Scheme, *infra*, Chapter 4.

46 For an examination of these programmes and a review of their progress to early 1991, see, Naya, Seiji and Michael G Plummer, 'ASEAN Economic Co-operation in the New International Economic Environment' (1991) 7 *ASEAN Economic Bulletin*, pp 261-276.

See also, Pangestu, Mari, Hadi Soesastro and Mubariq Ahmad, 'A New Look at Intra-ASEAN Economic Co-operation' (1992) 8 *ASEAN Economic Bulletin*, 333-352, especially at 335: 'Progress toward intra-ASEAN economic co-operation since the ASEAN Concord signed in Bali in 1976 has been at best slow and at worst negligible, even after the third ASEAN Summit held in Manila, which was aimed at providing the breakthrough for more effective economic co-operation.'

For other discussions of the ineffectiveness of these schemes, see Naronchai Akrasanee and David Stifel, 'The Political Economy of the ASEAN Free Trade Area', in Pearl Imada and Seiji Naya (eds), *AFTA, The Way Ahead*, (Singapore: ISEAS, 1992), pp 27-47; and Florian A Alburo, 'The ASEAN Summit and ASEAN Economic Co-operation', in KS Sandhu, et al (eds), *The ASEAN Reader* (Singapore: ISEAS, 1992) pp 203-207.

47 '...closer regional economic integration requires basing it on binding legal foundations if integration is to be stable, credible and effective. The commitments

undertaken must be clear, firm and enforceable, and those making them cannot lightly back out of them..': 'The ASEAN Way and the Rule of Law', Address by Rodolfo C Severino, Secretary-General of ASEAN, at the International Law Conference on ASEAN Legal Systems and Regional Integration, Kuala Lumpur, 3 September 2001. (http://www.aseansec.org/newdata/asean_way.htm).

• CHAPTER 4 •

THE NEW FRAMEWORK FOR ECONOMIC COOPERATION

The Framework Agreement on Enhancing ASEAN Economic Cooperation

ASEAN has made remarkable strides in economic cooperation since its very humble beginnings. Starting with bold and innovative approaches in the late 1980s and early 1990s, ASEAN leaders began to develop more ambitious means of economic cooperation. These were increasingly framed in terms of international agreements among the ASEAN members at the same time that political diplomatic imperatives were falling in importance. While many of these initiatives are only now being developed, they are indicative of the intentions of the ASEAN leaders to create a unified marketplace in a wider Southeast Asian region, and are indicative of a movement to more of a binding legal framework.[1]

A new framework for economic cooperation was agreed upon at the 1992 Singapore Summit. This framework is set out in the Framework Agreement on Enhancing ASEAN Economic Cooperation.[2] The Agreement is broadly-worded and embodies the general covenant among ASEAN member states to cooperate in a number of areas. As its name suggests, this agreement is not concerned with the details of implementing economic cooperation in ASEAN, but, rather, sets out a framework for enhancing ASEAN economic cooperation. As such, although it further addresses some of the issues set out above, its provisions are in very general terms. Agreements in more precise and specific terms need to be enacted by the ASEAN states to implement the mandate of the Framework Agreement. A number of areas of cooperation are set out.

1. Cooperation in trade

Article 2, Part A deals with cooperation in trade. This Part sets out the agreement of the Member States to establish and participate in the ASEAN Free Trade Area ("AFTA"). This part of the agreement has been implemented through the Common Effective Preferential Tariff ("CEPT") Agreement (see *infra*).

2. Cooperation in industry, minerals and energy[3]

Member States agree to increase investments, industrial linkages and complementarity by adopting new and innovative measures, as well as strengthening existing arrangements in ASEAN. They also agree to provide flexibility for new forms of industrial cooperation, to strengthen cooperation in the development of the minerals sector, and to enhance cooperation in the field of energy. The ASEAN Industrial Cooperation ("AICO") Scheme, discussed *infra*, is an example of the new approach to increased industrial linkages and complementarity.

With regard to cooperation in minerals, the Member Countries have focused on the development and utilization of industrial minerals. At the Fifth ASEAN Summit, they approved the Programme of Action for cooperation in minerals to promote trade and investment in industrial minerals in support of the industrialisation of Member Countries and to meet the demand of mineral-intensive manufacturing and construction sectors. The Bangkok Declaration of 1995 stated that, "ASEAN shall implement a programme of action that will further enhance trade and investment in industrial minerals ...(and) a mineral database shall be set in place and be immediately operationalized ...".[4] The First ASEAN Senior Officials Meeting on Minerals ("ASOMM") was held in October 1996 in Bali, Indonesia. ASOMM was established as a formal forum for ASEAN minerals cooperation. To realize the objectives of the Programme of Action, ASOMM established the ASEAN Industrial Minerals Information System ("AIMIS") to promote trade and investment in industrial minerals

There has been much activity in the area of cooperation in energy. The ASEAN Economic Ministers on Energy have held regular meetings and, in 1995, agreed to change the name of their meeting from the

ASEAN Economic Ministers' Meeting on Energy Cooperation ("AEMMEC") to the ASEAN Ministers on Energy Meeting ("AMEM").[5] Accordingly, the Senior Officials' Meeting on Energy Cooperation ("SOMEC") became the Senior Officials' Meeting on Energy ("SOME"). The most recent plan for cooperation is the "ASEAN Plan of Action for Energy Cooperation 1999-2004",[6] endorsed by the Senior Officials Meeting on Energy of the Seventeenth ASEAN Ministers on Energy Meeting, 1-2 July 1999, Bangkok, Thailand, and adopted by the Seventeenth ASEAN Ministers on Energy Meeting, 3 July 1999.

3. Cooperation in finance and banking[7]

Cooperation in trade and investment would be incomplete without providing for the free flow of capital and other financial resources. Therefore, the Member States agree to strengthen and develop further ASEAN economic cooperation in the field of capital markets, as well as to find new measures to increase cooperation in this area. They further agree to encourage and facilitate free movement of capital and other resources.

ASEAN finance cooperation has been strengthened with the various decisions made at the ASEAN Finance Ministers Meetings ("AFMM"). The first AFMM was held on 1 March 1997[8]. The Ministers signed the Ministerial Understanding on ASEAN Cooperation in Finance which provides a framework to enhance cooperation within their existing institutional arrangement in several areas of finance which include banking and finance; financial and capital markets; customs matters; insurance matters; taxation and human resouce development in the area of finance. The Ministers also signed the ASEAN Agreement on Customs which further enhances ASEAN cooperation in customs activities.

The Finance Ministers have established a network of bilateral swap arrangements ("BSA") and repurchase agreements between the ASEAN member countries and China, Japan and the Republic of Korea (ASEAN+3). Bilateral swap arrangements are to be complementary and supplementary to IMF facilities. The terms and modalities of the BSA take into account the different economic fundamentals, specific circumstances and financing needs of individual countries. These mechanisms aim to provide liquidity support to members in the event of temporary balance of payment difficulties.

4. Cooperation in food, agriculture and forestry:[9]

Agricultural products were originally excluded from the CEPT Scheme for AFTA (see *infra*). However, security of food supply within the region has always been a concern of the ASEAN Member States and in the Framework Agreement they agree to strengthen regional cooperation in the areas of development, production and promotion of agricultural products for ensuring food security and upgrading information exchanges in ASEAN. They further agree to enhance technical joint cooperation to better manage, conserve, develop and market forest resources.

Various measures have been implemented to promote the production and trade in agriculture and forestry products. A Memorandum of Understanding on ASEAN Cooperation and Joint Approaches on Agriculture and Forest Products Promotion Scheme has been designed to improve the competitiveness of ASEAN agriculture and forest products. At the Twentieth Meeting of The ASEAN Ministers on Agriculture And Forestry ("AMAF") held in Hanoi, 17-18 September 1998, the Ministers endorsed the Strategic Plan of Action on ASEAN Cooperation In Food, Agriculture and Forestry for the 1999-2004 period[10]. The Strategic Plan identifies strategic thrusts, action programmes and activities focused on enhancing food security, and the international competitiveness of ASEAN's food, agricultural and forest products, sustainable utilisation and conservation of natural resources, encouragement of the private sector's increased involvement, and enhancement of joint approaches on international and regional issues.

5. Cooperation in transportation and communications[11]

These are two further areas where cooperation is necessary in order to have effective economic cooperation. Member States have therefore agreed to further enhance regional cooperation for providing safe, efficient and innovative transportation and communications infra-structure networks. They also agree to continue to improve and develop the intra-country postal and telecommunications system to provide cost-effective, high quality and customer-oriented services.

With regard to cooperation in the transport sector, ASEAN Member Countries have signed the ASEAN Framework Agreement on the Facilitation of Goods in Transit[12], and at the Seventh ASEAN Transport Ministers Meeting held in Kuala Lumpur, Malaysia on 25-26 October 2001,[13] the Ministers agreed to request the member countries to study the desirability and feasibility of phased implementation to expedite the effective implementation of this Agreement. The Ministers also discussed signing the ASEAN Framework Agreements on Multimodal Transport and Facilitation of Inter-State Transport and the Protocols on Designation of Transit Transport Routes, Railways Border and Interchange Stations and Dangerous Goods, as well as the signing of the ASEAN Memorandum of Understanding on Air Freight Services.

In recognition of the emergence of info-communications issues in ASEAN, particularly in the context of the e-ASEAN Initiative, the first ASEAN telecommunications senior officials meeting ("TELSOM") was convened in Brunei Darussalam in October 2000, and the First ASEAN Telecommunications Ministers Meeting ("TELMIN") was held in Kuala Lumpur on 13-14 July 2001.[14] At the First TELMIN the Ministers also concluded a Ministerial Understanding on ASEAN Cooperation in Telecommunications and Information Technology.[15]

This Ministerial Understanding formalizes ASEAN cooperation in the telecommunications and IT sector and covers:

1. Establishment of the ASEAN Information Infrastructure ("AII") and the further advancement of the e-ASEAN initiative;
2. Facilitation of intra-ASEAN trade and investment;
3. Coordination and harmonization of policies and programs;
4. Promotion and development of indigenous content;
5. Promotion of private sector participation and enhancing public-private sector collaboration in regional programs and activities; and

6. Bridging the digital divide within ASEAN by encouraging capacity building and human resource development and enhancing access to and use of telecommunications and IT.

6. Other areas of cooperation:[16]

In addition to the above identified areas of cooperation, Member States also agree to increase cooperation in research and development, technology transfer, tourism promotion, human resource development and other economic-related areas, and to regularly consult and exchange views on regional and international developments and trends, and identify ASEAN priorities and challenges.

Areas which have seen progress in cooperation include tourism and intellectual property. Member Countries have signed the ASEAN Framework Agreement on Intellectual Property Cooperation,[17] and adopted the Programme of Action for 1996 — 1998 to carry out the activities of the Framework Agreement which included measures to enhance and strengthen intellectual property enforcement, protection, administration, legislation, and enhancement of public awareness of intellectual property. The Hanoi Plan of Action provided for further intellectual property cooperation, including to ensure adequate and effective protection, legislation, administration and enforcement, of intellectual property rights in the region based on the principles of Most Favoured Nation ("MFN") treatment, national treatment and transparency as set out in the TRIPS Agreement.[18]

ASEAN cooperation in tourism was formalised in 1976 following the formation of the Sub-Committee on Tourism ("SCOT") under the ASEAN Committee on Trade and Tourism. ASEAN SCOT was effective in initiating regional tourism projects in the functional areas of promotion, marketing and research. In 1998, the ASEAN Tourism Ministers signed the Ministerial Understanding on ASEAN Cooperation in Tourism and the Plan of Action on ASEAN Cooperation in Tourism.

In all these areas a number of agreements have been entered into. These agreements are legally binding and are forming a structure for economic cooperation exemplified by more of a legal framework.

The most significant step in enhancing cooperation in trade in ASEAN was the decision of the Fourth ASEAN Summit in 1992 to establish the ASEAN Free Trade Area. This is the most important development in the framework for economic cooperation.

The Asean Free Trade Area[19]

> ... the ASEAN Free Trade Area agenda is undoubtedly the most ambitious, and corollarily (sic), the most demanding [among all intra-ASEAN economic co-operation programmes devised by the ASEAN member states]. Imposing relatively more specific and strict obligations on the parties thereto, the Agreement on the Common Effective Preferential Tariff (CEPT) Scheme for the ASEAN Free Trade Area in fact ended ASEAN's 25-year selfimposed prohibition against "binding economic targets and schedules".[20]

Background to AFTA:

Initially the concept of a free trade area or customs union within ASEAN was rejected and, as discussed above, other methods of more limited economic cooperation were adopted. Neither the efforts of ASEAN preferential trading arrangements ("PTA"), nor attempts at industrial cooperation achieved many results to increase intra-regional trade and investment. It was only recently that ASEAN has tried to revive institutionalized integration within the grouping.[21] Support for the concept caught hold when the idea was revived in early 1991 by the then Thai Prime Minister, Anand Panyarachun, and endorsed by Prime Minister Goh Chok Tong of Singapore. The ASEAN Free Trade Arrangement represented an evolution of ASEAN from a forum aimed mainly at promoting peace and stability in the region to one aimed at deepening the economic partnerships in the region.

In preparation for the January 1992 Summit in Singapore, the Secretary-General of the ASEAN Secretariat was requested by the ASEAN Standing Committee to organize a study to yield ideas for economic cooperation for the future. Their report[22] was submitted to the ASEAN Economic Ministers meeting in October 1991 and served as input to the Fourth ASEAN Summit in Singapore in January 1992. In sum, the report stressed "the need for ASEAN to enhance its regional cooperation efforts in a rapidly-changing international economic environment.[23] To accomplish this, the study recommend[ed] that ASEAN move forward in its ASEAN economic cooperation programs by eventually creating an "ASEAN Free Trade Area Plus" arrangement...."[24]

The purpose of AFTA is, not so much to increase intra-ASEAN trade, but it is a way for members of ASEAN to cooperate to increase their international competitiveness and integration with the world.[25] By increasing the free flow of goods in the ASEAN region, ASEAN would be increasingly attractive as an area for trade and international investment. ASEAN owes much of its prosperity and progress to the open multilateral trading system and it is in the interest of ASEAN to ensure that multilateralism is not usurped by regionalism.

The concept of a free trade area was agreed to by the AEM at their October 1991 meeting and received official acceptance by the Heads of Government at the 1992 ASEAN Summit. At the Summit, the guiding principles, mechanism, product coverage, and timetable for AFTA were set. The main texts were: the Singapore Declaration of 1992; the Framework Agreement on Enhancing ASEAN Economic Cooperation; and the Agreement on the Common Effective Preferential Tariff ("CEPT") Scheme.[26] It was agreed that:

> ASEAN shall establish the ASEAN Free Trade Area using the Common Effective Preferential Tariff (CEPT) Scheme as the main mechanism within a time frame of 15 years beginning 1 January 1993 with the ultimate effective tariffs ranging from 0% to 5%.[27]

Thus, the primary instrument for implementing the AFTA is the CEPT Agreement.[28] It has been decided that the CEPT Scheme should take precedence over the AIJV and that products covered under the ASEAN PTA may be transferred to the CEPT. The objective of AFTA was, originally, to reduce AFTA tariff rates to between 0% and5 % within fifteen years beginning 1 January 1993. The member states of ASEAN have agreed to speed up implementation (see *infra*).

Products Covered under the CEPT Agreement

In principle, the free trade area now covers all manufactured and agricultural products although the time limits for including individual products may vary.

1. Inclusion list

Products in the Inclusion List are those that have to undergo immediate liberalization through reduction in intra-regional tariff rates, removal of quantitative restrictions and other non-tariff barriers. Tariffs on these products are to be brought down to 0-5% by the year 2002 for the ASEAN-6. The new Members of ASEAN have up to 2006 (Vietnam), 2008 (Laos and Myanmar) and 2010 (Cambodia) to meet this deadline.

2. Temporary Exclusion List ("TEL")

Products in the Temporary Exclusion List can be excluded from trade liberalization for a temporary period. However, the Temporary Exclusion List was eliminated at the 26th AEM in September 1994, and all these products eventually have to be transferred into the Inclusion List and begin a process of tariff reduction so that tariffs on these products are reduced to 0%-5%. For the ASEAN-6, products in the Temporary Exclusion List will be transferred to the Inclusion List in five equal installments of 20% beginning 1 January 1996.[29] The new Members of ASEAN have been given a longer period to begin the transfer process — beginning in 1999 (Vietnam), 2001 (Laos and Myanmar) and 2003 (Cambodia).

ASEAN has also agreed on a Protocol Regarding the Implementation of the CEPT Scheme Temporary Exclusion List,[30] which is intended to provide some flexibility to countries facing real problems on their last tranche of manufactured TEL products. The Protocol allows countries to temporarily delay the transfer of these TEL products or suspend concessions on those TEL products already transferred into the Inclusion List. The mechanism is based on Article XXVIII (Modification of Schedules) of GATT 1994.

3) Sensitive list

The Sensitive List contains unprocessed agricultural products, which are given a longer period for integration into the free trade area. The commitment to reduce tariffs to 0%-5%, remove quantitative restrictions and other non-tariff barriers is extended up to the year 2010 for the original ASEAN-6. The new members of ASEAN have up to 2013 (Vietnam), 2015 (Laos and Myanmar) and 2017 (Cambodia) to meet this deadline.

4. General Exception (GE) List

The General Exception List contains products which are permanently excluded from the free trade area for reasons of national security, protection of human, animal or plant life and health and articles of artistic, historic and archaeological value.

Rules of Origin

Rules of origin are necessary in a free trade area in order to prevent trade deflection when partner countries maintain different external tariff levels. Without such rules, third country goods will enter the free trade area via the lowest tariff point and then move duty free to other countries within the free trade area. To ensure that the benefit of the Agreement accrues to those products produced or manufactured within ASEAN and not to third party goods, the Agreement sets out rules of origin which a product must satisfy in order to receive preferential treatment under the Agreement. Article 2(4) provides:

> A product shall be deemed to be originating from ASEAN Member States, if at least 40% of its content originates from any Member State.

Thus, to be recognized as originated in ASEAN countries, goods must have a local content of not less than 40% which can be either from a single ASEAN country or cumulative.

Emergency Measures

Emergency measures, to limit the flow of trade, are provided for along the lines of what is available under the GATT. Article 6 of the CEPT Agreement provides that:

1. If, as a result of the implementation of this Agreement, import of a particular product eligible under the CEPT Scheme is increasing in such a manner as to cause or threaten to cause serious injury to sectors producing like or directly competitive products in the importing Member States, the importing Member States may, to the extent and for such time as may be necessary to prevent or to remedy such injury, suspend preferences provisionally and without discrimination, subject to Article 6(3) of this Agreement....

3. Where emergency measures are taken pursuant to this Article, immediate notice of such action shall be given to the Council [created by the Agreement] and such action may be the subject of consultation as provided....

Operation of the CEPT Scheme[31]

Full implementation of the scheme became possible only in mid-July 1993 when all six countries had come up with their respective lists of products for inclusion in the Common Effective Preferential Tariff and programmes for tariff cuts.*

The main mechanism to achieve AFTA is the CEPT Scheme.[32] The CEPT Scheme provides for tariff reductions to take place according to two schedules.

---

*   'ASEAN set to implement fully scheme for reducing tariffs', *Straits Times*, 15 July 1993, p.15.

1. Normal Track Reduction of Tariffs

The schedule of effective "normal track" preferential tariff reductions is set out in Article 4 of the CEPT Agreement and may be divided into two parts. The first relates to imports with existing tariff rates in excess of 20%; the second to those with existing tariff rates of 20% or below as at 1 January 1993.

For products with existing tariff rates in excess of 20%, the original CEPT Scheme called for a two-tier process of reduction of tariffs. First, the reduction from existing tariff rates to 20% was to be done within a time frame of five to eight years starting 1 January 1993. This reduction was to take place subject to a programme of reduction to be decided by each member state.[33] After this initial phase, the subsequent reduction of tariff rates from 20% or below to the target rate of between 0%-5% was to be done within a time frame of seven years. The rate of reduction during this phase was to be at a minimum of 5% quantum per reduction and a programme of reduction was to be decided by each Member State at the start of the programme.

For products with existing tariff rates of 20% or below as at 1 January 1993, tariffs were to be reduced to the 0%-5% target range within the 15-year implementation period for AFTA according to a programme of tariff reductions to be decided upon by each individual Member State.

In either case, Member States could reduce their tariffs to the 0%-5% range within a period of less than fifteen years, following an accelerated schedule of tariff reduction.

At the AEM held in Singapore in 1993, it was agreed to advance the implementation of tariff reductions to 2 January 1994. The original scheme, allowing countries to formulate their own tariff reduction programmes in terms of starting dates, frequency and depth of cuts as long as tariffs were reduced to no more than 5% by 2008, had resulted in significant differences in each country's start-up dates for the tariff cuts.

2. Fast Track Reduction of Tariffs

At the Singapore Summit, the ASEAN member states identified the following 15 groups of products to be included in the CEPT Scheme for accelerated tariff reductions:[34]

1. vegetable oils;
2. cement;
3. chemicals;
4. pharmaceuticals;
5. fertiliser;
6. plastics;
7. rubber products;
8. leather products;
9. pulp;
10. textiles;
11. ceramic and glass products;
12. gems and jewellery;
13. copper cathodes;
14. electronics; and
15. wooden and rattan furniture.

Import duties on these products were to be reduced to 0%-5% within seven to ten years, rather than the 15-year period for normal reductions. For products with existing import duties above 20%, the duties were to be reduced to 0%-5% within ten years; for products with import duties of 20% and below, the duties were to be reduced to 0%-5% within seven years.

The Accelerated AFTA

1. The 1994 acceleration

ASEAN has decided to speed up the AFTA.[35] At the 26th AEM in September 1994, the time-frame for the implementation of AFTA was revised as follows:

(i)   Normal Track
- to reduce tariff rates above 20% to 20% by 1 January 1998 and subsequently from 20% to 0-5% by 1 January 2003;
- to reduce tariff rates at or below 20% to 0-5% by 1 January 2000.

(ii) Fast Track
- to reduce tariff rates above 20% to 0-5% by 1 January 2000;
- to reduce tariff rates at or below 20% to 0-5% by 1 January 1998.[36]

At their December 1995 summit meeting in Bangkok the Heads of State and Government of ASEAN agreed that ASEAN should further accelerate the progress toward the actualisation of AFTA before the target date of the Year 2003 set at their 1994 meeting, and agreed that Member Countries would maximise the number of items with tariffs reduced to 0%-5% by the year 2000 as well as expand the number of products with tariffs reduced to 0% by the year 2003.[37] Although there was some reservation that it might be difficult for some countries to comply within this time-frame, no ASEAN country openly rejected this proposal.[38]

2.   The 1998 acceleration

At the Sixth Summit in December 1998, the members adopted the Statement on Bold Measures[39] which included provisions for the Acceleration of AFTA. To accelerate AFTA, the Leaders agreed that the six original signatories to the Agreement on the Common Effective Preferential Tariff (CEPT) Scheme for AFTA — Brunei Darussalam, Indonesia, Malaysia, the Philippines, Singapore and Thailand — would advance the implementation of AFTA by one year from 2003 to 2002. They also agreed to achieve a minimum of 90% of their total tariff lines with tariffs of 0%-5% by the year 2000, which would account for 90% of intra-ASEAN trade, and that individually, each country would commit to achieve a minimum of 85% of the Inclusion List with tariffs of 0%-5% by the year 2000. Thereafter, this would be increased to a minimum of 90% of the Inclusion list in the 0%-5% tariff range by the year 2001. By 2002, 100% of items in the Inclusion List would have tariffs of 0%-5% with some flexibility. Member Countries also agreed to deepen, as soon as possible, tariff reduction to 0% and to accelerate the transfer of products, which are currently not included in the tariff reduction scheme, into the Inclusion List.

It was further agreed that Vietnam will maximise its tariff lines between 0%-5% by 2003 and that Laos and Myanmar will maximise theirs by 2005; also that the number of tariff lines in the 0% category will be expanded by 2006 for Vietnam and by 2008 for Laos and Myanmar.

Much of this acceleration, has been in response to the recent financial crisis in ASEAN.[40] ASEAN's heads of government issued a mandate to this effect during their informal summit in December 1997.[41]

Much of the goal of an AFTA has now been achieved. As of 1 January 2002, six of the ten member nations of ASEAN have eliminated duties on almost all products they had pledged under the tariff liberalization scheme. "January 1, 2002, is very significant because effectively, most of Southeast Asia will be a free-trade area by then."[42]

ASEAN Integration System of Preferences

In order to narrow the development gap within ASEAN, members of ASEAN have decided to implement an ASEAN Integration System of Preferences for newer members.[43] This will allow Cambodia, Laos, Myanmar and Vietnam to gain tariff-free access to the more developed ASEAN markets earlier than the agreed target date of 2010 for all members. It has been agreed to implement this by the beginning of January 2002. This represents a further development in the legal framework for economic cooperation in ASEAN similar to the preferences given developing members within the WTO and parallels developments in the broader international legal framework.

Other Obligations

The CEPT provides for a number of other obligations as part of the implementation of the AFTA in order that the concessions will not be nullified by other measures.[44]

1. Elimination of quantitative restrictions and non-tariff barriers

Member States are bound to eliminate all quantitative restrictions in respect of products under the CEPT Scheme upon enjoyment of the concessions applicable to those products. Moreover, all other non-tariff barriers are to be eliminated on a gradual basis within five years after the enjoyment of concessions applicable to those products.

2. Foreign exchange restrictions

In order to ensure that the benefits of free trade are not restricted due to foreign exchange conditions, member states are obligated to make exceptions to their foreign exchange restrictions relating to payments for the products under the CEPT Scheme, as well as for repatriation of such payments.

3. Other areas of cooperation

Member States further agree to explore other measures on border and non-border areas of cooperation to supplement and complement the liberalization of trade, including, among others, the harmonization of standards, reciprocal recognition of tests and certification of products, removal of barriers to foreign investments, macroeconomic consultations, rules for fair competition, and promotion of venture capital.

4. Maintenance of concessions

Finally, member states agree that they will not nullify or impair any of the concessions agreed upon in the CEPT Agreement through the application of methods of customs valuation, any new charges or measures restricting trade, except in cases provided for in the Agreement.

Institutional Arrangements

In order to oversee the operation of the Agreement and to ensure that steps towards an AFTA take place and obstacles to its operation are overcome, the Agreement provides for the creation of a supervisory mechanism. This supervisory mechanism is the AFTA Council which is a ministerial-level Council established by the Fourth Summit and comprising one nominee from each Member State and the Secretary-General of the ASEAN Secretariat.[45] The Council meets as and when necessary, but at least once a year, and is mandated to report to the ASEAN Economic Ministers ("AEM"). The ASEAN Secretariat provides support to the Council for supervising, coordinating and reviewing the implementation of the Agreement, and assisting the AEM in all matters relating thereto. The Senior Economic Officials' Meeting ("SEOM") also provides support to the AFTA Council.

As well, the ASEAN Secretariat is to monitor and report to the SEOM on the implementation of the Agreement.

At the 26th AEM in September 1994, the Ministers agreed to form an AFTA unit within the ASEAN Secretariat by January 1995 and agreed that AFTA units should be set up in the ASEAN countries to ensure better coordination of CEPT and CEPT-related matters.[46] These have been established.[47]

Ultimate Target of Zero Tariff Rates

ASEAN Member Countries are working towards the elimination of import duties on all products to achieve the eventual objective of a free trade area. Initially, the AFTA Council agreed that the target dates to achieve this objective would be the year 2015 for the six original ASEAN Member Countries and the year 2018 for the new Members of ASEAN.[48] At the 3rd Informal Summit on 28 November 1999, The Heads of State/Government committed the Members of ASEAN to eliminate all import duties by 2010,* ahead of the original schedule, for

---

* The ASEAN Secretary-General, Rodolfo Severino, has proposed that South-east Asian nations should advance their 2010 deadline to cope with rising competition for investments, "Bring down trade barriers earlier, Asean told", *The Straits Times Interactive*, May 29, 2002.

the six original members of ASEAN, and they also agreed in principle to advance the schedule from 2018 to 2015 for the new members of ASEAN, but allowing some sensitive products to follow the original date of 2018.[49]

As the above discussion demonstrates, the move to closer economic cooperation has necessitated the development of detailed rules to allow for, and to regulate, this process. These "rules" are one element of an evolving legal framework. The other element of a legal framework is a mechanism for resolving disputes that arise pursuant to those rules.

Dispute Settlement:[50]

As Member States move to closer economic cooperation under the provisions of the CEPT Agreement it is inevitable that disputes will arise. In order to provide for the settlement of these disputes the following mechanism is provided for in the CEPT Agreement.[51]

1. Member States shall accord adequate opportunity for consultations regarding any representations made by other Member States with respect to any matter affecting the implementation of this Agreement. The Council referred to in Article 7 of this Agreement may seek guidance from the AEM in respect of any matter for which it has not been possible to find a solution during previous consultations.

2. Member States which consider that any other Member State has not carried out its obligations under this Agreement, resulting in the nullification or impairment of any benefit accruing to them, may, with a view to achieving satisfactory adjustment of the matter, make representations to the other Member States concerned, which shall give due consideration to the representations or proposals made to it.

3. Any differences between the Member States concerning the interpretation or application of this Agreement shall, as far as possible, be settled amicably between the parties. If such differences cannot be settled amicably, it shall be submitted

to the Council referred to in Article 7 of this Agreement,
and, if necessary, to the AEM.

At the 27th AEM in September 1995, "In facilitating the
implementation of the CEPT Scheme for AFTA and enhancing
greater economic cooperation, the Ministers agreed to the
establishment of a specific Dispute Settlement Mechanism ("DSM")
for CEPT-AFTA and an umbrella DSM which will cover disputes
arising from all ASEAN agreements on economic cooperation."[52]
This Dispute Settlement Mechanism is discussed in more detail in
Chapter Seven. The new Dispute Settlement Mechanism contains
more detailed procedures for resolving economic disputes that arise,
and demonstrates a movement toward the establishment of a more
"legalistic" approach to economic cooperation. This is a further
example of the development of a legal framework for the regulation
of ASEAN economic relations which will be discussed further in
Chapter 8.

Relation of AFTA to the PTA

As discussed above, the Agreement on ASEAN Preferential Trading
Arrangements ("PTA") was the initial agreement providing for
economic cooperation in the ASEAN region and provides for various
mechanisms to achieve its goal of trade liberalization, including
"other measures" upon which the PTA parties may agree. The CEPT
Agreement in its Preamble notes "that the Agreement on ASEAN
Preferential Trading Arrangements (PTA) ... provides for the
adoption of various instruments on trade liberalization on a
preferential basis" and further states that the CEPT Agreement is
entered into "DESIRING to effect improvements on the ASEAN
PTA in consonance with ASEAN's international commitments".
Thus, the CEPT Agreement is in effect an implementing instrument
of the PTA.[53]

However, the CEPT Agreement goes beyond being simply another
method to achieve trade liberalization through preferential trade
mechanisms, to the creation of a new trading arrangement based on the
concept of a "free trade area". Unlike the preferential tariffs under the

PTA which required further negotiations and agreements among the ASEAN member states for their implementation, the CEPT provides an automatic application on an across-the board basis to a wide range of products and contains a specific time frame to achieve the goal of establishing a virtual "free trade area".

The Seventh AFTA Council in Brunei Darussalam in September 1995 agreed that products in the Preferential Trading Arrangement ("PTA") would be phased in to the CEPT Scheme effective 1 January 1996.[54] A Protocol to Amend the Agreement on ASEAN Preferential Trading Agreements was agreed to at Bangkok on 15 December 1995.[55] The Protocol provided that the Rules of Origin of the PTA would be substituted by the Rules of Origin for the Common Effective Preferential Tariff Scheme for AFTA.

The main difference between the PTA and CEPT was that under the former, preferences were granted only by the nominating country and there was no reciprocity. Under the latter, there is reciprocity in that once the goods are accepted to be under the CEPT by all countries then all must give the preferential tariff. The CEPT is, therefore, potentially more encompassing[56] and, illustrates the development of more of a "rules-based" approach to economic cooperation.

The evolution from the PTA to AFTA is reflected in the development of the legal framework for economic cooperation. Law is dynamic and changes to reflect, inter alia, changes in the underlying economic structure of society. As economic cooperation in ASEAN became closer and more complex, it was necessary to develop more detailed "rules" to enable this economic cooperation to take place. The development of these rules has contributed to an evolving legal framework for regulation of economic activity among ASEAN partners.

From the outset, AFTA was aimed at enhancing ASEAN's attractiveness as an investment location, a production platform for the global markets. It is widely recognized that the AFTA scheme alone is not viable unless the liberalization process is supplemented by a comprehensive "AFTA-Plus" programme, which goes beyond trade liberalization measures.[57] Thus, ASEAN has also adopted a number of other measures aimed at other aspects of economic cooperation. These measures have also necessitated "rules" which have contributed to the evolving legal framework. The following discussion looks at some of these rules. As can be seen, as the members of ASEAN have moved toward closer economic cooperation, more detailed rules to regulate this cooperation have evolved.

Cooperation in Investment

ASEAN places a high emphazis on luring Direct Foreign Investment ("DFI") and has a commitment to providing and maintaining a highly competitive and conducive investment environment. Many of the early economic cooperation schemes were aimed at making ASEAN more attractive to DFI by providing a larger market for manufactured goods by allowing greater margin of preferences on intra-regional trade. Hence the perceived need for such schemes as the BBC and the AIJV. In addition to these measures, ASEAN has adopted a number of agreements at a regional basis which deal specifically with the ASEAN Member Countries' commitment to investment liberalisation and their collective efforts in attracting and protecting FDI.

Agreements Relating to Investment Protection

The first category of investment agreements are those agreements relating to investment protection which cover protection against expropriation and guarantee repatriation of capital, profits and dividends. The main agreement in this category is the 1987 ASEAN Agreement for the Promotion and Protection of Investments, as amended by the 1996 Protocol to Amend the 1987 Agreement for the Promotion and Protection of Investments.[58]

Agreement for the Promotion and Protection of Investments

The third ASEAN Summit held in Manila on 14-15 December 1987 focussed on intra-regional economic cooperation. In addition to changes to the AIP and AIJV schemes, the Summit also concluded an agreement on Promotion and Protection of Investments to further promote intra-ASEAN investments. The objective of this Agreement was:

> to create favourable conditions for investments by nationals
> and companies of any ASEAN member state in the territory of

the other ASEAN member states and to facilitate the desired flow of private investments therein to increase prosperity in their respective territories.[59]

The Agreement applies only to investments which are brought into, derived from or directly connected with investments brought into the territory of one ASEAN state by nationals or companies of another ASEAN state and which are specifically approved in writing and registered by the host country and upon such conditions as it deems fit for the purposes of the Agreement.[60]

All investments to which the Agreement relates are, subject to the terms of the Agreement, governed by the laws and regulations of the host country, including rules of registration and valuation of such investments.[61] Such investments are to be at all times accorded fair and equitable treatment and enjoy full protection and security in the territory of the host country.[62] Such treatment shall be no less favourable than that granted to investors of the most-favoured nation.[63] Any two or more States may negotiate to accord national treatment within the framework of the Agreement, but this is *not* extended automatically on a Most Favoured Nation basis.[64]

The Agreement contains an Article dealing with expropriation and compensation which provides that investments shall not be subject to expropriation or nationalization or any equivalent measure except for public use or public purpose or in the public interest, and under due process of law, on a non-discriminatory basis and upon payment of adequate compensation;[65] as well as an Article dealing with repatriation of capital and earnings.[66]

The 1996 Protocol to Amend the 1987 Agreement for the Promotion and Protection of Investments

Given the rapid development of the global and region's investment environment, together with the strengthened investment cooperation among the ASEAN countries, the 1987 Agreement was amended to improve and to make it a more appropriate instrument. The Protocol added the following commitments of the member countries to:

1. Endeavour to simplify and streamline investment procedures and approval process to facilitate investment flows; and
2. Ensure the provision of up-to-date information on all laws and regulations pertaining to direct investment and take appropriate measures to ensure that such information be made as transparent, timely and publicly accessible as possible.

Regarding dispute settlement, the Protocol provides that the provisions of the ASEAN Dispute Settlement Mechanism will apply to the settlement of investment disputes between the Contracting Parties. Disputes between any contracting party and a national or company of any other contracting party are to be settled amicably as far as possible, and if not so settled, then either party can elect to submit the dispute for conciliation or arbitration.[67] Vietnam, the Lao People's Democratic Republic and the Union of Myanmar have also acceded to the Agreement.

Agreements Relating to Enhancing Investment

The second category of investment agreements are those agreements relating to enhancing investment cooperation, facilitation, promotion and liberalization. This type of agreement aims to develop ASEAN into a highly competitive and conducive investment area by providing investors with greater opportunities for economies of scale, synergies and lower transaction cost environment. The relevant agreements are, the ASEAN Industrial Cooperation ("AICO") Scheme, the ASEAN Free Trade Area ("AFTA") and the ASEAN Investment Area ("AIA") Agreement. AFTA has been discussed above in the context of trading arrangements; the following discussion will consider the AICO Scheme and the AIA Agreement.

The ASEAN Industrial Cooperation ("AICO") Scheme[68]

The acceleration of AFTA's implementation goes beyond tariff-reductions. It also involves other ways of liberalizing trade. ASEAN has placed a high emphasis on luring DFI as seen, for example, in the AIJV scheme. However, with the advent of AFTA, industrial cooperation in these areas is becoming less important, as the main attraction of earlier schemes was the greater margin of preferences granted on intra-regional trade. With the view to enhancing ASEAN's industrial competitive edge and maintaining the attractiveness of ASEAN as an investment region and a premier global production base, ASEAN began looking for a new form of industrial cooperation scheme to replace the previous Schemes.

The new scheme which was introduced on 1 November 1996, is the AICO Scheme. This scheme retains some of the features of the BBC and AIJV scheme but offers more in terms of tariff and non-tariff incentives. The new scheme is based on the CEPT Scheme for AFTA, promotes investment from technology-based industries, and enhances value-added activities. It is essentially an intermediate step giving favoured industries a "head start" in attracting DFI before the full implementation of AFTA. The AICO is part of an on-going process within ASEAN to create an ASEAN Investment Area (AIA) (see below).

The ASEAN industrial cooperation scheme has the following objectives:

1. Increased ASEAN industrial production
2. Closer ASEAN integration
3. Increased investments from ASEAN and non-ASEAN sources
4. Increased intra-ASEAN trade
5. Improved economies of scale in production and scope
6. Enhanced technology base
7. Internationally competitive ASEAN industries
8. Increased private sector participation
9. Increased industrial complementation.

The new industrial cooperation scheme is to operate on the following principles:

1. Mutually beneficial and equitable benefits
2. CEPT-AFTA based
3. Simplified and uniform application, approval and administrative procedures

4. Private sector driven
5. Attractive and manageable to SMEs
6. Offer incentives other than tariff and local content accreditation
7. Promote resource pooling and sharing
8. Regionally acceptable and workable.

The AICO Scheme is a scheme to encourage companies located and operating in different ASEAN countries to cooperate with one another in the manufacture of approved AICO products. A minimum of two companies in two different ASEAN countries is required to form an "AICO arrangement"[69]. Since February 1999, an AICO arrangement in the form of an intra firm transaction is allowed.[70] Manufacturing companies that belong to the same group of companies or are administered by the same principal can now apply to form intra-firm AICO arrangements among themselves to exchange products in which they specialize.

The major privilege of the new scheme is that approved AICO products will enjoy preferential tariff rates of 0%-5% immediately upon approval of the AICO arrangement. This tariff represents the final CEPT rate to be reached by ASEAN by the year 2002. The immediate application of the 0%-5% preferential tariff rate will provide a head start to AICO products compared to non-AICO products. Other incentives include local content accreditation where applicable, and other non-tariff incentives to be provided by the participating member countries.

Initially, the scheme required a minimum 30% ASEAN national equity. This requirement has been waived for those who qualify and opt for the ASEAN Industrial Cooperation Scheme prior to 31 December 2001.[71]

The AICO Agreement supersedes the Basic Agreement on ASEAN Industrial Joint Ventures ("AIJVs") and the Memorandum of Understanding on the Brand-to-Brand Complementation ("BBC") Scheme.[72]

The ASEAN Investment Area ("AIA")

Since the Fifth ASEAN Summit, held in December 1995 in Bangkok, ASEAN cooperation in the area of investment has made significant developments. One notable development, is the progress made towards realising the decision of the ASEAN Heads of Government on establishing a bold regional arrangement for investment known as the ASEAN Investment Area ("AIA"). The objective of AIA is to help ASEAN attract greater and sustainable levels of FDI flows into and within the region. This is to be achieved by undertaking collective measures that would enhance the attractiveness, competitiveness and the complementarity of the region for FDI.

The present form and scope of ASEAN investment cooperation emanated from the Meeting of the ASEAN Heads of Investment Agencies in Bangkok on 14-15 December 1995. The December 1995 ASEAN Summit endorsed in principle the concept of an AIA, in which barriers to intra-regional investment would be lowered and removed, regulations would be liberalized, streamlined, and made more transparent, and incentives would be offered to boost regional investment. The basic concept is to substantially increase the flow of investment into ASEAN from both ASEAN and non-ASEAN sources by enhancing the region's competitiveness. The AIA aims to enhance the competitiveness of the region for attracting higher and sustainable levels of direct investment flows into and within ASEAN. Three broad-based programmes of action form the thrust of the AIA arrangement — Cooperation and Facilitation, Promotion and Awareness, and Liberalisation Programme.

The Cooperation and Facilitation Programme is to enhance ASEAN's competitiveness and provide investors with an efficient and low-transaction cost investment environment. It includes activities aiming at facilitating investment flows, human-resource development and the upgrading of skills of ASEAN investment agencies.

The Promotion and Awareness Programme is to promote ASEAN as a single investment destination. It aims to give investors a better understanding and awareness of the region's investment opportunities. This programme includes regular high-level outward ASEAN Joint Investment Promotion Missions, the creation of investment websites and databases, and the publications of timely and useful investment information.

The Liberalization Programme is to open up investment regimes throughout the region by eliminating investment barriers, liberalizing investment rules and policies, and granting national treatment.

The Framework Agreement on the ASEAN Investment Area was signed on 8 October 1998 in Manila and entered into force on 21 June 1999.[73] The objectives of this Agreement are:

1. to establish a competitive ASEAN Investment Area with a more liberal and transparent investment environment amongst Member States in order to;
    i.   substantially increase the flow of investments into ASEAN from both ASEAN and non-ASEAN sources;
    ii. jointly promote ASEAN as the most attractive investment area;
    iii. strengthen and increase the competitiveness of ASEAN's economic sectors;
    iv. progressively reduce or eliminate investment regulations and conditions which may impede investment flows and the operation of investment projects in ASEAN; and
2. to ensure that the realization of the above objectives would contribute towards free flow of investments by 2020.[74]

The Framework Agreement provides that the ASEAN Investment Area shall be an area where:

(a) there is a coordinated ASEAN investment cooperation programme that will generate increased investments from ASEAN and non-ASEAN sources;

(b) national treatment is extended to ASEAN investors by 2010, subject to exceptions as specified in the Temporary Exclusion List ("TEL") and the Sensitive List ("SL"), and to all investors by 2020;

(c) all industries are opened for investment to ASEAN investors by 2010 and to all investors by 2020, subject to the exceptions provided for under this Agreement;

(d)   the business sector has a larger role in the cooperation efforts in relation to investments and related activities in ASEAN; and

(e)   there is freer flow of capital, skilled labour and professionals, and technology amongst Member States.[75]

The Agreement further provides that subject to certain exceptions, each Member State will accord immediately and unconditionally to investors and investments of another Member State, treatment no less favourable than that accorded to investors and investments of any other Member State with respect to all measures affecting investment including but not limited to the admission, establishment, acquisition, expansion, management, operation and disposition of investments.[76]

"ASEAN investor" under the Agreement means a national of a Member State or any juridical person of a Member State.[77] An ASEAN investor is defined as being equal to a national investor in terms of the equity requirements of the member country in which the investment is made. Thus, a foreign firm with a majority interest can avail itself of national treatment and investment market access privileges, in addition to the other benefits provided under the AIA Agreement and other regional economic schemes.

A ministerial-level ASEAN Investment Area Council has been established to oversee the implementation of the Framework Agreement. The Council is assisted by the ASEAN Coordinating Committee on Investment.

At the Sixth Summit in Hanoi, the Heads of State and Government of ASEAN adopted the Hanoi Plan of Action.[78] In the plan it was agreed to implement the three programmes of the AIA (Cooperation and Facilitation, Promotion and Awareness, and Liberalization Programme) through individual and collective action plans, within agreed schedules and timetable.

The Framework Agreement has been amended by the Protocol to Amend the Framework Agreement, signed in Hanoi on 14 September 2001. The Protocol, inter alia, shortens the end date for the Temporary Exclusion List of the manufacturing sector to 2003 instead of 2010 for the original six member countries and Myanmar.

Lao People's Democratic Republic, Cambodia and Vietnam will have no later than 1 January 2010 to phase out the Temporary Exclusion List of the manufacturing sector. The protocol also expands the coverage of the AIA agreement to include agriculture, fishery, forestry and mining sectors, and services incidental to manufacturing and these sectors.

The AICO and the AIA are new concepts which constitute vital components of the efforts within ASEAN to create a more attractive business environment. The AIA is aimed at enabling the region to attract FDI by creating a more open, liberal and competitive investment environment. Proponents are hopeful that the signing of the agreement will assure investors of ASEAN's firm resolve to revitalise the region and inspire confidence among investors.

The complexity of the schemes and the need for detailed rules is reflected in the evolving legal framework for economic cooperation in ASEAN.

Cooperation in Services

In addition to the measures for cooperation in trade in goods and in investment, ASEAN members are moving ahead on negotiations to open up trade in services to one another.

The ASEAN Framework Agreement on Services was signed during the Fifth ASEAN Summit in December 1995 in Bangkok.[79] At the Summit, it was agreed that a process of negotiations commence beginning 1 January 1996 and ending 31 December 1998. The negotiations were aimed at producing commitments on increased market access and national treatment from Member Countries in seven priority service sectors — air transport, business services, construction, financial services, maritime transport, telecommunications and tourism. A Coordinating Committee on Services ("CCS") was established with seven working groups under it, and Member Countries exchanged information on their General Agreement on Trade in Services ("GATS") commitments and service regime under the WTO framework.[80] Member States carried out an initial round of negotiations and concluded a set of commitments embodied in the Protocol to Implement the Initial Package of Commitments under the ASEAN

Framework Agreement on Services signed on 15 December 1997 in Kuala Lumpur, Malaysia.[81] They carried out subsequent negotiations and finalised the second package of commitments at Hanoi, Vietnam, on 16 December 1998.[82]

At the Sixth ASEAN Summit in Hanoi in December 1998, the Leaders agreed to initiate a new round of negotiations beginning 1999 and ending 2001. The Plan of Action, adopted by the Summit provided that Members would:

1. Progressively liberalise trade in services by initiating a new round of negotiations beginning 1999 and ending 2001;
2. Expand the scope of negotiations in services beyond the seven priority sectors, identified at the Fifth ASEAN Summit, to cover all services sectors and all modes of supply;
3. Seek to accelerate the liberalisation of trade in services through the adoption of alternative approaches to liberalization; and
4. Accelerate the free flow of professional and other services in the region.[83]

Futher to this Plan of Action, a third package of commitments was agreed to on 31 December 2001.*

The Framework Agreement seeks to integrate the ASEAN market for services by eliminating restrictions on trade in services among member countries. This involves liberalizing trade in services beyond the commitments undertaken by member countries under the WTO's General Agreement on Trade in Services. The final goal of the Framework Agreement is to realise a free-trade area in services.

Cooperation in Intellectual Property

In order to take advantage of new technologies, developing countries are finding that they must establish strong intellectual property

---

* Protocol to Implement the Third Package of Commitments under the ASEAN Framework Agreement on Services, *TAPR* Document I.B.7.1 (1).

protection laws and enforcement of these laws. Without a stable environment in which multinationals can operate and in which domestic firms can invest in new innovations, the process of technology transfer is significantly inhibited. Regional co-operation agreements are useful in creating a strong underlying framework for the protection of intellectual property.

In order to provide a framework for the protection of intellectual property rights ("IPR") within ASEAN, the ASEAN countries agreed to the ASEAN Framework Agreement on Intellectual Property Cooperation in December 1995.[84] This Agreement commits ASEAN countries to strengthening cooperation in protecting intellectual property and creating ASEAN standards and practices which are consistent with international standards. Furthermore, the Agreement notes that ASEAN countries should explore the possibility of setting up an ASEAN patent system and an ASEAN Patent Office, in which ASEAN countries could promote region-wide protection of patents; and an ASEAN trademark system and an ASEAN Trademark Office to promote the region-wide protection of trademarks. Other proposals include training and human resource development programs, and education campaigns. The Program of Action on ASEAN Intellectual Property Cooperation for the period 1996-1998 was adopted to carry out the activities of the ASEAN Framework Agreement on Intellectual Property Cooperation.

At the 13th ASEAN Economic Ministers Meeting in October 1998, the Ministers endorsed the proposal on the establishment of the ASEAN Regional Filing Systems for Trademarks and Patents by 1 January 2000. The Ministers noted that the system would enable the filing of trademarks and patent registration at any ASEAN intellectual property office. The Ministers agreed that participation of Member Countries in this regional scheme would be on a voluntary basis.[85]

The Hanoi Plan of Action, adopted at the Sixth Summit in Hanoi in December, 1998, provides:

2.7   Further intellectual property cooperation
        To ensure adequate and effective protection, including
        legislation, administration and enforcement, of intellectual

property rights in the region based on the principles of Most Favoured Nation (MFN) treatment, national treatment and transparency as set out in the TRIPS Agreement.

2.7.1 Protection

1. Strengthen civil and administrative procedures and remedies against infringement of intellectual property rights and relevant legislation; and

2. Provide and expand technical cooperation in relation to areas such as patent search and examination, computerisation and human resource development for the implementation of the TRIPS Agreement;

2.7.2 Facilitation

1. Deepen Intellectual Property policy exchange among ASEAN Member States;

2. Survey the current status of intellectual property rights protection in each ASEAN Member State with a view to studying measures, including development principles, for the effective enforcement of intellectual property rights;

3. Develop a contact point list of public and business/private sector experts on intellectual property rights and a list of law enforcement officers, the latter list for the purpose of establishing a network to prevent cross-border flow of counterfeits;

4. Exchange information on well-known marks as a first step in examining the possibility of establishing a region-wide trademark system;

5. Exchange information on current intellectual property rights administrative systems with a view to simplifying and standardising administrative systems throughout the region;

6. Ensure that intellectual property legislation conform to the TRIPS Agreement of the World Trade Organisation through the review of intellectual property laws and introduction of TRIPS-consistent laws. This would begin with a comprehensive review of existing legislation to be completed by the year 2000; and

7. Strengthen intellectual property administration by setting up an ASEAN electronic database by the year 2004 on patents, designs, geographical indications, trademarks and information on copyright and layout design of integrated circuits.

2.7.3 Cooperation

1. Implement an ASEAN Regional Trademark and Patent Filing System by the year 2000;

2. Establish an ASEAN Regional Fund for Trademark and Patent by the year 2000;

3. Finalise and implement an ASEAN Common Form for Trade Mark and Patent Applications;

4. Establish a regional trademark and patent registration system; or establish a regional trademark or patent office (on voluntary basis);

5. Promote accession of Member States to international treaties;

6. Promote Intellectual Property public and private sector awareness;

7. Introduce Intellectual Property as a subject in the curriculum of higher learning institutions;

8. Develop training programmes for Intellectual Property officials; and

9. Enhance intellectual property enforcement and protection through establishing mechanisms for the dissemination of information on ASEAN intellectual property administration, registration and infringement; facilitating interaction among legal and judicial bodies through seminars, etc.; facilitating networking among intellectual enforcement agencies; encouraging bilateral/plurilateral arrangements on mutual protection and joint cooperation in enforcement of Intellectual Property Rights.[86]

The ASEAN Working Group on Intellectual Property Cooperation ("AWGIPC") has been established under the purview of ASEAN Senior Economic Officials ("SEOM") to implement the activities of the Program of Action and to serve as a forum for regular consultations to monitor regional and international developments in intellectual property. The Working Group has continued to implement the activities of the ASEAN Programme of Action on Intellectual Property Cooperation and the Hanoi Plan of Action ("HPA").

Non-Tariff Barriers

AFTA laid out a comprehensive programme of regional tariff reduction. In order to ensure that these tariff reductions were not frustrated by other measures, the members of ASEAN have also initiated efforts to eliminate non-tariff barriers ("NTB"s). The CEPT Agreement for AFTA provides for the immediate elimination of quantitative restrictions for products included in the CEPT Scheme, and the elimination of other non-tariff barriers within a period of five years upon enjoyment of the CEPT concession (Article 5).

Member countries are in the process of verifying a list of NTBs and products covered by these measures compiled by the ASEAN Secretariat. ASEAN agreed in December 1995 that NTBs should be eliminated no later than the year 2003.

ASEAN Customs Initiatives

One type of non-tariff barrier which has received particular attention has been custom matters. These issues are spelled out in an ASEAN Agreement on Customs, which was approved at a March 1997 meeting of the ASEAN Ministers of Finance.[87] At the May 1997 Customs Directors-General meeting, an "ASEAN Customs Vision 2020"[88] was adopted, which reiterates the commitment to harmonizing customs procedures and working toward world class standards and excellence in efficiency, professionalism and service, to promote trade and investment in the region. An ASEAN Customs Policy Implementation and Work Programme has been developed for the purpose of managing the implementation of the ASEAN Customs Vision 2020.[89]

The Directors-General of Customs have endorsed the ASEAN Harmonised Tariff Nomenclature ("AHTN") and agreed on its implementation beginning 1 January 2002. The AHTN will create a harmonised tariff nomenclature at the eight-digit level for the ten ASEAN countries. The AHTN will contain 10,800 tariff lines from all ten Member Countries. Its implementation in the year 2002 will coincide with the implementation of the latest Harmonised System ("HS") code of the World Customs Organisation, upon which it is based.

A "Green Lane" system for the expedited clearance of CEPT-eligible products was launched in 1996 at customs clearance points in ASEAN. The Ministers at the 13th ASEAN Economic Ministers Meeting in October 1998, noted that, as a contribution towards enhancing intra-ASEAN trade, the customs authorities of ASEAN have agreed to expand the scope of the Customs Green Lane to cover all ASEAN products.[90]

Endnotes

1   'This may be an indication of ASEAN's growing realization that closer regional economic integration requires basing it on binding legal foundations if integration is to be stable, credible and effective. The commitments undertaken must be clear, firm and enforceable, and those making them cannot lightly back out of them.': Severino, Rodolfo C, Secretary-General of ASEAN, 'The ASEAN Way and the Rule of Law', address at the International Law Conference on ASEAN Legal Systems and Regional Integration, Kuala Lumpur, 3 September 2001. (http://www.aseansec.org/newdata/asean_way.htm).

2   *TAPR*, Document I.B.8, see Appendix 4.

3   Article 2, Part B.

4   *TAPR*, Document I.B.5.e.

5   See *TAPR*, Documents in I.B.4.d, for the Joint Press Statements of these meetings.

6   *TAPR*, Document I.B.11.e.

7   Article 2, Part C.

8   See *TAPR*, Document I.B.4.c(1).

9   Article 2, Part D.

10   See *TAPR*, Document I.B.15.a.

11   Article 2, Part E.

12   See *TAPR*, Document I.B.17.a.

13   See *TAPR*, Document I.B.4.j(7).

14   See *TAPR*, Document I.B.4.i.

15   See *TAPR*, Document I.B.4.i(2).

16   Article 3.

17   See *TAPR*, Document I.B.10.

18   See *TAPR*, Document I.B.5.j, Article 2.7.

19   For a report of a 1992 Roundtable on AFTA, see, Pearl Imada and Seiji Naya (eds), *AFTA The Way Ahead* (Singapore: ISEAS, 1992).

20   Joseph Sedfrey S Santiago, 'Postscript to AFTA's False Start — The Loss of Sovereignty Issue' (1995) 12 ASEAN Economic Bulletin, p 19.

21   Suthiphand Chirathivat, 'ASEAN Economic Integration with the World through AFTA', Chapter.2, in Tan, Joseph (ed), *AFTA in the Changing International Economy* (Singapore: ISEAS, 1996), p 22.

22   *ASEAN Economic Cooperation for the 1990s – A Report Prepared for the ASEAN Standing Committee* (Philippines: Philippines Institute for Development Studies and ASEAN Secretariat, 1992).

23   'In the years prior to 1992, there were a number of fundamental changes in the global and regional economic environment which stimulated the formation of AFTA. These include: (1) the emergence and consolidation of economic blocs in Europe and North America; (2) within the Southeast Asian region, the adoption of trade/economic liberalization policies since the mid-1980s and the growing emphasis on growth strategies based on attracting foreign direct investment; and (3) the more favourable perceptions of regional governments and the private sectors in the need for forging deeper economic co-operation in the light of greater competitive pressures coming from outside the region.' Tan, Joseph, 'AFTA in the Changing International Economy', in Tan, Joseph (ed), *AFTA in the Changing International Economy* (Singapore: ISEAS, 1996), pp 1-2.

24   *Supra*, note 12, at pp v-vi.

25   Suthiphand Chirathivat, 'ASEAN Economic Integration with the World through AFTA', Chapter 2, in Tan, Joseph (ed), *AFTA in the Changing International Economy* (Singapore: ISEAS, 1996), p 29: 'This reasoning would mean that ASEAN is integrating among themselves in order to integrate with the world and AFTA would be a means for achieving this.' At p 32: 'AFTA, seen in another way, is created by ASEAN as a response to the changing world environment, in order to increase ASEAN's competitive position for trade and production in the global economy. The advantages here should be stated clearly without too many expectations in the narrow sense of increasing intra-ASEAN trade through AFTA. Overall, the results of trade increases from the implementation of the Uruguay Round are much greater than the potential ones to be realized by the present static gains of the AFTA scheme.'

     See also, Mohamed Ariff, "APEC and ASEAN: "Complementing or Competing"", Chapter 7, in Chia Siow Yue (ed), *APEC: Challenges and Opportunitie* (Singapore: ISEAS, 1994).

26   See Appendices 4-6.

27   Singapore Declaration of 1992, para 5, *TAPR*, Document I.B.8; see Appendix 5.

28   Agreement on the Common Effective Preferential Tariff (CEPT) Scheme for the ASEAN Free Trade Area (AFTA), *TAPR*, Document I.B.8; see Appendix 6.

Although this is the primary instrument for implementing AFTA, it is not envisaged as the sole instrument for this purpose: 'The Common Effective Preferential Tariff (CEPT) Scheme shall be the main mechanism for the AFTA. For products not covered by the CEPT Scheme, the ASEAN Preferential Trading Arrangements (PTA) or any other mechanism to be agreed upon, may be used.' (Article 2A, para 2, Framework Agreement on Enhancing ASEAN Economic Cooperation, Singapore, 28 January 1992, *TAPR*, Document I.B.8; see Appendix 4.) 'All products under the PTA which are not transferred to the CEPT Scheme shall continue to enjoy the MoP existing as at 31 December 1992.' (CEPT Agreement, Article 2(6).)

29   Joint Press Statement of the 26th Meeting of the ASEAN Economic Ministers, 22-23 September 1994, Chiangmai, Thailand, *TAPR*, Document I.B.4.b(26).

30   Protocol Regarding the Implementation of the CEPT Scheme Temporary Exclusion List, The Fourth ASEAN Informal Summit, 22-25 November 2000, Singapore.

31   For a brief statement on the scope of the CEPT scheme within each country as of the implementation of AFTA on 1 January 1993, see, 'Documentation — Press Releases on the CEPT Scheme' (1993) 9 ASEAN *Economic Bulletin*, pp 364-374.

32   The name 'Common Effective Preferential Tariff' Scheme originates from the original approach to tariff reduction within ASEAN which was a proposal for harmonizing internal tariff rates of ASEAN countries. The basic idea of the original CEPT Scheme was that a common internal tariff rate would be set for selected ASEAN products. This common rate would represent a maximum internal tariff and would gradually be reduced to zero. Although the scheme which was finally adopted abandoned this approach, the name 'Common Effective Preferential Tariff' scheme was retained.

33   Member states were encouraged to adopt an annual rate of reduction of $(x-20)\%/$ 5 or 8, where X equals the existing tariff rates of individual Member States (Article 4(1)(a)).

34   Singapore Declaration of 1992, para 5.

35   See, 'Ministers accelerate implementation of AFTA', ASEAN *Update*, October 1994, pp 1-3. The original AFTA schedule of 15 years apparently seemed to be too long. The Uruguay Round had been concluded and allowed ten years for implementation; APEC was to start trade liberalization by the year 2000; regional agreements in the European Union ("EU") and the North American Free Trade Agreement ("NAFTA") suggested rapid transition within the groups. The members of ASEAN felt it was necessary to advance implementation of AFTA in order to ensure that ASEAN kept abreast of new conditions of international competitiveness.

36   Joint Press Statement of the 26th Meeting of the ASEAN Economic Ministers, 22-23 September 1994, Chiangmai, Thailand, *TAPR*, Document I.B.4.b(26).

37   Bangkok Summit Declaration of 1995, para 8; Joint Press Statement of the 27th ASEAN Economic Ministers Meeting, Brunei Darussalam, 7-8 September 1995, para 8, *TAPR*, Document I.B.4.b(27).

38 Tan, Joseph, 'AFTA in the Changing International Economy, in Tan, Joseph (ed), *AFTA in the Changing International Economy* (Singapore: ISEAS, 1996), p 8.

39 *TAPR*, Document I.B.5.k.

40 'It was advanced to 2002 as a result of the regional financial and economic crisis of 1997-1998 and greater competition pressure from other countries. "That decision clearly demonstrated Asean's commitment to maintain Southeast Asia's economic competitiveness through economic integration," Mr Abad [ASEAN spokesman] said.' ('Region achieves landmark goal', South China Morning Post, 1 January, 2002).

41 HE Rodolfo C Severino, Jr, ASEAN Secretary-General, 'The Financial Crisis and ASEAN's Private Sector', Briefing at the 55th ASEAN-CCI Council Meeting, Kuala Lumpur, 10 April 1998.

42 Mr. Abad, *supra*, note 40.

43 Press Statement by the Chairman of the Seventh ASEAN Summit and the Fifth ASEAN + 3 Summit, 5 November 2001, Bandar Seri Begawan.

44 Article 5.

45 Article 7(1); see documents in *TAPR*, section I.B.8(aa) for Joint Press Statements of AFTA Ministerial Council meetings.

46 See, 'Ministers accelerate implementation of AFTA', *ASEAN Update*, October 1994, pp 1-3, at 2, and Joint Press Statement of the 26th Meeting of the ASEAN Economic Ministers, 22-23 September 1994, Chiangmai, Thailand, *TAPR*, Document I.B.4.b(26).

47 For information on the AFTA Unit in the ASEAN Secretariat and the National AFTA Units, see 'AFTA and National AFTA Units', on the ASEAN website, http://www.aseansec.org.

48 Joint Press Statement, the 13th Meeting of the Asean Free Trade Area (AFTA) Council, 29 September 1999, Singapore.

49 Chairman's Press Statement, ASEAN Third Informal Summit, 28 November 1999, Manila.

50 For a further discussion of dispute settlement within ASEAN and a critique of the CEPT provisions, see Chapter 7, *infra*.

51 Article 8.

52 Joint Press Statement of the 27th Meeting of the ASEAN Economic Ministers, Brunei Darussalam, 7-8 September 1995, para 13, *TAPR*, Document I.B.4.b(27); see Protocol on Dispute Settlement, *TAPR*, Document I.B.7.o, and Chapter 7, *infra*.

53 'The PTA is a policy-making instrument while the AFTA Agreement, as the latter's own preamble indicates, is an implementing instrument of the PTA.' (Joseph Sedfrey S Santiago, 'The ASEAN Free Trade Area (AFTA): Preliminary Legal Implications for the Philippines' (1992) ASEAN Law Association Proceedings, 179 at 186.)

54 *TAPR*, Document I.B.8.aa(7).

55 *TAPR*, Document I.B.7.a.

56 It should also be noted that the other schemes for industrial cooperation which have been discussed which rely on tariff preferences will become redundant once

tariff levels within ASEAN are reduced under the CEPT scheme. For example, as noted above, it has been decided that the CEPT Scheme should take precedence over the AIJV and that products covered under the ASEAN PTA will be phased in to the CEPT.

57 Suthiphand Chirathivat, 'ASEAN Economic Integration with the World through AFTA', Chapter 2, in Tan, Joseph (ed), *AFTA in the Changing International Economy* (Singapore: ISEAS, 1996), pp 29-30.

58 Agreement Among the Governments of Brunei Darussalam, The Republic of Indonesia, Malaysia, The Republic of the Philippines, The Republic of Singapore, and The Kingdom of Thailand for the Promotion and Protection of Investments, Manila, 15 December 1987, as amended, *TAPR*, Document I.B.12.a. The newer members of ASEAN have also acceded to this Agreement.

59 From the Preamble to the Agreement.

60 Article II, paragraph 1.

61 Article III(1).

62 Article III(2) and Article IV.

63 Article IV(2).

64 Article IV(4).

65 Article VI.

66 Article VII.

67 Article X.

68 The Basic Agreement on The ASEAN Industrial Cooperation Scheme, Singapore, 27 April 1996, *TAPR*, Document I.B.7.n (see Appendix 9); and, see also, Secretariat note on the AICO scheme at *TAPR*, Document I.B.7.m.

69 A cooperative arrangement consisting of a minimum of two participating companies from two different countries. It is not a legal entity but merely an 'umbrella association' under the scheme that entitles the participating companies to enjoy the AICO privileges. This would mean that existing companies meeting the AICO eligibility criteria may apply to form an AICO Arrangement without having to create a new entity.

70 *TAPR*, Document I.B.7.m(1) – 'A More Attractive AICO Scheme: Intra-Firm Transaction Allowed'.

71 The initial waiver was granted by the ASEAN Statement on Bold Measures for applications received between 1 January 1999 and 31 December 2000. The waiver was extended to 31 December 2001 by the 32nd AEM on 5 October 2000. See *TAPR*, Documents I.B.5.k and I.B.4.b(32).

72 Article 12 of the Agreement establishing the AICO scheme (*TAPR*, Document I.B.7.n).

73 *TAPR*, Document I.B.12.f (see Appendix 10).

74 Article 3.

75 Article 4.

76 Article 8.

77 Article 1.

78 Hanoi Declaration of 1998, 16 December 1998, *TAPR*, Document I.B.5.i; and Hanoi Plan of Action, *TAPR*, Document I.B.5.j (see Appendix 3).

79 *TAPR*, Document I.B.7.l.

80 This is an example of the limiting role of prior international obligations discussed in Chapter One.

81 *TAPR*, Document I.B.7.l.

82 Protocol to Implement the Second Package of Commitments Under the ASEAN Framework Agreement on Services, *TAPR*, Document I.B.7.l.

83 Hanoi Plan of Action, 16 December 1998, *TAPR*, Document I.B.5.j, para.2.3.1. It should be noted that a significant number of the offers involved opening up new service sectors that were not previously included in the GATS. This is an example of a regional framework going beyond the obligations of the broader 'international' framework.

84 *TAPR*, Document I.B.10.a.

85 Joint Press Statement of the 13th Asean Economic Ministers Meeting, Makati City, Philippines, 7-8 October 1998, para 24, *TAPR*, Document I.B.4.b(30).

86 Hanoi Plan of Action *TAPR*, Document I.B.5.j.

87 *TAPR*, Document I.B.14.c.

88 *TAPR*, Document I.B.14.d.

89 See ASEAN website, www.aseansec.org, at 'economic cooperation/customs'.

90 Joint Press Statement of the 13th Asean Economic Ministers Meeting, Makati City, Philippines, 7-8 October 1998, para 10, *TAPR*, Document I.B.4.b(30).

CHAPTER 5

BROADER ECONOMIC COOPERATION

> The propensity for government summit meetings ...is obviously not unrelated to ... world economic trends of interdependence. Likewise, the attempts of governments to combine their efforts through international organizations have a similar result. The question is not whether a government will play on the international scene; the question is, where will it play and with whom (that is, what forum will it work in and which other governments is it willing to let into its "club")? The problem of international economics today, then, is largely a problem of "managing" interdependence.[1]

In addition to the establishment of a framework for economic cooperation at the ASEAN regional level, there have also been movements to establish economic cooperation at a broader Asia Pacific level. Although these have been of a much "looser" nature, ie, not as rules-based, they will have an effect on the evolving legal framework for economic cooperation in the region and will contribute to it. In looking at the form that these groups take, one must keep in mind that they are evolving within an existing legal framework and may be limited by or may precipitate changes to it. Also, in analysing the evolution of institutions in the region, it is important to recognise constraints put on the future evolution by the underlying economic, political and social differences in the countries in the region.

Two developments within the broader region are particularly noteworthy and require some discussion. The first is the Asia

Pacific Economic Cooperation ("APEC") forum, and the second is the East Asia Economic Caucus ("EAEC"), which appears to be evolving into the ASEAN+3. This chapter provides a brief overview of these.[2]

The Asia Pacific Economic Cooperation ("APEC") Forum[3]

Introduction

Increased economic interdependence leads to an increased likelihood of disputes and the need for a forum to discuss common problems. As the economies of the Asia Pacific became more interdependent, there arose a need for a forum for airing grievances, discussing issues of common interest, seeking amicable solutions to disputes, and undertaking studies for mutual benefits. Begun as an informal dialogue group with limited participation, APEC has since become the primary regional vehicle for promoting open trade and practical economic cooperation in the Asia Pacific.

The question of regional economic cooperation in the Pacific Rim has been an issue for some time now[4]. However, it really came to the fore with the Hawke initiative in 1989. In January 1989, Australian Prime Minister Hawke proposed the need for more effective Asia Pacific economic cooperation.

> That proposal stemmed from a recognition that the increasing interdependence of regional economies indicated a need for effective consultations among regional decision-makers to:
>
> - help strengthen the multilateral trading system and enhance the prospects for success in the Uruguay Round;
> - provide an opportunity to assess prospects for, and obstacles to, increased trade and investment flows within the Asia Pacific region; and
> - identify the range of practical common economic interests.[5]

This led to a major Ministerial meeting in Canberra in November of 1989 which established APEC. Participants included ministers from Australia, Brunei Darussalam, Canada, Indonesia, Japan, the Republic of Korea, Malaysia, New Zealand, The Philippines, Singapore, Thailand, and the United States of America.

Organization

Participants at the APEC Ministerial Meeting in Canberra reaffirmed their commitment to the GATT legal framework and asserted that they had no desire to create an Article XXIV type trading bloc.[6] The question as to the legal framework which would emerge to regulate this developing cooperation was left open. "Ministers agreed that it was premature at this stage to decide upon any particular structure either for a Ministerial-level forum or its necessary support mechanism." However, they did agree it "was appropriate for further consultative meetings to take place and for work to be undertaken on matters of common interest and concern".[7]

Reflecting the importance of ASEAN to the APEC structure, at the 1989 Canberra Ministerial Meeting, it was agreed that every alternate Ministerial Meeting be held in an ASEAN economy.

The early years of APEC were marked by a clash of preferences for its development. The Australians saw APEC as the embryo of an eventual regional free trade agreement, while the Japanese preferred establishment of an architecture for international economic cooperation across the region. The American vision, at least initially, was for APEC to acquire something of the character of an Asian OECD, or consultative forum. The ASEAN members of APEC insisted that APEC would not be converted into a negotiating forum, but would remain a forum whose decision-making is based on consensus among equal members.[8]

As a result of its participants' divergent views regarding its very utility and mission, APEC's first few years were spent in search of an acceptable organization and agenda. The initial work plan, established in Canberra and approved the following year in Singapore, was one of 'functional cooperation'.

The Third APEC Ministerial Meeting was held in Seoul, Korea. At the Seoul Ministerial Meeting, the Ministers agreed that the APEC process had reached a stage where a firm foundation for its future development should be established, and the Meeting adopted the *Seoul APEC Declaration*[9] which established a number of parameters for APEC. The Declaration includes sections setting out

1. Objectives
2. Scope of activity
3. Mode of operation
4. Participation
5. Organisation, and
6. The future of APEC.

It is interesting to note that in their Joint Statement the Ministers stated, "The Declaration *...endows APEC with a clear international personality...*" (emphasis added).

Cooperation within APEC is based on the principle of mutual benefit and a commitment to open dialogue and consensus-building. In 1991, members committed themselves to conducting their activities and work programmes on the basis of open dialogue with equal respect for the views of all participants. These are the same principles upon which ASEAN functions, and indicate the influence of ASEAN within the APEC process.

The Seoul Declaration established an institutional framework for APEC and enunciated agreed organizational objectives, including:

> To reduce barriers to trade in goods and services and investment among participants in a manner consistent with GATT principles, where applicable, and without detriment to other economies.[10]

At the Fourth Ministerial Meeting held in Bangkok in September 1992, further steps were taken towards institutionalization when it was agreed to establish an APEC Secretariat to be located in Singapore and a fund to support APEC's activities. 'The Secretariat ... has been described as an "epoch-making event", turning APEC's previously loose arrangements of meetings into a full-fledged international organization.'[11] Although the members have not given over any real decision-making powers to the Secretariat, the evolution of the Secretariat indicates the maturation of APEC as an entity and may be considered as an initial step in formalizing the legal personality of APEC as a corporate entity governed by its own constitution and by-laws.

Although steps have been taken to create more of an institutional structure for the APEC process, APEC is not an organization so much as it is a forum through which the political leaders and officials of member economies can interact. As such, it is non-hierarchical, and highly process-oriented and is characterized by the promotion and use of inter- and intra-organizational linkages. APEC was conceived by most of its founders as an open, information-generating, consensus-building forum. For most of its member economies, it was never intended to evolve into a rules-based regime. The ad hoc character of its institutional evolution has, at times, caused APEC to function rather haphazardly.[12]

The OECD model was dismissed early in the discussion of what APEC should become.[13] APEC members deliberately chose not to create a large bureaucracy to serve as its secretariat. Whereas the OECD secretariat carries on the bulk of that organization's work, APEC work plans are carried out almost exclusively through the contributions of member economies which means that APEC activities are more tightly controlled by its membership, and by the individuals who occupy sub-committee chairs and working-group shepherd roles. It also engenders a degree of community-building within member bureaucracies that cannot be accomplished in situations in which much of the work is performed by international civil servants.[14]

While APEC has become more structured as an organization, and has elements of 'rules', the APEC members have clearly indicated that these are to be non-binding. These have been of a much 'looser' nature, ie, not as rules-based, they will have an effect on the evolving legal framework for economic cooperation in the region and will contribute to it.

Membership

The original members of APEC were Australia, Brunei Darussalam, Canada, Indonesia, Japan, the Republic of Korea, Malaysia, New Zealand, The Philippines, Singapore, Thailand, and the United States of America. Following an agreement at the Singapore meeting in 1990, consultations were conducted with the People's Republic of China, Hong Kong[15] and Chinese Taipei and an agreement was reached enabling them to participate in APEC; the three were invited to participate in the third Ministerial Meeting held in Seoul in 1991. Because APEC includes political entities other than countries, such as Hong Kong and Taiwan, the term "member economies" is used in place of "countries". In addition, as part of the negotiations which allowed simultaneous entry to Taiwan and China, Taiwan agreed to use the name Chinese Taipei within APEC. APEC's membership was increased from 15 to 18 with the admission of Mexico and Papua New Guinea in 1993 and Chile in 1994, and to 21 in 1998 with the admission of Peru, Russia and Vietnam.

Trade in goods

APEC members have stated that a regional free trade agreement is not feasible. However, free trade has been a subject of consideration. One of APEC's most important objectives has been to 'achieve free and open trade in the Asia-Pacific Region by:

1. Progressively reducing tariffs; and
2. Ensuring the transparency of APEC economies' respective tariff regimes.'[16]

Open regionalism

The approach which has been taken is *not* the creation of a GATT Article XXIV free trade area, but rather, what has been termed "open regionalism". This is defined by APEC as regional economic integration without discrimination against outsiders, through gradual elimination of internal barriers and lowering of barriers towards non-members, consistent with the rules of the WTO, particularly with the Most Favoured Nation ("MFN") principle of GATT Article 1. Under this approach, all benefits affecting WTO obligations will be available to economic partners outside APEC, to maintain consistency with GATT MFN obligations. The goal of free trade is to be achieved through specific measures by every country, consistent with the MFN Principle, which basically boils down to an acceleration of the Uruguay Round commitments. "The very concept of "open regionalism" hinges on the notion that APEC undertakings will be consistent with multilateral rules."[17]

However, the extension of the benefits to all WTO members on a MFN-basis raises doubts about its long-term feasibility, as economic rationale shows that no region will allow for free-riding by extending trade concessions to others automatically; regions and countries will tend to restrict trade benefits to others offering reciprocal concessions, either through multilateral trade negotiations or under Article XXIV in the framework of a free trade area or a customs union.[18] The EPG Report of 1994[19] provides that APEC members should include, as an element of their regional liberalization programme, "an offer to extend the benefits of APEC liberalization to non-members on a mutually reciprocal basis" and "recognition that any individual APEC member can unilaterally extend its APEC liberalization to non-members on a conditional basis or on an unconditional basis". "The suggestion that APEC members would be permitted to discriminate against non-member countries by offering them conditional, instead of unconditional, MFN treatment, reflects the views of the EPG chairman, Dr Fred Bergsten, and other American policy makers and has a long tradition in US trade policy behind it."[20]

Investment[21]

Steps have also been taken in APEC towards creating a more structured approach to investment liberalization in the region. Investment is an activity which currently is not extensively regulated within the WTO framework. While the WTO sets the legal framework for trade relations, it does not generally govern international investment (aside from the Agreement on Trade-Related Investment Measures ("TRIMs") to reduce or eliminate the trade-distortive effects of certain *trade-related* investment measures and some provisions in the General Agreement on Trade in Services ("GATS") related to the provision of services).

The Second Report of the EPG (1994)[22] recommended the "early adoption of an APEC Concord on Investment Principles, a voluntary code to further improve the environment for international direct investment…".The EPG Report recommended that the Concord begin as a voluntary instrument, "in the sense that each member can decide for itself whether or when to apply the agreed principles", but stipulated that APEC should adopt the investment principles as a group in the first instance. This is in keeping with the approach that APEC is *not* intended to become a rules-based organization, so that any agreement of the APEC members is not binding. However, the fact that the members are able to agree on certain principles may be argued to have a 'soft law'[23] effect, in that members, although not *bound by*, may nevertheless be expected to follow the principles.*

At the APEC Ministerial Meeting in Indonesia in November 1994, APEC members agreed on a set of non-binding investment principles designed to remove obstacles to foreign investment.[24] These principles, covering issues such as transparency, non-discrimination and repatriation of funds, have helped to establish the framework and direction of the investment liberalization agenda. These principles were designed not to prejudice existing multilateral obligations such as the investment-related provisions in the GATS accord under the WTO or the provisions of the Agreement on Trade-Related Investment Measures ("TRIMs"). It has been argued that "[t]he APEC non-binding investment principles are not only weak but are weaker in some respects than the investment commitments already agreed to in the context of the Uruguay Round

---

* Paul Davidson, "Ralesabased: APEC's role in the Evoloving International Legal Framework for Regulating International Economic Relations", paper presented at APEC Study Centre Consortium Meeting, Merida, Mexico, May 22-24, 2002.

Trade Related Investment Measures ("TRIMs") — which is itself quite limited in scope."[25]

The scope of these principles has been constrained by pre-existing international obligations. As discussed, pre-existing international obligations may have the effect of constraining the development of a subsequent legal framework among members of an existing legal framework.

Intellectual Property

Another area of concern to members of APEC is intellectual property rights. Intellectual property rights is another area which had not been traditionally regulated within the GATT framework. The regulation of intellectual property only came within the ambit of the GATT/WTO framework with the conclusion of the Agreement on Trade-Related Aspects of Intellectual Property Rights ("TRIPs") as part of the Uruguay Round negotiations. The Intellectual Property Rights ("IPR") experts within APEC have carried out a work programme since 1996 to achieve the planned Collective Actions as well as to enhance APEC-wide cooperation in the following areas: deepening the dialogue on intellectual property policy; surveying and exchanging information on the current status of intellectual property rights protection and administrative systems; studying measures for the effective enforcement of intellectual property rights; fully implementing the TRIPS Agreement no later than 2000; and facilitating technical cooperation to that end.

ASEAN and APEC[26]

The ASEAN countries are important participants within the APEC process and have had an impact on decisions within APEC. However, ASEAN members have been a bit reluctant about their role in APEC, fearing a diminution of their influence in the region. APEC has not yet developed its own legal framework. Although it has become more structured as an organization, and has elements of "rules" and a "dispute settlement mechanism", the APEC members have clearly indicated that these are to be non-binding. However, as APEC has more influence within the region, and develops more "principles" for "consideration" by its members, ASEAN may be more limited in the rules it can develop for ASEAN trade and investment. For example, the ASEAN members may have to balance their desire to create an ASEAN Free Trade Area with the creation of an APEC free trade area, and their development of a framework to regulate investment within ASEAN with the development of principles to regulate investment within all APEC countries.

Will APEC and ASEAN compete with or complement each other as institutions? Will APEC render ASEAN irrelevant? APEC includes nearly all the Dialogue partners of ASEAN and provides a forum for the ASEAN countries to take a common position on regional issues. It has been argued that APEC will complement ASEAN only if the former remains a loosely structured organization.[27]

The APEC framework is still at an early stage of development. As has been seen, although steps have been taken to create more of an institutional structure for the APEC process, APEC is not an organization so much as it is a forum through which the political leaders and officials of member economies can interact. Nevertheless, there has been the development within APEC of a framework to govern economic cooperation of APEC members. While "non-binding" at its outset, this framework is evolving into an international framework which regulates conduct among its members and, "...in order to maintain liberalization commitments that are made on a voluntary basis, an enhanced enforcement mechanism may be necessary."[28] Distinct views of Asia-Pacific economic cooperation have vied to shape the institutionalization of APEC with the United States pushing for a more legalistic approach and an adherence to timetables, while several Asian countries prefer a consultative forum for discussion.[29]

The "North American" or "American institutional" approach to AsiaPacific economic co-operation is epitomized by the views of Fred Bergsten, chairman of the APEC EPG. Although the recommendations of the EPG Report to the APEC ministers were agreed to unanimously by the EPG members, certain recommendations — such as

clear endorsement of free trade and setting a target date for
reaching that goal — bear the imprint of an "American
legalistic approach". The conflict of such an approach with
the more cautious Asian one was evident in the APEC
leaders ignoring the proposal to set a date for regional trade
liberalization.[30]

The latter reflects the view of the ASEAN members of APEC.

The East Asia Economic Caucus ("EAEC")

An East Asian Economic Grouping ("EAEG") was proposed by
Malaysian Prime Minister Mahathir Mohamad in December 1990. He
suggested the formation of an Asian bloc to counter the formation of
trading blocs in North America and the European Community. It was
proposed that the group should include the ASEAN countries, Japan,
and South Korea, as well as China, Hong Kong and Taiwan[31] and
possibly Burma, Laos, Vietnam and Cambodia (which were not members
of ASEAN at the time). Notably absent were the United States,
Canada, Australia and New Zealand.

The use of the term "bloc" aroused misapprehension among some
of the proposed participants, and in the United States and the EC, and
further statements were made to clarify that the EAEG was not intended
to be a trade bloc. The proposal was further explored in a round of talks
by the Malaysian Minister of International Trade and Industry, Datuk
Seri Rafidah Aziz, in the other ASEAN capitals and this initial round
of talks led to an emerging broad consensus in ASEAN that whatever
form EAEG should take, it should:

1. be consistent with the principles of free trade laid down in the
    GATT;
2. not affect the APEC initiative, which has a wider scope and
    coverage; and
3. not undermine the solidarity of ASEAN.[32]

At an international conference on "The ASEAN Countries and
the World Economy: Challenges of Change", in Denpasar, Bali,

Indonesia in early March 1991, Dr Mahathir presented a paper "From Confrontation to Cooperation: Asean's Agenda for a Productive Peace", in which he said the countries of East Asia must speak with one voice. "It will be impossible to do this unless we consult each other, unless we can have some form of group which is recognisable." He added that a formal grouping intended to facilitate consultation and seek consensus prior to negotiation with Europe or America or in multilateral forums such as GATT would therefore not be too far-fetched, but ideal.[33]

After much further discussion, the concept proposed under the EAEG was accepted by a meeting of the ASEAN Economic Ministers in Kuala Lumpur on 9 October 1991, but it was decided to change its name to East Asia Economic Caucus ("EAEC") to avoid any misconceptions. The Ministers agreed to "convening of East Asian economies and to meet as and when the need arises". They further agreed that such a Caucus would:

1. expand intra-regional cooperation in East Asia ...The initiative would provide the necessary collective approach in areas of mutual concern in international economic fora; and
2. not be an institutionalized entity and would not be a trading bloc.[34]

The concept was further discussed at the Singapore Summit in January 1992. In his opening statement, Prime Minister Mahathir, said:

> The East Asia Economic Caucus (EAEC) will not be any kind of trade or economic bloc but a Caucus, an informal getting together of nations in East Asia for the purpose of consultation and to seek consensus so as to speak with one voice at international trade conferences.[35]

At the conclusion of the Singapore Summit, the Singapore Declaration contained the following reference to the EAEC:

> With respect to an EAEC, ASEAN recognizes that consultations on issues of common concern among East Asian economies, as and when the need arises, could contribute to

expanding cooperation among the region's economies, and the promotion of an open and free global trading system.[36]

One of the most difficult problems with forming the EAEC has been the role to be played by Japan. Japan is seen as a critical member of an EAEC. However, Japan has been reluctant to endorse the concept because it is uncomfortable with the exclusion of the US, Canada and Australia.[37]

For its part, the United States was critical of and generally opposed to the EAEC arguing that it is anti-West and undermines the role of APEC.[38] On the one hand, Japan is reluctant to disturb the delicate equilibrium in US-Japan relations. On the other hand, Japan feels that it should not be left out of an Asian grouping particularly as many of its markets and sources of raw materials are there.

On 25 July 1994, in Bangkok during the 27 AMM/PMC, the ASEAN Foreign Ministers met their counterparts from China, Japan and the Republic of Korea (6 + 3) and discussed aspects of the EAEC.[39] These informal meetings continued and in November 1999, a Joint Statement on East Asia Cooperation was issued in Manila, the Philippines in which, inter alia, the Leaders of ASEAN, China, Japan and the Republic of Korea agreed to enhance the dialogue process among themselves and strengthen cooperation with a view to advancing East Asian collaboration in priority areas of shared interest and concern. The Joint Statement provides a set of broad guidelines for cooperation in economic, financial, political, security and transnational issues. In November 2000 it was agreed to establish a study group of government officials from the 13 Asian nations to examine two proposals: firstly, the establishment of a formal East Asian summit meeting to replace the existing informal ASEAN+3 meetings, and secondly, the setting up of a regional free trade and investment area.[40] At the fifth "ASEAN + 3" summit on November 5 2001 in Bandar Seri Begawan, the ASEAN + 3 leaders considered the *Report of the East Asia Vision Group* which contains key proposals and concrete measures to broaden East Asia cooperation, and a proposal was made to establish an ASEAN+3 secretariat in order to promote ASEAN+3 cooperation further.[41] These moves towards closer East Asian ties have been sparked to a large extent by the 1997-98 Asian financial collapse. The grouping was brought together in part by mutual resentment of the aggressive intervention by the US and the International Monetary Fund during the Asian financial meltdown.[42] "[T]he rapid development of the ASEAN-plus-three strongly suggests that it is in the process of developing into an important institution for East Asia and a valuable tool for the sharing of economic information."[43] ASEAN+3 seems to be the current manifestation of the EAEC.[44]

In developing further, the EAEC/ASEAN+3 will be limited by its members' international legal obligations within the existing international legal framework as well as by political and economic considerations. While ASEAN seems to be developing its own legal framework to govern relations amongst its members, the EAEC/ ASEAN+3 seems to be a much looser "caucus" without, at present, the intention of having a formalized legal framework to govern economic relations among its members.

Endnotes

1   John H Jackson, *The World Trading System – Law and Policy of International Economic Relations* (Cambridge/ London: The MIT Press, 1989), p 4.

2   For further discussion of APEC, see, inter alia, PJ Davidson, 'Asia Pacific Economic Cooperation: An Introductory Note', *TAPR*, Document II.A.

3   See, inter alia: Wendy Dobson and Lee Tsao Yuan, 'APEC – Co-operation amidst Diversity' (1994) 10 *ASEAN Economic Bulletin*, pp 231-244; and, Martin Rudner, 'APEC: The Challenges of Asia Pacific Economic Cooperation' (1995) 29 *Modern Asian Studies*.

4   For examples of early proposals, see H Edward English, ''An OECD of the Pacific? A Canadian Perspective', APRRC W/P-1 (Ottawa: Asian Pacific Research and Resource Centre, Carleton University, 1990); and, Senator Gareth Evans, 'Interdependence and Cooperation in the Asia Pacific Region: An Australian Perspective', Address by the Australian Minister for Foreign Affairs and Trade to the Canadian Institute of International Affairs, Montreal, 10 October 1989.

5   Ministerial-level Meeting, Asia Pacific Economic Cooperation, Canberra, 7 November 1989, Summary Statement by the Chairman, Senator the Honourable Gareth Evans, QC, Minister for Foreign Affairs and Trade of Australia.

6   See, Ministerial-Level Meeting, Joint Statement, Canberra, November 1989, *TAPR*, Document II.B.4.a(1). See also, 'APEC countries should set themselves up as examples of good GATT-abiding citizens of the world.' (Then Prime Minister of Singapore, Lee Kuan Yew at APEC's second

Ministerial Meeting in Singapore in July 1990, as quoted in The Straits Times, 1 May 1993: 'Apec countries gearing up to promote freer trade and investment in region'.) But a report prepared by an Eminent Persons Group created by APEC (Eminent Persons Group Report, November 1993), *TAPR*, Document II.B.1.b, recommended the creation of a free trade area in the region (see discussion, *infra*).

7   Joint Statement, *ibid*.

8   Michael Hart and Todd Weiler, 'An Assessment of the Prospects for Trade Liberalization in APEC', paper prepared for the Canadian Senate Foreign Affairs Committee in October 1997 by the Centre for Trade Policy and Law, Carleton University, Ottawa, Canada (CTPL Occasional Paper No 47), p 6.

9   Seoul APEC Declaration, Seoul, 14 November 1991, *TAPR*, Document II.B.2.a.

10 Seoul APEC Declaration, para 1.

11 Shaun Seow and Phua Kok Kim, 'Apec to focus on freer trade for region', Straits Times, 12 September 1992, at 1.

12 Michael Hart and Todd Weiler, 'An Assessment of the Prospects for Trade Liberalization in APEC', *op.cit.* , p 10.

13 Martin Rudner, 'APEC: The Challenges of Asia Pacific Economic Cooperation' (1995) 29 *Modern Asian Studies*, p 410. But see, Yuen Pau and David MDuff, "APEC Study Centre Consortium Meeting, Merida mexico, May 22-24, 2002 for a discussion of aspects of the OECD model that may be adopted by APEC to reinvigorate its economic cooperation mandate.

14 Michael Hart and Todd Weiler, 'An Assessment of the Prospects for Trade Liberalization in APEC', *op. cit.*

15 Following the 1 July 1 1997 transition in Hong Kong, Hong Kong changed its APEC name to 'Hong Kong, China'.

16 The Osaka Action Agenda, 19 November 1995, *TAPR*, Document II.B.2.b, Part I, Section C, para 1.

17 Merit E Janow, 'Symposium — Institutions for International Economic Integration: Assessing APEC's Role in Economic Integration in the Asia-Pacific Region' (1997) 17 *J Intl L Bus* 947.

18 Lopez, Carolina Albero, and Jacint Soler Matutes, 'Open Regionalism versus Discriminatory Trading Agreements: Institutional and Empirical Analysis' (1998) 14 *ASEAN Economic Bulletin*, p 256.

19 Eminent Persons Group Report – *Achieving the APEC vision: Free and Open Trade in the Asia Pacific*, August 1994 – Executive Summary, *TAPR*, Document II.B.1.b.

20 Heinz W Arndt, chapter 3, 'AFTA and After', in Joseph Tan (ed) *AFTA in the changing international economy* (Singapore: ISEAS, 1996) p 46.

21 See, Chia Siow Yue (ed) APEC – Challenges and Opportunities (Singapore: ISEAS,1994) Chapter 6: 'Asia-Pacific Foreign Direct Investment: An APEC Investment Code?'.

22 Eminent Persons Group Report, *op.cit.*

23 For a more detailed discussion of 'soft law', see, inter alia, Roessler, Frieder, 'Law,

DeFacto Agreements and Declarations of Principle in International economic relations' (1978) 21 *German YB Int'l Law*, pp 27-59; Bothe, Michael, 'Legal and Non-Legal Norms – A Meaningful Distinction in International Relations?' (1980) 11 *Neth YB Int'l Law*, pp 65-95; Tadeusz Gruchalla-Wesierski, 'A Framework for Understanding "Soft Law"' (1984) 30 *McGill LJ*, pp 37-88; Martha Finnemore, 'Response: Are Legal Norms Distinctive?' (2000) 32 *NYUJ Int'l L & Pol* 699.

24 *TAPR*, Document II.B.3.a.

25 Merit, *op. cit.*, at 983.

26 See, Mohamed Ariff, 'APEC and ASEAN: Complementing or Competing', chapter 7 in Chia Siow Yue (ed), *APEC: Challenges and Opportunities* (Singapore: ISEAS, 1994). See also Garnaut, Ross, 'ASEAN and the Regionalization and Globalization of World Trade' (1998) 14 *ASEAN Economic Bulletin*, pp 215-223, especially at 223, 'ASEAN, APEC and the Years Ahead'.

27 Mohamed Ariff, *ibid*, p 169.

28 Jennifer L Haworth and Mark D Nguyen, 'Law and Agreement in APEC', *TAPR*, Document II.C.10, p.2. The authors discuss, *inter alia*, APEC's non-legally binding nature and the issue of 'to bind or not to bind'.

29 Seiji Finch Naya and Pearl Imada Iboshi, chapter 4: 'A Post-Uruguay Round Agenda for APEC: Promoting Convergence of North American and Asian Views', in Chia Siow Yue (ed), *APEC — Challenges and Opportunities* (Singapore: ISEAS,1994).

30 *Ibid*, p 72.

31 China has objected to Taiwan's inclusion in the EAEC: 'China's Objection to Taiwan's Inclusion Could Delay Start of East Asian Caucus', The Asian Wall Street Journal Weekly, 20 December 1993, p 4.

32 *Ibid*, at 11. But see, 'Malaysia Extends its Run as the Rogue of APEC', Asia Wall Street Journal Weekly, 28 November 1994, p 16.

33 As reported in Malaysian New Straits Times, 5 March 1991.

34 Joint Press Statement, the 23rd Meeting of the ASEAN Economic Ministers, Kuala Lumpur, Malaysia, 7-8 October 1991, *TAPR*, Document I.B.4.b(23).

35 Opening Statement by HE Dato' Seri Dr Mahathir Bin Mohamad the Prime Minister of Malaysia at the Fourth Meeting of the ASEAN Heads of Government, Singapore, 27 January 1992, in *Meeting of the ASEAN Heads of Government, Singapore, 27-28 January 1992* (Jakarta: ASEAN Secretariat, 1992), at 19.

36 Singapore Declaration of 1992, *TAPR*, Document I.B.8.

37 'The EAEC has been discussed at ASEAN ministerial meetings, but I don't see it taking shape because Japan doesn't want to come in,' reckons political scientist Dr P Ramasamy of the National University of Malaysia. The US, which was not invited to participate in the EAEC, he says, has been advising Japan and South Korea not to join. 'Japan still wants the US as a security umbrella (in the region) so it won't participate without the US giving it the green light,' Ramasamy says. 'It has a huge trade surplus in the US and none in Southeast Asia. You have to consider the political economy.' (Santha Oorjitham, 'ASEAN+3 = 'EAEC' -

Building ties across the region', 15 March 2000, www.asiaweek.com/asiaweek/toc/ 2000/03/15/.).

38   See, eg, 'US Seeks to Blunt Division of APEC on Ethnic Lines', The Asian Wall Street Journal, 25 July 1994 at 8; but see also, 'It is Time for Washington to Embrace the EAEC', The Asian Wall Street Journal, 25 July 1994 at 16.

39   In referring to the developments with China, Japan and South Korea, the Former President of the Republic of the Philippines, Fidel Valdez Ramos, has said, '[this] resurrects the "East Asian Economic Caucus (EAEC)" idea conceived by Malaysia's prime minister Mahathir Mohamad, which the United States had opposed'. 'The World to Come: ASEAN's Political and Economic Prospects in the New Century', Address at The Economic Strategy Institute's (ESI) Global Forum 2000: 'The World to Come — Value and Price of Globalization', Ronald Reagan International Trade Center, Washington DC, USA, 17 May 2000.

40   Singapore's Prime Minister Goh Chok Tong has emphasised: 'This is not, I repeat, an attempt to shut Washington from East Asia.' These assurances are in response to the fears which had been expressed to the earlier proposals for an EAEC. Peter Symonds, 'ASEAN makes tentative moves toward an East Asian economic bloc', 30 November 2000, WSWS: News & Analysis: Asia, World Socialist Web Site http://www.wsws.org/articles/2000/nov2000/asea-n30.shtml.

41   Press Statement by the Chairman of the Seventh ASEAN Summit And the Fifth ASEAN + 3 Summit, 5 November 2001, Bandar Seri Begawan.

42   'The latest moves towards closer East Asian ties have been sparked by the 1997-98 Asian financial collapse, which has fueled political and economic instability throughout the region.' (Ibid).

43   Marc Lanteigne, 'ASEAN Plus Three and the Changing Roles of Economic Institutions in the Post-Crisis Asia Pacific Region', TAPR, Document I.C.12.

44   '"It is for Malaysia and Mahathir to judge whether ASEAN+3 is what they had in mind (when they proposed the EAEC)," says a diplomat from one of the "plus-three" countries.' Santha Oorjitham, op. cit.

CHAPTER 6

GROWTH TRIANGLES

Introduction

Because of the unsatisfactory rate of progress in ASEAN industrial and economic cooperation aimed at the integration of ASEAN as a whole, considerations for economic cooperation have to some extent shifted to focus on sub-regional economic cooperation.[1] In sub-regional economic cooperation, the parties seek to create an environment that will facilitate the efficient flow of goods, services, investment and human resources within a more limited sphere. This form of development can progress more rapidly than broad-based economic cooperation because it is aimed at specific areas where the benefits for all participating countries are visible and rapid enough.

> These zones aim not only at market sharing, but also at resource-pooling amongst the ASEAN partners to increase their competitive advantages *vis-a-vis* the extra-regional competition.[2]

These sub-regional zones also form part of the evolving legal framework within ASEAN, and it is necessary to consider these zones, and how they fit in the evolving legal framework. A detailed examination of these zones is beyond the purview of this book, and the following discussion will be limited to their impact on and place in the developing legal framework for economic cooperation in ASEAN.

In his paper presented at the First ASEAN Economic Congress, held in Kuala Lumpur from 13-22 March 1987, Chee Peng Lim noted:

> A review of ASEAN industrial co-operation schemes, post-AIP, seems to indicate that such schemes are moving from larger to smaller projects, from public to more private sector participation and from complete participation of all member countries to participation of only interested ASEAN countries. In short, the basis for ASEAN industrial co-operation appears to have grown more flexible and realistic since the implementation of the AIP scheme.[3]

He suggested that "it may be desirable...to place more emphazis on cooperation rather than integration in new schemes for ASEAN's consideration" and that "in view of the reluctance to move towards a common market, ASEAN industrial schemes may be more successful if they are based on the pooling of resources rather than market sharing". He also suggested that, "For the same reason, we will assume that ASEAN schemes will be easier to implement if they are oriented towards the outside rather than the domestic ASEAN markets." "Finally, in view of the importance of the private sector and the role of TNCs, co-operation schemes should involve private sector participation at all levels and new institutional arrangements may be necessary."[4]

Professor Chee may have been foreseeing the recent development of growth triangles when he noted:

> The integration of industries in the ASEAN region can also proceed horizontally to facilitate the establishment of an Asean common market, should this be a long-term objective. For example, Indonesia, Singapore and Malaysia can jointly develop Batam Island into an Asean processing zone; or Indonesia, Malaysia and Thailand can jointly develop their plantation-based agro industries...[5]

The Indonesia-Malaysia-Singapore Growth Triangle ("IMS-GT")

The economic "Growth Triangle" of Indonesia, Malaysia, and Singapore is an interesting example of the development of sub-regional economic cooperation.[6] Originally, this Growth Triangle linked Singapore to the Malaysian state of Johor and to Indonesia's Riau Islands to establish a region which could maximize the benefits of resource complementarity of the three partners (often referred to as SIJORI). When contiguous provinces joined the Growth Triangle, the arrangement became known as the Indonesia-Malaysia-Singapore Growth Triangle ("IMS-GT"). The SIJORI economic zone was proposed in December 1989 by Singapore's then Deputy Prime Minister Goh Chok Tong as a new form of sub-regional economic cooperation within ASEAN to exploit economic complementarities in the region.

> The aim is to lure multinational companies seeking the right mix of cheap labour, skilled professionals and efficient infrastructure to an economic zone provided by all three.[7]
>
> This triangle is important for ASEAN because it illustrates an obvious point: small plans are much more likely to succeed than big ones .... It is far better ... to concentrate on speeding up sub-regional economic cooperation.[8]

Singapore possesses excellent infrastructure, well-developed financial markets, comprehensive sea and air transport, and advanced telecommunication facilities. It has easy access to world markets for investors and is an important financial and business services centre for the region. However, Singapore faces shortages of labour, land and water as well as rising production costs. Malaysia and Indonesia have low-cost land and labor available. Under a growth triangle arrangement, the products of plants in Malaysia and Indonesia can be designed, marketed, and distributed by service industries in Singapore, where they will benefit from the excellent infrastructure.

The Legal Framework[9]

Much has been written on the economic reasons for the development of the "Growth Triangle"[10], but little consideration has been given to developing a legal framework within which the Growth Triangle can operate. In order for the Triangle concept to operate it requires agreement among the participating states to establish the legal framework within which cooperation is to take place.

SIJORI developed effectively through the links between Singapore and Johor on the one hand, and between Singapore and Riau on the other. Singapore and Johor had had a long history of economic interaction driven mainly by market forces, whereas the Singapore-Riau link was created by government-led initiatives. A key agreement was struck between Singapore and Indonesia in October 1989, allowing full foreign ownership of Batam-based companies which export their production, for the first five years and 95% for the life of the project. On 28 August 1990, a further agreement was signed to extend the triangle beyond Indonesia's existing export zone on Batam Island, to the whole of the surrounding Riau province. The agreement included the following provisions:

1. simplification of product distribution, payment, and delivery procedures between Singapore and Riau province;
2. joint tourism promotion and development;
3. cooperation in water supply and transportation to Singapore;
4. cooperation in development and maintenance of infrastructure for joint development projects;
5. cooperation in industrial and technological development in the Riau province, including trade, agriculture, and warehousing;
6. exchange of visits by advisers, specialists, and trainees;
7. simplification of the tax system to facilitate investments; and,
8. simplification of entry and exit procedures.[11]

An Indonesian-Singaporean ministerial committee on the development of Riau was set up and, an *ad-hoc* coordination board made up of officials from the Riau province regional development agency ("BAPPEDA"), the provincial-level Board of Investment ("BKPMD"), and Singapore's Economic Development Board ("EDB"), was set up to assist companies investing in Riau.[12] However, the major factor behind the movement of investment from Singapore to Batam was the fact that the EDB and government-linked-companies ("GLCs") were actively involved in developing and managing the industrial parks and resorts on Batam. The

GLCs gave security through their dealings with higher authorities in Indonesia and provided a key interface between the Indonesian bureaucracy and investors.[13]

The two governments signed a bilateral investment guarantee agreement[14], and in June 1991, a further agreement was signed to develop jointly and share Riau's water resources.

Development of the Johor arm of the triangle has been slower. What development there has been, has primarily been in the form of investment from Singapore into Johor. As regards the link in the growth triangle between Johor and Riau, economic links hardly existed before 1993. However, the emerging shortage of labour in Johor led it to consider the possibility of firms in the plantation sector investing in Indonesia.

The federal government in Malaysia officially endorsed Johor's participation in the triangle, giving Johor powers to deal with Singapore and Indonesia on Malaysia's behalf on bilateral matters involving Singapore and Batam; however, in areas such as taxes and immigration which come under federal purview, Johor would need to consult the federal Ministry.[15]

At the Fourth ASEAN Summit which was held in Singapore from 27-28 January 1992, the leaders of the ASEAN countries agreed on a "Framework Agreement on Enhancing ASEAN Economic Cooperation"[16] (see discussion, *supra*, chapter 4) which binds ASEAN members to strengthening economic cooperation. Recognizing that a past stumbling block to cooperation has been the difficulty of achieving a full consensus on how to proceed, the agreement states that although "All Member States shall participate in intra-ASEAN economic arrangements", "two or more Member States may proceed first" with the implementation of cooperative measures "if other Member States are not ready to implement these arrangements".[17] As well as covering cooperation in trade, industry, finance, banking, transport and communications, the agreement also recognises the development of sub-regional growth areas, both within ASEAN and between ASEAN and non-ASEAN states.[18] Thus, the evolving legal framework within ASEAN provides for sub-regional groupings.

In addition to the bilateral agreements and the Framework Agreement which established the initial framework for economic cooperation, it was also necessary to have trilateral agreement if the area was to be considered as a distinct location with its own framework that would attract investment. Official trilateral agreement on the development of the Indonesia-Malaysia-Singapore Growth Triangle was signed in December 1994. The Memorandum of Understanding ("MOU") on Economic Cooperation in relation to IMS-GT was signed in Johor Bahru on 17 December 1994. The objectives of the agreement, as stated in Article 1 of the MOU, are to promote development, expansion and integration in the areas of trade and transport, tourism, shipping and communications, agriculture, forestry, development of industrial infrastructure, and supporting industries. The MOU provides that the development of the Triangle is to be private sector-led and market-driven, and that the private sector is to be the "engine of growth" for the Triangle. In this regard any collaborative effort by the private sector to enhance their participation is to be supported, encouraged and facilitated by the parties to the agreement. The role of the three governments will be to support, encourage and facilitate the successful implementation of the collaborative projects under the MOU, and adopt the necessary measures to promote and facilitate among others the exchange of personnel and the conduct of training activities under the MOU, and the expeditious and smooth flow of goods and services as well as people and investments within the Triangle.

The MOU also provided for an institutional structure for the Triangle. The national coordinating authorities for the MOU are as follows: for the Government of Indonesia, the Office of the Coordinating Minister of Industry and Trade; for the Government of Malaysia, the Ministry of International Trade and Industry; and for the Government of Singapore, the Ministry of Trade and Industry. Ministerial meetings are to be convened at least once a year to review the progress of the collaborative undertakings. The Terms of Reference for the Ministerial Meeting are as follows:

1. function as the formal apparatus of the Consultative Mechanism defined in the MOU Article V;
2. monitor process in implementation of the MOU, including review of reports presented by the Senior Officials Meeting;

resolve outstanding policy issues affecting trade, investment and other areas of collaboration within the Triangle, including specifically policy questions and issues referred from the Senior Officials Meeting;

3. review major cooperation projects covered under the MOU;

4. establish and/or revise the scope of Working Groups, upon the recommendation of the private sector or as otherwise necessary.

Senior Officials are to meet at least once a year, prior to the Ministerial Meeting, to review the progress of the projects under the MOU and to provide the necessary facilitation by resolving outstanding issues and to prepare policy recommendations to be submitted to the Ministerial Meeting for its consideration. The Terms of Reference for the Senior Officials Meeting are as follows:

1. function as the liaison between the Working Groups as the operational level of the Consultative Mechanism and the Ministerial Meeting as the formal apparatus of the Consultative Mechanism;

2. update each party on matters pertaining to trade, investment and other areas of collaboration under the MOU;

3. identify joint promotion and marketing programs to promote trade, investment and other areas of collaboration under the MOU;

4. review relevant policy issues which affect trade, investment and other areas of collaboration under the MOU, to ensure that policies support trade, investment and such other areas of collaboration. Among others, these include immigration, customs and fiscal policies, regulations and procedures.

The Terms of Reference for the Working Groups are as follows:

1. function as the operational level of the Consultative Mechanism defined in the MOU, in particular as the mechanism through which to integrate the private sector director into the formal sub-regional economic cooperation;

2. review and discuss the relevant policy issues affecting a particular field/sector of cooperation;

3. initiate policy actions, such as negotiations leading to international agreements (bilateral or trilateral) in their particular fields/sectors of cooperation;

4. review the progress of the projects in a particular sector/field of cooperation under the MOU, identify outstanding issues which require resolution and prepare policy recommendations to be submitted to the Senior Officials Meeting for its consideration.

The MOU emphasizes the participation of the private sector. The private sector is to participate at all levels of the formal institutional structure of the consultative mechanism. At the level of the Ministerial and Senior Officials Meetings, the private sector is to be invited to present its views on policy issues affecting the success of the IMS-GT cooperation. At the level of the Working Groups, the private sector can make proposals and register complaints which are to be discussed and then taken directly to the most senior levels of the relevant government agencies, through the Senior Officials Meeting and subsequent Ministerial Meeting.

This formal institutionalizing of links provides a useful channel for enabling both public and private sectors to participate in the Growth Triangle. However, further agreements are necessary to further develop the legal framework to provide for changes to laws and regulations to speed up the movement of goods, capital and labour among the participants. Provision has to be made for the duty-free movement of goods and the harmonization of customs procedures. There has to be harmonization of investment, tax and land regulations amongst others. There also has to be simplification and harmonization of immigration regulations to allow for the free movement of people.[19] Much of this framework is being established at the broader, regional level within AFTA or the AIA, and to the extent that the larger framework encompasses these provisions, obviously it will be unnecessary to establish separate rules for the Triangle. However, if additional provisions are necessary, or it is desired to advance the Triangle faster than the regional agreements, it will be necessary to have a separate framework for the growth triangle.

Whatever approach is taken to establishing a special legal framework within which "growth triangles" can develop, careful consideration must be given to making sure that the framework accords with other international legal obligations which the participants may have. Consideration must be given to ensuring that the framework is consistent with the evolving legal framework within ASEAN. As well, one must bear in mind that aspects of a multilateral international legal framework for regulating trade and investment already exist and that the ASEAN countries are participants to varying degrees in this framework which may put constraints on or may assist the future development of the legal framework.

Growth areas were discussed at the Sixth ASEAN Summit in Hanoi in December 1998. The Hanoi Plan of Action, which was adopted, contains the following provisions:[20]

2.11   Further development of growth areas.
      To narrow the gap in the level of development among Member States and to reduce poverty and socio-economic disparities in the region.

2.11.1 Actively expedite the implementation and further development of growth areas such as the Brunei-Indonesia-Malaysia-Philippines East ASEAN Growth Area (BIMP-EAGA), Indonesia-Malaysia-Singapore Growth Triangle (IMS-GT), Indonesia-Malaysia-Thailand Growth Triangle (IMT-GT), and the inter-state areas along the West-East Corridor (WEC) of Mekong Basin in Vietnam, Laos, Cambodia and North-eastern Thailand within the ASEAN-Mekong Basin Development Cooperation Scheme.

In the Hanoi Declaration on Narrowing Development Gap for Closer ASEAN Integration, adopted in Hanoi on 23 July 2001, the Foreign Ministers of the ASEAN Member countries renewed their call for the development of the region through sub-regional cooperative programmes, including the Indonesia-Malaysia-Singapore Growth triangle.

Endnotes

1. 'Such arrangements, a new phenomenon among developing countries, are designed to complement overall ASEAN economic cooperation.' 'On Regional Development Efforts', Statement by HE Mr Ali Alatas, Minister for Foreign Affairs, Republic of Indonesia, at the PMC 9+10 Session, Manila, 28 July 1998.

2. Suthiphand Chirathivat, 'ASEAN Economic Integration with the World through AFTA', chapter 2, in Tan, Joseph (ed), *AFTA in the Changing International Economy* (Singapore: ISEAS, 1996), p 30.

3. Chee Peng Lim, 'Asean co-operation in industry: Looking back and looking forward', in Sopiee, Noordin et al (eds), *ASEAN at the Crossroads* (Malaysia: Institute of Strategic and International Studies, 1987), p 112.

4. *Ibid.*

5. *Ibid*, at 118.

6. Other arrangements are also developing, eg, the so-called 'Northern Triangle' comprising Sumatra, north Malaysia and southern Thailand. The discussion here will be limited to the 'Growth Triangle' which is at a more advanced stage.

7. Vatikiotis, Michael, 'Search for a hinterland', Far Eastern Economic Review, 3 January 1991, pp 34-35, at 34.

8. Holloway, Nigel, 'Development 1', Far Eastern Economic Review, 3 January 1991, p 34.

9. See also, Paul J Davidson, 'Regional Economic Zones in the Asia-Pacific: An Economic Law Perspective', in Toh Mun Heng and Linda Low (eds), *Regional Cooperation and Growth Triangles in ASEAN* (Singapore: Times Academic Press, 1993), pp 193-209.

10. See, for example, Lee Tsao Yuan (ed), *Growth Triangle – The Johor-Singapore-Riau Experience* (Singapore: ISEAS, 1991), for a good discussion of the development of the 'Southern' 'Growth Triangle' from the perspective of the three different participant countries.

11. *Ibid*, at 80.

12. *Id.*

13. Lee Tsao Yuan (ed), *Growth Triangle — The Johor-Singapore-Riau Experience* (Singapore: ISEAS, 1991), at 12-13.

14. Vatikiotis, Michael, 'Bet on Batam', Far Eastern Economic Review, 6 September 1990, at 13.

15. 'KL officially endorses Johor's participation in Growth Triangle', The Sunday Times (Singapore), 23 May 1993.

16. *TAPR*, Document I.B.8.

17. Article 1, para 3.

18. Article 4.

19. It is recognised that there may be difficulties in achieving this degree of harmonization and freedom of movement within the area because of the policy implications, but a detailed discussion of these difficulties is beyond the scope of

this paper. For a more detailed treatment see, Lee Tsao Yuan (ed), *Growth Triangle — The Johor-Singapore-Riau Experience* (Singapore: ISEAS, 1991), especially at 108-113 and Toh Mun Heng and Linda Low (eds), *Regional Cooperation and Growth Triangles in ASEAN* (Singapore: Times Academic Press, 1993).

20 Hanoi Plan of Action, *TAPR*, Document I.B.5.j.

CHAPTER 7

DISPUTE SETTLEMENT

Introduction

An important aspect of any legal system is a mechanism for settling disputes which arise between or among participants within that system. When parties enter into a relationship, it is almost inevitable that disagreements will arise, and it is important to have a mechanism in place to resolve these disputes in an efficient and effective manner so that the parties can continue their relationship. Thus, with enhanced economic cooperation among states and the increased economic activity which results, comes a need for a mechanism for quickly and effectively resolving any differences that may arise.

This chapter discusses the evolution of dispute settlement mechanisms within ASEAN for the settlement of economic disputes. The development of an effective dispute settlement mechanism is an important element in the development of a legal framework. In discussing the settlement of disputes arising from international economic activity, there are three levels of disputes which must be considered. First, in looking at the international framework for regulating international economic activity, one must consider disputes which may arise among the member states in interpreting their rights and obligations arising from treaties or other agreements which form part of the legal framework. Unless special arrangements are made to provide for the resolution of such disputes, the parties run the risk that differences between states may lead to major disagreements that weaken the system as a whole and, if serious enough, may lead to the dissolution of the whole system. An effective dispute settlement mechanism is therefore an important aspect of any institutional structure and of any cooperative framework.

Second, disputes may arise between states and private parties in the former's dealings with foreign traders and investors. These disputes may arise from the implementation and administration of the various measures agreed to by the states as part of the framework, or may arise out of commercial relations between private and state parties. In either case, it is important for the private party to have recourse to some form of dispute settlement procedure which is objective and unbiased, so that the private party will not be deterred from engaging in economic activity.

Third, disputes may arise between private parties in their relations within the established framework. Although these disputes may be resolved completely within the domestic realm of one of the parties, the international framework may provide a mechanism to recognise the international character of these disputes and to provide for their settlement and the enforcement of any ensuing awards. To the extent that the international legal framework provides such a mechanism, it may facilitate and encourage trade and investment to take place within the framework.

The following discussion will not deal in detail with the original General Agreement on Tariffs and Trade/World Trade Organization ("GATT/WTO") mechanisms for settlement of trade disputes nor the mechanisms under the International Convention for the Settlement of Investment Disputes between States and Nationals of Other States (the ICSID Convention) as these have been dealt with in detail elsewhere.[1] Rather, it will concentrate on the mechanisms for resolution of disputes within the existing legal frameworks for economic cooperation within ASEAN. This will include reference to mechanisms for settling disputes between states and private parties, and between private parties where appropriate. Mention will also be made of dispute settlement within APEC as this may affect member countries of ASEAN.

'International' Mechanisms

Before turning to "regional" dispute settlement mechanisms in ASEAN and APEC, the following is a brief look at dispute settlement mechanisms at the "international" level, to which most of the ASEAN states are parties. These mechanisms expressly create decision-making bodies that can independently adjudicate cases and whose decisions are binding on all state parties concerned, including those ASEAN member states which are parties to these mechanisms.[2] These are examples of mechanisms that each deal with one of the three categories of disputes mentioned, ie, state-state disputes, state-private party disputes, private party-private party disputes. These treaties or agreements are:

1. The World Trade Organization Agreement;
2. The Convention on the Settlement of Investment Disputes Between States and Nationals of Other States (ICSID Convention); and,
3. The Convention on the Recognition and Enforcement of Foreign Arbitral Awards.

Various members of ASEAN participate in these mechanisms as part of their interaction in the broader, international legal framework for regulating international economic activity.

1. The dispute settlement mechanism in the World Trade Organization[3]

The GATT/WTO has significantly strengthened and streamlined the GATT rules on dispute settlement, through the creation of an integrated dispute-settlement mechanism. Dispute resolutions are accelerated, with strict time limits established. Other improvements to the rules reduce the ability of any one member to block the adoption of a panel or an appellate body report (also established by the new rules). All WTO members are committed to avoiding the use of unilateral retaliatory measures.

The WTO mechanism is administered by a Dispute Settlement Body ("DSB") which has the authority to establish panels that can examine matters referred to it by the DSB. Panels can make findings to assist the DSB in making recommendations or in the issuance of rulings. Once the panel report has been adopted by the DSB or, in cases of appeals, where the Appellate Body's report has been adopted, the DSB is also authorized to maintain surveillance to ensure that its rulings and recommendations are being implemented. If the party at fault refuses to implement the DSB ruling, the DSB has the power to authorize the suspension of concessions and other obligations due the erring party. This procedure clearly demonstrates a supra national body that can both decide with binding effect on cases involving states and ensure to a significant degree that its decisions are enforced.

ASEAN countries did not generally participate in the old dispute-settlement procedures of the GATT. The strengthened disciplines of the new agreement and the WTO provide the basis for an effective dispute-settlement mechanism that should encourage more use of the system.[4]

2. Convention on the Settlement of Investment Disputes Between States and Nationals of Other States ("ICSID Convention")[5]

The International Centre for Settlement of Investment Disputes ("ICSID") was established by the Convention on the Settlement of Investment Disputes between States and Nationals of other States, which came into force on 14 October 1966. ICSID is an international organization which is closely associated with the World Bank, and was established inter alia, to promote a climate of mutual confidence between states and investors that would be conducive to increasing the flow of private international investment to countries seeking it. ICSID comprises an Administrative Council and Secretariat and maintains a Panel of Conciliators and a Panel of Arbitrators.

No Contracting State is by the mere fact of its ratification of the Convention under any obligation to use the ICSID machinery. That obligation only arises once the State has specifically agreed to submit a particular dispute or class of dispute to ICSID procedures. Such consent may be given, either through a written agreement with the private investor entered prior to or after the dispute arises, or through national legislation, or through a bilateral or multilateral treaty with a contracting state of which the investor is a national. Once the parties have given their consent, such consent is irrevocable and may not be withdrawn unilaterally. Consent of the parties to ICSID arbitration is, unless the parties state otherwise, consent to such arbitration to the exclusion of any other remedy.

Awards given by an arbitration tribunal are final and binding on the parties and not subject to review by any national court. Each Contracting State is obligated to recognize the award as binding and to enforce the pecuniary obligations imposed by the award as if it were a final judgement of a court in the State.

An ASEAN member state which is a party to the Convention is bound in two ways: first, as a party to a dispute, the state is bound by the decision of the arbitration panel; and second, as a contracting party to the Convention, the state is bound, as in the case of the Convention on the Recognition and Enforcement of Foreign Arbitral Awards (see following), to recognize and enforce the award given under the ICSID Convention.

3. Convention on the Recognition and Enforcement of Foreign Arbitral Awards

One of the advantages of arbitration is the ease of enforcement of arbitral awards. Most countries, including most of the members of ASEAN, are parties to the United Nations Convention on the Recognition and Enforcement of Arbitral Awards (the New York Convention). The purpose of the New York Convention is to facilitate the recognition and enforcement of foreign arbitral awards by providing a simple mechanism for that purpose in member states. Under Article 11(1) of the Convention, state parties are obliged to "recognize an agreement in writing under which the parties undertake to submit to arbitration any differences which have arisen or which may arise between them in respect of a defined legal relationship, whether contractual or not, concerning a subject matter capable of settlement by arbitration." Thus, where a case is brought before the courts of a state party to the Convention and the parties to the case have previously entered into a written agreement that disagreements between them shall be subjected to arbitration, then the court concerned 'shall, at the request of one of the parties, refer the parties to arbitration....' Similarly, a 'Contracting State shall recognize arbitral awards as binding and enforce them in accordance with rules of procedure of the territory where the award is relied upon....'

All of the ASEAN member states, except for Myanmar, are signatories to the Convention.

Dispute Settlement within ASEAN

There has been little written concerning the mechanisms for dispute resolution within ASEAN. In addressing this question one must keep in mind the nature of ASEAN and the historical context within which economic cooperation within ASEAN arose. Although the founding instrument of ASEAN (the Bangkok Declaration) included reference to "collaboration and mutual assistance on matters of common interest in the economic...field", economic cooperation has not always been in the forefront of ASEAN relations. In early years, ASEAN relations were very much shaped by political and ideological undercurrents and economic cooperation was very much in the background. Even in the mid-seventies and eighties when various ASEAN initiatives were taken to promote greater economic cooperation there was still a strong desire to preserve the individuality of the member states and to recognise their national interests. It is not surprising therefore that where differences have arisen in the past, they have tended to be resolved through political and diplomatic means rather than through judicial or quasi-judicial organs.

Although ASEAN was established by the Bangkok Declaration in 1967, the first mention of general provisions for settlement of disputes[6] was not made until almost ten years later in the Declaration of ASEAN Concord and the Treaty of Amity and Cooperation, both of which were signed in Bali on 24 February 1976. At that time, the ASEAN member states adopted as part of the programme of action as a framework for ASEAN cooperation, set out in the Declaration of ASEAN Concord, "Settlement of intra-regional disputes by peaceful means as soon as possible".

This provision is expanded upon in the Treaty of Amity and Cooperation, Chapter IV of which contains five articles providing for the "Pacific Settlement of Disputes". These articles emphasize that parties 'shall at all times settle disputes among themselves through friendly negotiations' (Article 13), and only 'in the event no solution is reached through direct negotiations' are further steps to be taken (Article 15).

In order "to settle disputes through regional processes", the Treaty provides for the creation of "a High Council comprising a Representative at ministerial level from each of the High Contracting Parties to take cognizance of disputes...." (Article 14). In the event no solution is reached through direct negotiations, this High Council is directed to recommend to the parties in dispute, appropriate means of settlement such as good offices, mediation, inquiry or conciliation. In addition, the council may offer its good offices, or upon agreement of the parties in dispute, constitute itself into a committee of mediation, inquiry or conciliation (Article 15). However, a further limitation is put on the process in that "the foregoing provisions...shall not apply to a dispute unless all the parties agree to their application to that dispute" (Article 16).

The treaty also provides that nothing in it shall preclude recourse to the modes of peaceful settlement contained in Article 33(1) of the Charter of the United Nations.[7] However, parties should be encouraged to take initiatives to solve disputes by friendly negotiations before resorting to the other procedures provided for in the Charter of the United Nations (Article 17).

The treaty has been called a benchmark in ASEAN development in that it marks a maturation stage for the Association and that by providing a framework for settling disputes the members had acknowledged the existence of disruptive forces within the region which, if not dealt with, could erode whatever gains had been achieved.

> They had gone past the stage of building and nursing the fragile foundations of the early stages and in the now familiar "step-by-step ASEAN approach" to region-building they set out to shape the framework for peaceful solutions to outstanding conflicts. Thus, as an event the Treaty might well represent one of the major achievements of ASEAN.[8]

This mechanism has remained unused. However, the High Contracting Parties, at their meeting held on 23 July 2001 in Hanoi, adopted Rules of Procedure of the High Council.[9] This represents a further step in the "juridicization" of ASEAN.

These provisions are meant to deal with political disputes and are not really meant to provide a mechanism for resolving economic disputes. However, they are of interest in examining the development of the legal framework for economic cooperation as they indicate a general trend to a more "legalistic", rules-based framework for governing relations among members of ASEAN.

Following the Bali Summit, the attention of ASEAN turned more to issues of economic cooperation. As has been discussed in Chapter 3, Agreements were entered into, inter alia, to establish a Preferential Trade Area ("PTA") as well as to establish ASEAN Industrial Projects ("AIP"). Both these agreements contained provisions for settling disputes which might arise in their implementation.

Further developments in economic cooperation took place at the Manila meeting of the ASEAN Heads of Government in December 1987. At this meeting the Member countries signed the Agreement for the Promotion and Protection of Investments.[10] This Agreement also contains provisions dealing with the settlement of disputes. Article IX originally provided that:

(1) Any dispute between and among the Contracting Parties concerning the interpretation or application of this Agreement shall, as far as possible, be settled amicably between the parties to the dispute. Such settlement shall be reported to the ASEAN Economic Ministers (AEM).

(2) If such a dispute cannot thus be settled it shall be submitted to the AEM for resolution.

This was amended in 1996 by the 1996 Protocol to Amend the 1987 Agreement for the Promotion and Protection of Investments. The Protocol provides that the provisions of the ASEAN Dispute Settlement Mechanism (see *infra*) will apply to the settlement of investment disputes. This is another indication of the move towards more of a "legal" framework for ASEAN.

Article XI further provides for "Consultation":

> The Contracting Parties agree to consult each other at the request of any Party on any matter relating to investments covered by this Agreement, or otherwise affecting the implementation of this Agreement.

The Agreement also provides for the resolution of disputes between nationals of one of the Contracting Parties and a Contracting Party, ie, the second category of disputes referred to above. These provisions are interesting in that they provide for a detailed mechanism for the binding resolution of such disputes by arbitration. Article X provides as follows:

(1) Any legal dispute arising directly out of an investment between any Contracting Party and a national or company of any of the other Contracting Parties shall as far as possible, be settled amicably between the parties to the dispute.

(2) If such a dispute cannot thus be settled within six months of its being raised, then either party can elect to submit the dispute for conciliation or arbitration and such election shall be binding on the other party. The dispute may be brought before the International Centre for the Settlement of Investment Disputes (ICSID), the United Nations Commission on International Trade Law (UNCITRAL)[11], the Regional Centre for Arbitration at Kuala Lumpur or any other regional centre for arbitration in ASEAN, whichever body the parties to the dispute mutually agree to appoint for the purposes of conducting the arbitration.

(3) In the event that the parties cannot agree within a period of three months on a suitable body for arbitration, an arbitral tribunal consisting of three members shall be formed. The parties to the dispute shall appoint one member each, and these two members shall then select a national of a Third Contracting Party to be the Chairman of the tribunal, subject to the approval of the parties to the dispute. The appointment of the members and the

(4) chairman shall be made within two months and three months respectively, from the date a decision to form such an arbitral tribunal is made.

(4) If the arbitral tribunal is not formed in the periods specified in paragraph 3 above, then either party to the dispute may, in the absence of any other relevant arrangement, request the President of the International Court of Justice to make the required appointments.

(5) The arbitral tribunal shall reach its decisions by a majority of votes and its decisions shall be binding. The Parties involved in the dispute shall bear the cost of their respective members to the arbitral tribunal and shall share equally the cost of the chairman and other relevant costs. In all other respects, the arbitral tribunal shall determine its own procedures.

This mechanism has not been utilized, but is interesting in that it shows the development of more detailed mechanisms for the settlement of economic disputes as the parties have developed more rules to regulate their economic activity, and indicates a move towards more of a legalistic framework for governing their economic activity *inter se*.

With the increased steps towards economic cooperation which have taken place, particularly at the Singapore Summit, it has become necessary for ASEAN to consider the development of a more appropriate dispute resolution mechanism, at least for disputes involving economic matters. As intra-regional economic activity increases, the likelihood of disputes arising increases, and it becomes more important to have an efficient and effective mechanism for dealing with such disputes. As discussed in Chapter Two, the "ASEAN way" of consensus-building embodied in the ASEAN terms *Musyawarah* and *Mufakat* has been the principle underlying decision-making, and ASEAN has shunned supra-national mechanisms to make decisions or to resolve disputes. With this historical context in mind, it is unlikely that ASEAN would be prepared to move towards a mechanism such as the Court of Justice of the European Communities which can give decisions that are binding on member states and whose judgements overrule those of national courts. The question therefore arises as to what may be an appropriate and acceptable form for this mechanism to take.

In fact, there have been developments in this regard within ASEAN, flowing from the Singapore Summit of 1992. Much of the Singapore Summit was devoted to discussions of the importance of enhancing economic cooperation within ASEAN and one of the major Summit documents was the Framework Agreement on Enhancing ASEAN Economic Cooperation.[12] Article 9 of the Framework Agreement addresses the question of dispute settlement and provides that:

> Any differences between the Member States concerning the interpretation or application of this Agreement or any arrangements arising therefrom shall, as far as possible, be settled amicably between the parties. Whenever necessary, an appropriate body shall be designated for the settlement of disputes.

As part of the framework on enhancing ASEAN economic development, the ASEAN Heads of Government agreed to establish and participate in the ASEAN Free Trade Area ("AFTA") and agreed that the Common Effective Preferential Tariff (CEPT) scheme will be the main mechanism for AFTA (See discussion, *supra*). Article 8 of the Agreement on the CEPT Scheme for AFTA (hereafter referred to as the CEPT Agreement)[13] expands on the dispute settlement mechanism for differences arising under that Agreement.

These provisions drew from the original dispute settlement provisions of GATT 1947 and provided that Member States should accord adequate opportunity for consultations regarding any representations made by other Member States with respect to any matter affecting the implementation of the Agreement, or that Member States which considered that any other Member State had not carried out its obligations under the Agreement, resulting in the nullification or impairment of any benefit accruing to them, could, with a view to achieving satisfactory adjustment of the matter, make representations to the other Member States concerned. Any differences between the Member States concerning the interpretation or application of the Agreement were, as far as possible, to be settled amicably between the parties. If such differences could not be settled amicably, they were to be submitted to the Council set up by the agreement, and, if necessary, to the AEM.

However, over time, the original GATT provisions were found to be inadequate in themselves to provide for an efficient dispute settlement mechanism, and over the years a number of developments and refinements were made to provide more detailed rules and procedures to flesh out the original "bare-bones" provisions. This culminated in the new dispute settlement mechanism in the WTO which is briefly outlined above. The new mechanism provides a detailed process for dispute settlement, and is indicative of the movement to more "legalism" in the GATT/WTO framework.

Within ASEAN, the need for a more efficient, detailed dispute settlement was also becoming apparent as ASEAN expanded its membership and the level of economic cooperation deepened. At the Bangkok Summit in December 1995, the Heads of State and Government of ASEAN agreed that ASEAN would adopt a General Dispute Settlement Mechanism ("DSM") which will apply to all disputes arising from ASEAN economic agreements.[14] The Protocol on DSM was entered into on 20 November 1996 at Manila[15] in recognition of "the need to expand Article 9 of the [Framework] Agreement [on Enhancing ASEAN Economic Cooperation] to strengthen the mechanism for the settlement of disputes in the area of ASEAN economic cooperation".[16] This Protocol, is patterned after the WTO Dispute Settlement Understanding, and is expected to make the process of resolving economic disputes in ASEAN more expeditious and transparent. The Protocol is applicable to all past and future ASEAN economic agreements, including the CEPT Agreement. As with the new dispute settlement mechanism in the WTO, the new DSM provides much more detailed procedures for dispute settlement and, is indicative of the evolving legal framework in ASEAN.[17]

The Protocol provides rules and procedures to apply to disputes brought pursuant to the consultation and dispute settlement provisions of the Agreement as well as the agreements listed in Appendix 1 of the Protocol (a list of 47 prior agreements dealing with different economic matters — see list in Appendix 11) and future ASEAN economic agreements (the "covered agreements").[18] The rules and procedures of the Protocol apply subject to such special or additional rules and procedures on dispute settlement contained in the covered agreements. To the extent that there is a difference between the rules and procedures of the Protocol and the special or additional rules and procedures in the covered agreements, the special or additional rules and procedures shall prevail.[19]

Member States who have disagreements are encouraged to undertake bilateral consultations so as to reach an amicable settlement. Other Member States may offer good offices and mediation. Should no amicable settlement be reached, the issue is elevated to the Senior Economic Officials Meeting ("SEOM"). A panel of experts will be convened by SEOM to assist them in making rulings. The panel's task includes fact-finding and determining the applicability of relevant ASEAN agreements.

An important new element introduced by the DSM is that rulings by SEOM on disputes is by simple majority and not by consensus. Hence the ASEAN DSM represents the first formal use of non-consensual decision-making in ASEAN.[20]

Under the Protocol, the ASEAN Economic Ministers serve as the final appellate body. Its decisions on appeals shall be by simple majority. The decision shall be final and binding on all parties to the dispute.

Under the ASEAN DSM, the entire process of dispute settlement has a maximum length of 290 days. The Protocol also provides for a maximum of 30 days in which the parties concerned shall implement the ruling of SEOM or the decision of the AEM. Member States are also required to give a written report of the progress they have made in implementing these rulings or decisions.

Should parties concerned fail to implement the SEOM or AEM decision, the Protocol requires them to enter into negotiations to provide satisfactory compensation to the other parties. If no mutually acceptable compensation is worked out, then the party which has invoked the dispute settlement procedures may request authorization from the AEM to suspend the application to the Member State concerned of any applicable concessions.

The new ASEAN Industrial Cooperation ("AICO") Scheme discussed in Chapter Four, includes a dispute resolution process which makes reference to the DSM. Article 9 of the AICO Agreement provides that "Any differences between the ASEAN Member Countries concerning the interpretation or application of this Agreement shall, as far as possible, be settled amicably between the parties. If such differences cannot be settled amicably, it shall be submitted to the Dispute Settlement Mechanism."

As can be seen from these recent developments, the member states of ASEAN seem to be moving to more formalised dispute settlement mechanisms.[21] This is in keeping with the move towards the development of more of a legal framework to regulate economic activity *inter se*, and in keeping with the general trend internationally to 'legalism' in regulating international economic relations.[22]

Dispute Settlement in APEC

As discussed in Chapter 5, The Asia Pacific Economic Cooperation ("APEC") forum is the newest organization concerned with economic cooperation in the Asia-Pacific region. The members of ASEAN (except Cambodia, Laos and Myanmar which just joined ASEAN) are all members of APEC and will be affected by any dispute settlement mechanism developed there.

Since its formation in 1989, APEC has developed rapidly and although still in its formative stages, has established some framework for economic cooperation and taken steps toward an institutional structure with the establishment of a Secretariat in Singapore in 1992 (see discussion of APEC in Chapter 5).

At a meeting of the APEC Trade Ministers in 1994, it was noted:

> Both the Eminent Persons' Group and the Pacific Business Forum...look to the early adoption of ...an APEC dispute avoidance or mediation mechanism...[23]

and at the November 1994 Bogor Summit, APEC Leaders stated their interest in dispute mediation:

> Trade and other economic disputes among APEC economies have negative implications for the implementation of agreed cooperative arrangements as well as for the spirit of cooperation. To assist in resolving such disputes and in avoiding [their] recurrence, we agree to examine the possibility of a voluntary consultative dispute mediation service, to supplement the WTO dispute settlement mechanism, which should continue to be the primary channel for resolving disputes.[24]

The Third Report of The Eminent Persons Group, August 1995,[25] addressed the need for a dispute resolution mechanism recommending:

> the immediate creation of a voluntary APEC Dispute Mediation Service (DMS). It should:
> - Apply to all issues, thus ranging far beyond the dispute settlement mechanism in the World Trade Organization;
> - Emphasize mediation and conciliation rather than arbitration, in which the mediator tries to bring the parties together to arrive at their own settlement of the dispute or, failing that, offers his or her own proposals for a settlement;
> - Feature "shuttle diplomacy" by a mediator moving between the two sides in an effort to reconcile their differences and foster a settlement between them;
> - Be implemented by individual mediators chosen voluntarily by the APEC member economies that are parties to a dispute from a list originally nominated by each economy and maintained by the APEC Secretariat;
> - Enable third parties to make their views known at the outset of the process; and
> - Encompass a second stage through which, if mediation and conciliation fail, a special review panel would make

> an objective assessment of the dispute that would be released publicly if one or more of the parties failed to accept its proposals.

Mediation was recommended rather than arbitration as '[t]his approach would be in keeping with the growing sense of community in the region. It would offer an intermediate channel between bilateral negotiation and the "win or lose" confrontations of the WTO."[26] It was noted that mediation was frequently used in the resolution of private commercial disputes within several economies in the Asia Pacific region and that its success may be due in part to the ability of parties to "save face" through such a mechanism, which allows for resolution by consensus rather than by confrontation.[27]

A Dispute Mediation Experts' Group ("DMEG") was created by the Committee on Trade and Investment of APEC ("CTI") and met for the first time in Vancouver on 17-18 June 1995. The DMEG, chaired by Canada, examined the possibility for dispute mediation in APEC under four broad headings:

1. Government-to-government dispute mediation;
2. Private-to-government dispute mediation;
3. Private-to-private dispute mediation; and
4. Avoidance of disputes through increased transparency.

APEC Leaders expressed their continuing interest in dispute mediation at the November 1995 Osaka summit:

> Desiring that trade and economic tensions among APEC economies be resolved in a non-confrontational manner, we are committed to finding ways of ameliorating trade friction. We agree on the desirability of an APEC dispute *mediation service*, without prejudice to rights and obligations under the WTO Agreement and other international agreements.[28]

The DMEG met several times to discuss dispute mediation and reaffirmed the importance of the WTO dispute settlement procedures for disputes between governments and agreed on the need for education and training in the area of WTO dispute settlement and avoidance. The DMEG published *International Commercial Disputes: a Guide to Arbitration and Dispute Resolution in APEC Member Economies*, and conducted a training seminar on the WTO Dispute Settlement Understanding and policy discussions and information-sharing on dispute issues.

Although the Experts discussed options for a dispute mediation service, including, in particular, the use of the "Trade Policy Dialogue" of the Committee on Trade and Investment for disputes between APEC economies, the main emphasis in the Dispute Mediation Experts Group was on facilitating the resolution of private disputes.

At its meeting in May 1999, the CTI decided to realign work to enable the substantive work on dispute mediation to be carried out under the direct responsibility of the CTI Chair. The CTI will continue consideration of government-to-government dispute mediation in keeping with the evolution of APEC's work on trade and investment liberalization and facilitation.

Different traditions and practices among APEC countries have made the issue of a dispute settlement mechanism in APEC controversial. North American countries tend to prefer a legalistic solution to investment disputes; for example, NAFTA has an elaborate dispute settlement mechanism. On the other hand, ASEAN countries are known to favour a less formal mechanism, even though the recent developments within ASEAN may indicate the development of more formalised mechanisms.

APEC regards WTO dispute settlement as the primary channel for solving disputes. Although APEC can have a role in helping to resolve and avoid disputes through non-adversarial and voluntary approaches, APEC is not a rules-based organization, so it is not possible for it to establish a formal, binding dispute settlement mechanism.

Endnotes

1   See, eg, on the WTO mechanism, Palitha TB Kohona, 'Dispute Resolution Under the World Trade Organization: An Overview', in *Journal of World Trade* (1994) vol 28, no 2, pp 23-47; and on the ICSID system, Aron Broches, 'Convention on the Settlement of Investment Disputes Between States and Nationals of Other States of 1965: Explanatory Notes and Survey of Its Application', in *XVIII Yearbook of Commercial Arbitration* (1993) at p 627.

2   See discussion in Joseph Sedfrey S Santiago, 'A Postscript to AFTA's False Start — The Loss of Sovereignty Issue' (1995) 12 *ASEAN Economic Bulletin*, p 18, especially at pp 23ff, 'ASEAN Member States' Experiences on Sovereignty Diminution'.

3   Brunei Darussalam, Indonesia, Malaysia, Myanmar, the Philippines, Singapore and Thailand are currently members of the WTO. Cambodia, Laos and Vietnam have observer status and are seeking membership in the WTO.

4   In fact, the first WTO dispute involved Singapore and Malaysia: 'Developing countries are becoming active users of WTO dispute-settlement rules', *WTO Focus*, No 9, March-April 1996.

5   Indonesia, Malaysia, the Philippines and Singapore have signed and ratified the ICSID Agreement. Thailand signed the Convention on 6 December 1985 but has not deposited its ratification; Cambodia signed the Convention on 5 November 1993 but has not deposited its ratification.

6   There had been provisions for dispute settlement in the Multilateral Agreement on Commercial Rights on Non-Scheduled Services Among the Association of Southeast Asian Nations, signed at Manila on 13 March 1971, but they were specific to that agreement. (See, *ASEAN Documents Series 1967-1988* (Jakarta: ASEAN Secretariat, 1988), pp 332-334.) Article 4 provides, inter alia:

    If any dispute arises between Member States relating to the interpretation or application of the present Agreement, they shall, in the first place, endeavour to settle it by negotiation between themselves.

    If they fail to reach a settlement they may agree to refer the dispute for decision firstly, to the Permanent Committee on Civil Air Transportation, secondly, to the ASEAN Standing Committee and, lastly, to the ASEAN Ministers whose decisions shall be final.

7   Article 33(1) of the UN Charter provides:

    The parties to any dispute,...shall, first of all, seek a solution by negotiation, enquiry, mediation, conciliation, arbitration, judicial settlement, resort to regional agencies or arrangements, or other peaceful means of their own choice.

8   Purificacion Valera-Quisumbing, 'Can ASEAN Forge a Viable Legal Regime for regional Cooperation?' (1981) 56 Philippine Law Journal, 209 at 221.

9   *TAPR*, Document I.B.3.j.

10   Agreement among the Governments of Brunei Darussalam, The Republic of Indonesia, Malaysia, The Republic of the Philippines, The Republic of Singapore,

and The Kingdom of Thailand for the Promotion and Protection of Investments, Manila, 15 December 1987, *TAPR*, Document I.B.12.a.

11　It should be noted that, although UNCITRAL has developed uniform rules for arbitration and conciliation which parties may agree to use, and has also developed a model arbitration law which countries may use in developing their own arbitration laws, UNCITRAL itself does not act as an institution for assisting with arbitration or conciliation proceedings.

12　*TAPR*, Document I.B.8; see Appendix 4.

13　*TAPR*, Document I.B.8; see Appendix 3.

14　Bangkok Summit Declaration of 1995, Bangkok, 15 December 1995, para 8, *TAPR*, Document I.B.5.e.

15　The Protocol on Dispute Settlement Mechanism, Manila, 20 November 1996, *TAPR*, Document I.B.7.o; see Appendix 7.

16　From the Preamble, *ibid.*

17　The following is a very brief discussion of the mechanism. For a more detailed discussion of the new DSM see, Paul J Davidson, 'Dispute Settlement in ASEAN', *TAPR*, Document I.C.4.

18　Article 1, para 1.

19　Article 1, para 2.

20　APEC Secretariat, Economic Committee, *The Impact of Subregionalism in APEC* (Singapore: APEC Secretariat, 1997).

21　'In 1996, the ASEAN economic ministers decided to set up a dispute-settlement mechanism that would cover disagreements on AFTA and other significant ASEAN economic agreements, an important step toward a more rules-based regime.': Severino, Rodolfo C, Secretary-General of ASEAN, Asia Policy Lecture: 'What ASEAN is and what it stands for', The Research Institute for Asia and the Pacific, University of Sydney, Australia, 22 October 1998.

22　'...the ASEAN mechanism is less legalistic in nature than the WTO dispute settlement mechanism and leaves much discretion to its political organs. However, its establishment is a testament to the growing legalism in the fora of international commerce, especially in a region that has long resisted such efforts.': Jennifer L Haworth and Mark D Nguyen, 'Law and Agreement in APEC', *TAPR*, Document II.C.10, p 13.

23　Notes for an Address by the Honourable Roy MacLaren, Minister for International Trade (Canada) at the Meeting of APEC Trade Ministers, Jakarta, 6 October 1994.

24　APEC Economic Leaders' Declaration of Common Resolve, Bogor, Indonesia, 15 November 1994, para 9, *TAPR*, Document II.B.2.a.

25　*Implementing the APEC Vision* (Singapore: the APEC Secretariat, 1995).

26　*Ibid.*, at p 10-11.

27　*Ibid.*, p 12.

28　APEC Economic Leaders' Declaration of Common Resolve, Osaka, Japan, 19 November 1995, para 4, *TAPR*, Document II.B.2.a(1).

• CHAPTER 8 •

THE EVOLVING
LEGAL FRAMEWORK

Introduction

As discussed in Chapter 1, a legal framework is comprised of two basic elements: (1) rules; and (2) a mechanism for dealing with disputes that may arise under those rules. At the international level, many different frameworks exist, governing the relations among the participants to a particular legal community. Different frameworks exist, comprising different members and governing various elements of their relationship, eg, a framework governing trade relations or a framework governing investment. A hierarchy of frameworks may exist — multilateral (comprising a large number of participants and having a broad membership), plurilateral (comprising a more restricted membership, and often of a regional nature), or bilateral (two participants). Rules of frameworks lower in the hierarchy must accord with those of frameworks higher in the hierarchy if they have members which are also participants in a "higher" framework. Thus, participants of a regional grouping must comply with the rules of multilateral frameworks of which they are also members.

The Evolving Legal Framework in ASEAN

ASEAN is undergoing an evolution of the framework regulating economic relations in the region. Just as at the broader international level there has been a move to more of a rules-based system to regulate international economic relations (as exemplified by the developments within the World Trade Organization)[1], so too there have been

155

developments within ASEAN which have led to more "legalism" in regulating the economic relations of the members. Initially, ASEAN had a very loose framework for cooperation and the members were reluctant to be too "legalistic" in their relations with each other. Although the members of ASEAN still prefer to conduct their relations in the "ASEAN way"[2], there has nevertheless been a development of a legal framework for regulating their economic relations *inter se*.

The evolution of ASEAN as an entity and the development of a framework to govern relations among its members can be seen in part by looking at the evolution of the institutional structures within ASEAN.[3]

ASEAN was initially formed with mainly political objectives at a time of recent military conflict and considerable continuing tension amongst several of ASEAN's members. It was a time of political instability on the borders of the original ASEAN, in particular with the war in Indochina, and it was a time of political uncertainty within several of the ASEAN members, as they sought a firm basis for development.[4] Although collaboration in the economic field was mentioned in its founding document,[5] little was done in this area, and the Association concentrated on political concerns. The political objectives were met splendidly, and ASEAN performed a valuable role in keeping peace in the region. Gradually, objectives of economic cooperation became more prominent in ASEAN. With the development of closer economic relations, the need for more of a legal framework to govern these relations grew.

ASEAN was initially established with a structure which was organizationally loose and avoided the trappings of a strong regional organization. The creation of the ASEAN Secretariat in 1976 to act as a central administrative organ to promote greater efficiency in the coordination of the ASEAN organs and more effective implementation of ASEAN projects and activities was an important step in the evolution of ASEAN as a legal entity. In January 1993, the ASEAN Secretariat was restructured and vested with an expanded set of functions and responsibilities to initiate, advise, coordinate and implement ASEAN activities. In accordance with the Protocol restructuring the Secretariat, the Secretary-General was redesignated as the Secretary-General of ASEAN and given an enlarged mandate to initiate, advise coordinate and implement ASEAN activities, and also accorded ministerial status.[6] Although the members have not given over any real decision-making powers to the Secretariat, the evolution of the Secretariat indicates the maturation of ASEAN as an entity and "may be considered as an initial step in formalizing the legal personality of ASEAN as a corporate entity governed by its own constitution and by-laws".[7]

The "summit meetings" are the supreme organ of ASEAN. Until the Singapore meeting of Heads of State in 1992, the Heads of State had been following the practice of meeting as and when necessary to give directions to ASEAN; there was no institutionalisation of the meetings. The Singapore summit regularized these meetings as part of the restructuring of ASEAN institutions and decided to meet on a regular basis every three years, with informal meetings in between. In 1995, the Fifth ASEAN Summit in Bangkok decided to hold annual Informal Summits. At their informal meeting in Singapore in 2000, the ASEAN leaders decided to devote more time to important matters of substance and reduce ceremonial proceedings, in favour of working summits, and agreed to meet in an annual summit without the distinction of it being either an informal or formal summit.

However, ASEAN remains an inter-governmental regional organization without a supranational objective. The member countries still maintain ASEAN as a forum for consultation and cooperation only, with each member retaining its individual identity. Unlike the European Community, ASEAN as an entity in its present form does not have any legal controls over the regional economy. There has been a slow movement towards more structure in the institutions and organization of ASEAN as an entity, although the emergence of a strong ASEAN identity has been constrained by a preoccupation with consensus and the mistrust of a strong ASEAN identity with powers parallelling the member states in some areas.[8]

Concern has been expressed in ASEAN that becoming more "legalistic" and having a supranational structure would involve a loss of sovereignty. One can say that the sovereignty of a state is practically restricted when it enters into an international agreement and assumes legal obligations thereunder, since treaties and international agreements create legal regimes and, in many cases, structures, which impose obligations on states that are party to such treaties and agreements. A state, party to a treaty or international agreement, must act in accordance with its treaty obligations since non-compliance with treaty obligations would put the erring state at the risk not only of legal sanctions where sanctions are provided in case of breach, but isolation from the community of nations which form the legal community. However, ASEAN member states have already entered into a number of treaties and international agreements and so may be said to have voluntarily and repeatedly caused the diminution of their sovereignty.[9]

This book has traced the development of the framework for regulating economic relations in ASEAN through the various agreements into which the members have entered for regulating their economic relations. These schemes, such as the Agreement on ASEAN Preferential Trading Arrangements, the ASEAN Industrial Projects and the ASEAN Industrial Complementation Scheme,[10] were initially quite limited in their scope and application and reflected the hesitancy of the members of ASEAN to enter into economic relations. However, there has been a move to more economic cooperation in the region and this has necessitated the development of more of a legal framework to govern these closer economic relations.

'Rules'

Within ASEAN, a rationalization of the framework for economic cooperation and the development of rules to set the guidelines within which this cooperation can take place is occurring. This is taking place within the context of The Framework Agreement for Enhancing ASEAN Economic Cooperation.[11] Although it is a framework agreement and does not set out any details for implementing and supervising economic cooperation in the region, it is important in that it sets out an agreement to cooperate in a number of areas and envisages a number of agreements arising from the Agreement. These agreements are forming the "rules" of an evolving legal framework.

To date, the most important agreement to come within this evolving framework is the Agreement on the Common Effective Preferential Tariff ("CEPT") Scheme for the ASEAN Free Trade Area ("AFTA").[12] This Agreement is a further implementation of the earlier Agreement on ASEAN Preferential Trading Arrangements and indicates a movement towards more liberalization of trade in the region. This move to the creation of a more formalized free trade area has, in turn, necessitated the development of more formalized relations among the members and hence the evolution of the legal framework and more "legalism" in their relations with each other.

The ASEAN Industrial Cooperation Scheme ("AICO") "fleshes out" the Framework Agreement in the area of industrial cooperation and further expands the legal framework for economic cooperation within ASEAN. As was seen in Chapter 4, the AICO Scheme provides a framework for industrial cooperation to replace the previous schemes. The ASEAN Industrial Cooperation Scheme is one of the agreements implementing the new framework for economic cooperation set out in the Framework Agreement on Enhancing ASEAN Economic Cooperation. As discussed, it is based on the CEPT Scheme for AFTA and is essentially an intermediate step giving favoured industries a "head start" in attracting foreign direct investment ("FDI") before the full implementation of AFTA. The AICO is part of an on-going process within ASEAN to create an ASEAN Investment Area.

The legal framework has also been developed in the area of investment. The objective of the ASEAN Investment Area ("AIA") is to help ASEAN attract greater and sustainable levels of FDI flows into and within the region. This is to be achieved by undertaking collective measures that would enhance the attractiveness, competitiveness and the complementarity of the region for FDI. The Framework Agreement on the ASEAN Investment Area which was signed on 8 October 1998 in Manila entered into force on 21 June 1999 and has been amended by the Protocol to Amend the Framework Agreement, signed in Hanoi on 14 September 2001. This Agreement sets out "rules" for the implementation of the AIA and is a further example of the evolving legal framework for economic cooperation in ASEAN.

Another part of the framework regulating economic cooperation among the members of ASEAN is the 1987 Agreement for the

Promotion and Protection of Investments as amended by the 1996 Protocol. Although the original agreement was entered into before the Framework Agreement on Enhancing ASEAN Economic Cooperation, the provisions of the Agreement are consistent with the Framework Agreement's objectives of creating strengthened investment cooperation among the ASEAN countries, and have been amended to improve the Agreement, and to make it a more appropriate instrument. The 1996 Protocol provides that the provisions of the ASEAN Dispute Settlement Mechanism will apply to the settlement of investment disputes.

In addition to the measures for cooperation in trade in goods and in investment, ASEAN members have established a framework to open up trade in services to one another.[13] The ASEAN Framework Agreement on Services was signed during the Fifth ASEAN Summit in December 1995 in Bangkok. Further negotiations have been undertaken and commitments made by member countries which further contribute to the international legal framework for regulating economic cooperation among the members of ASEAN.

Another part of the evolving legal framework relates to another important issue in economic cooperation, ie intellectual property.[14] In order to provide a framework for the protection of intellectual property rights within ASEAN, the ASEAN countries agreed to the ASEAN Framework Agreement on Intellectual Property Cooperation in December 1995. This Agreement commits ASEAN countries to strengthening cooperation in protecting intellectual property and creating ASEAN standards and practices which are consistent with international standards. Further steps have been taken towards developing more of an ASEAN legal framework to deal with this aspect of economic cooperation.

Thus, within ASEAN, a rationalization of the framework for economic cooperation and the development of rules to set the guidelines within which this cooperation can occur is taking place. This is happening within the context of The Framework Agreement for Enhancing ASEAN Economic Cooperation. The above discussion illustrates how economic cooperation has evolved in ASEAN, and, as can be seen, more rules are being put in place to facilitate this economic cooperation. These rules form the basis of a legal framework for economic cooperation among the members of ASEAN.

'Dispute Settlement'

A further indication that a legal framework is evolving within ASEAN is the move to a more formalized dispute settlement mechanism. A mechanism for settling disputes which arise among members of a community is the second element of a legal framework. As discussed in Chapter Seven, the Heads of State and Government of ASEAN have agreed that ASEAN will adopt a General Dispute Settlement Mechanism ("DSM") which will apply to all disputes arising from ASEAN economic agreements with specific mechanisms tailored to various economic agreements. The new DSM provides detailed procedures for dispute settlement and, is indicative of the evolving legal framework in ASEAN. As noted, the ASEAN DSM represents the first formal use of non-consensual decision-making in ASEAN. The ASEAN Industrial Cooperation ("AICO") Scheme includes a dispute resolution process which makes reference to the DSM, and the Agreement for the Promotion and Protection of Investments was amended in 1996 to provide that the provisions of the ASEAN DSM will apply to the settlement of investment disputes.

The ASEAN mechanism is less legalistic in nature than the WTO dispute settlement mechanism and leaves much discretion to its political organs. However, its establishment is a testament to the growing legalism in the field of international economic cooperation and is a promising development towards a more transparent approach to dispute settlement in the region.

Proposals have been made to create more of a legal framework for ASEAN including a restructuring of the ASEAN decision-making process. One author has even argued that,

> the central problem to be considered for making the ASEAN an effective instrumentality for economic... development of the region is the creation of legal structures that will operate as its implementing arms in providing for the

common basic needs of the region. Such legal structures must be *authorities*, equipped with the necessary powers on the region-wide basis, for taking over resources, carrying on operations, and for engaging in transactions essential to the accomplishment of the ASEAN objectives of cultural and economic development... such authorities cannot exist and operate, except on the basis of legal instruments participated in by all countries in the ASEAN. They can be set up *only* through agreements in treaty form, implementation of ASEAN declarations of objectives, policies and strategies to meet the basic needs of the ASEAN populations.[15]

As part of this proposal, the setting up of an ASEAN Court of Arbitration to settle disputes which may arise among these authorities is suggested. Such a Court of Arbitration, it is argued, would lead to the creation of an appropriate legal order on the regional level and would systematize and develop an ASEAN legal order.[16]

While it is unlikely that ASEAN will adopt such an extreme legalistic form for economic cooperation, it is clear that some steps must, and are, being taken towards providing a clearer legal framework within which economic cooperation can take place.

Compliance with the Existing International Framework

In developing a legal framework, the members of ASEAN have to keep in mind that they may be constrained by their obligations as members of other international organizations, for example, the WTO and Asia Pacific Economic Cooperation ("APEC"),[17] or that elements of the existing framework may assist the future development of the legal framework for regional economic cooperation. It is therefore necessary to examine how the emerging legal framework for economic cooperation in ASEAN accords with the existing international legal framework.[18]

Trade

The present regional framework has, to a large extent, been based on the exceptions to the Most Favored Nation ("MFN") obligation allowed to developing countries by the "enabling clause" agreed to by the Contracting Parties at the Tokyo Round of the GATT. For example, in examining AFTA, the first thing one must keep in mind is that this "free trade area" is not being established within the provisions of Article XXIV of GATT; rather, AFTA has been established, as was the Preferential Trading Arrangments ("PTA"), relying on the exception given to developing countries to enter into preferential trading arrangements by the Tokyo Round "enabling clause".[19] Articles 1 and 2 of that Declaration state:

1.   Notwithstanding the provisions of Article I of the General Agreement, contracting parties may accord differential and more favourable treatment to developing countries, without according such treatment to other contracting parties.

2.   The provisions of paragraph 1 apply to the following:

(c) Regional or global arrangements entered into amongst less-developed contracting parties for the mutual reduction or elimination of tariffs and, in accordance with criteria or conditions which may be prescribed by the CONTRACTING PARTIES, for the mutual reduction or elimination of non-tariff measures, on products imported from one another.

As has been noted in Chapter 4, the CEPT Agreement is in effect an implementing instrument of the PTA. However, while the PTA scheme was approved by the Contracting Parties under the enabling clause, the economic position of the ASEAN member states has changed since that time and will change even more over the course of the implementation of AFTA. The "enabling clause" contains a provision that:

Less-developed contracting parties expect that their capacity to make contributions or negotiated concessions...

would improve with the progressive development of their
economies... and they would accordingly expect to participate
more fully in the framework of rights and obligations under the
General Agreement.[20]

Thus, other members of GATT may expect countries claiming the
benefits of the enabling clause to "graduate" at some point. The
"developing country" status of Singapore[21] is certainly questionable and
other ASEAN member states are also rapidly reaching the point where
their claim to this status will be untenable.

The issue is essentially one of the role of a developed country
participating in a scheme for preferential trade with developing
countries. The enabling clause provides for "regional or global
arrangements entered into *amongst less-developed contracting
parties*..."[22] (emphazis added). Although the enabling clause allows a
developed country to give preferences to trade coming from
developing countries,[23] it does not permit the reverse, ie, preferences
to be given by a developing country to trade coming from a
developed country. Moreover, such preferences have to be on a non-
discriminatory basis 'in accordance with the Generalized System of
Preferences'. Thus, it would appear that a developed country cannot
enter into a "free trade area" on the basis of the enabling clause.

In order to have a free trade area comprising both
developing and developed countries, such a free trade area would
have to comply with the provisions of Article XXIV of the
GATT in order to be compatible with the parties' GATT
obligations. As the member states within ASEAN reach
developed country status, therefore, the structure of AFTA will
have to change to bring it within the provisions of Article XXIV
and provisions of other agreements.

The "enabling clause" continues in the WTO[24], although the
situation continues with even more ambiguity.[25]

Changes to the GATT Framework?

With the development of more regional economic groupings, it may be
time to re-examine the legal framework for such groupings. Article

XXIV was enacted originally at a time when few such groupings existed. Article XXIV is part of an agreement which was originally entered into as a temporary agreement among like-minded (mostly developed) economies. While the goal of MFN treatment on a universal basis may be the ideal, with preferential agreements being considered as an impediment to the development of world trade, such agreements among certain developing economies may be necessary to enable them to develop to a position where they are able to fully participate on an equal basis with more developed economies. This is the basis for the "enabling clause". It may be necessary to further develop the international framework to "legitimise" such groupings where they comprise more-developed economies entering into arrangements with less-developed economies, such as Singapore with the other members of ASEAN. Law is not something that is static but is dynamic — it must be certain enough to provide stability but flexible enough to adapt to changing social and economic conditions.

Investment

Investment has not been regulated internationally to the same extent as trade and, the framework regulating investment within ASEAN has, therefore, been less constrained in its development by international rules. Although some attempts have been made to formulate multilateral rules on investment, the international legal framework for regulating investment has not developed to the same extent as the rules regulating trade in goods. In 1977 the United Nations Centre for Transnational Corporations began protracted negotiations on a Code of Conduct for transnational corporations to provide a comprehensive global framework on direct investment to govern the behaviour of multinational corporations and governments. However, there was failure to agree on a multilateral investment code. Discussions have taken place in an attempt to negotiate a Multilateral Agreement on Investment ("MAI"), but these have also failed.

Limited elements of a framework for investment have been implemented. For example, the International Centre for Settlement of Investment Disputes ("ICSID") was established to provide the institutional framework for dispute settlement between host governments and foreign investors and the Multilateral Investment Guarantee Agency ("MIGA") was established under the aegis of the World Bank to provide protection for investors against non-commercial risks. However, most of the international framework that currently exists is in the form of bilateral investment treaties or in regional agreements such as NAFTA or the EU.

The Trade-related Investment Measures ("TRIMs") Agreement is currently the only binding multilateral investment agreement. The TRIMs agreement deals with trade-related investment measures and was enacted I July 1995. The agreement on TRIMs addresses only those measures that are inconsistent with existing GATT principles, eg, the accord restricts the use of local content requirements, trade balancing requirements, and foreign exchange balancing requirements. Broader aspects of the international regulation of investment are currently being considered by the WTO. As most of the members of ASEAN are also members of the WTO, any investment rules in ASEAN will have to comply with the WTO rules. ASEAN nations are largely in compliance with the current GATT standards on investment measures.[26]

The Pacific Basin Economic Council adopted a Pacific Basin Charter on International Investments in 1972, and revised it in 1978 and more recently in 1995. The charter sets forth important basic principles for both governments and investors which, if fully implemented, would make significant progress toward the goal of investment liberalization. Although voluntary in nature, the Charter provides a building block for the evolution of more formal regional cooperation. Thus, this Charter will have to be taken into account in the evolving legal framework in ASEAN. "The PBEC Charter expresses the needs of regional businesses and governments with respect to cross-border investment. Full adoption would be a major step toward improving the investment climate in the region."[27]

Another consideration is the APEC grouping. As discussed above, APEC members, adopted a set of non-binding investment principles in 1994. While APEC itself is still developing its own framework and is not a rules-based institution, it is important to ASEAN, as any framework which ASEAN develops should accord with any codes developed in APEC. While not binding, the APEC codes reflect the expectations of other APEC members, and may develop into binding rules of international law.

The Pacific Basin Economic Council has recommended that Pacific economies should consider negotiating a *binding* regional investment agreement that meets strong requirements of market access, protection for foreign investment, and effective dispute settlement.[28]

The current Secretary-General of the Association of Southeast Asian Nations has said "that it is about time that people looked upon ASEAN in terms of legal obligations and norms".[29] A legal framework to regulate economic relations among members of ASEAN has evolved as indicated. However, ASEAN still has further to go in developing this framework.[30] The evolution has been from a loose organisation to a more "legalistic" framework as illustrated by the development of the various schemes for economic cooperation which have been discussed.

Endnotes

1   See, Jackson, John H, *The World Trading System — Law and Policy of International Economic Relations*, 2nd ed (Cambridge/London: The MIT Press, 1997); Trebilcock, Michael J, and Robert Howse, *The Regulation of International Trade*, 2nd ed. (London and New York: Routledge, 1999).

2   See Chapter Two.

3   *Ibid.*

4   Garnaut, Ross, 'ASEAN and the Regionalization and Globalization of World Trade' (1998) 14 *ASEAN Economic Bulletin*, p 215.

5   The ASEAN Declaration, 1967, *TAPR*, Document I.B.2.

6   See, 'Secretariat restructuring completed', *ASEAN Update*, September 1993, at 4.

7   Ingles, Jose D, 'Problems and Progress in Regional Integration: The Case of ASEAN', in RP Amand and PV-Quisumbing (eds), *ASEAN Identity, Development and Culture* (Manila: UP Law Center and East-West Center Culture Learning Institute, 1981), 217 at 224.

8   Vitit Muntarbhorn, 'ASEAN and the Treaty-Making Process', in *ASEAN Economic Cooperation for the 1990s*, A Report prepared for the ASEAN Standing Committee (Philippines: Philippine Institute for Development Studies and ASEAN Secretariat, 1992), 106 at 116. See also, Joseph Sedfrey S Santiago, 'A Postscript to AFTA's False Start — The Loss of Sovereignty Issue' (1995) 12 *ASEAN Economic Bulletin*, pp 18-28.

9   Joseph Sedfrey S Santiago, 'A Postscript to AFTA's False Start — The Loss of Sovereignty Issue' (1995) 12 *ASEAN Economic Bulletin*, 18 at 25: 'Despite its

avowed aversion to legal structures, upon which is based the ASEAN member states' refusal to create a judicial organ, ASEAN member states have ratified treaties and conventions which impose more stringent legal regimes. If the definition of sovereignty were to be accepted as either 'the international independence of a state, combined with the right and power of regulating its internal affairs without foreign dictation' or the more terse 'freedom from external control', then certainly, the agreements and conventions aforecited have invariably and repeatedly diminished ASEAN states' sovereignty.'

10 See Chapter Three.

11 See Chapter Four for a discussion of this agreement.

12 *Ibid.*

13 *Ibid.*

14 *Ibid.*

15 Perfecto V Fernandez, 'Law and Culture in the ASEAN: Towards New Structures for Economic-Cultural Development', in RP Anand and PV-Quisumbing (eds), *ASEAN Identity, Development and Culture* (Manila: UP Law Center and East West Center Culture Learning Institute, 1981), 319 at 323-324.

16 *Ibid*, at 328-329.

17 In the Preamble to the Framework Agreement on Enhancing ASEAN Economic Cooperation the members 'Reiterat[ed] their commitment to the principles of the General Agreement on Tariffs and Trade'.

18 'Increasingly, ASEAN would find itself reacting to APEC as well as the new WTO. As small players in international trade, ASEAN decision makers see strong advantages in having internationally agreed rules, with procedures for enforcing them and non-arbitrary methods of changing them. Being members of both the WTO and APEC, ASEAN leaders have the responsibilities to ensure regional economic co-operation is consistent and coherent with respect to international practices.' (Tob Mun-Heng, 'AFTA and Uruguay Round of Multilateral Trade Negotiations', Chapter 4 in in Tan, Joseph (ed), *AFTA in the Changing International Economy* (Singapore: ISEAS, 1996), p 63.

19 Differential and More Favourable Treatment Reciprocity and Fuller Participation of Developing Countries, Decision of 28 November 1979 (L/4903). Notification under Enabling Clause in 1982 (L/5243); notification in 1989 (L/6569). The PTA was approved initially by the GATT CONTRACTING PARTIES in Decision of 29 January 1979 (L/4768): Agreement on ASEAN Preferential Trading Arrangements.

20 *Ibid*, para 7.

21 Singapore has been 'graduated' from the US's GSP plan (John H Jackson, *The World Trading System* (2nd ed), (Cambridge: The MIT Press,1997), p 322, note 19.

22 *Supra*, note 19, para 2(c).

23 *Ibid*, para.2(a).

24 The WTO website, www.wto.org, states that 'The Enabling Clause is...the legal basis for regional arrangements among developing countries'.

25 John H Jackson, *The World Trading System* (2nd ed), (Cambridge: The MIT Press,1997), p 324.

26 Konan, Denise Eby, 'The Need for Common Investment Measures within ASEAN' (1996) 12 *ASEAN Economic Bulletin*, 339 at 346.

27 PBEC, *Implementing Free Trade and Investment in the Pacific Region*, http://www.pbec.org/home/.

28 *Ibid.*

29 Rodolfo C Severino, Secretary-General of the Association of Southeast Asian Nations, 'The ASEAN Way and the Rule of Law', Address at the International Law Conference on ASEAN Legal Systems and Regional Integration sponsored by the Asia-Europe Institute and the Faculty of Law, University of Malaya, Kuala Lumpur, 3 September 2001.

30 'ASEAN should explore the possibility of undertaking more legally binding agreements to promote cooperation in various fields, such as economic dispute settlement, the environment, and transnational crime. As ASEAN economies integrate and as more serious transnational problems emerge more binding agreements rather than informal understandings may be needed to manage the integrated economy and the problems that transcend national boundaries.' (Report of the Secretary-general of ASEAN to the 32nd ASEAN Ministerial Meeting, Singapore 22-24 July 1999)

APPENDIX 1: THE ASEAN DECLARATION, 1967 BANGKOK, AUGUST 8, 1967

The Presidium Minister for Political Affairs/ Minister for Foreign Affairs of Indonesia, the Deputy Prime Minister of Malaysia, the Secretary of Foreign Affairs of the Philippines, the Minister for Foreign Affairs of Singapore and the Minister of Foreign Affairs of Thailand:

MINDFUL of the existence of mutual interests and common problems among countries of South-East Asia and convinced of the need to strengthen further the existing bonds of regional solidarity and cooperation;

DESIRING to establish a firm foundation for common action to promote regional cooperation in South-East Asia in the spirit of equality and partnership and thereby contribute towards peace, progress and prosperity in the region;

CONSCIOUS that in an increasingly interdependent world, the cherished ideals of peace, freedom, social justice and economic well-being are best attained by fostering good understanding, good neighbourliness and meaningful cooperation among the countries of the region already bound together by ties of history and culture;

CONSIDERING that the countries of South-East Asia share a primary responsibility for strengthening the economic and social stability of the region and ensuring their peaceful and progressive national development, and that they are determined to ensure their stability and security from external interference in any form or manifestation in order to preserve their national identities in accordance with the ideals and aspirations of their peoples;

AFFIRMING that all foreign bases are temporary and remain only with the expressed concurrence of the countries concerned and are not intended to be used directly or indirectly to subvert the national independence and freedom of States in the area or prejudice the orderly processes of their national development;

DO HEREBY DECLARE:

FIRST, the establishment of an Association for Regional Cooperation among the countries of South-East Asia to be known as the Association of South-East Asian Nations (ASEAN).

SECOND, that the aims and purposes of the Association shall be:

1. To accelerate the economic growth, social progress and cultural development in the region through joint endeavours in the spirit of equality and partnership in order to strengthen the foundation for a prosperous and peaceful community of South-East Asian Nations;

2. To promote regional peace and stability through abiding respect for justice and the rule of law in the relationship among countries of the region and adherence to the principles of the United Nations Charter;

3. To promote active collaboration and mutual assistance on matters of common interest in the economic, social, cultural, technical, scientific and administrative fields;

4. To provide assistance to each other in the form of training and research faclities in the educational, professional, technical and administrative spheres;

5. To collaborate more effectively for the greater utilization of their agriculture and industries, the expansion of their trade, including the study of the problems of international commodity trade, the improvement of their transportation and communications facilities and the raising of the living standards of their peoples;

6. To promote South-East Asian studies;

7. To maintain close and beneficial cooperation with existing international and regional organizations with similar aims and purposes, and explore all avenues for even closer cooperation among themselves.

THIRD, that to carry out these aims and purposes, the following machinery shall be established:

(a) Annual Meeting of Foreign Ministers, which shall be by rotation and referred to as ASEAN Ministerial Meeting. Special Meetings of Foreign Ministers may be convened as required.

(b) A Standing committee, under the chairmanship of the Foreign Minister of the host country or his representative and having as its members the accredited Ambassadors of the other member countries, to carry on the work of the Association in between Meetings of Foreign Ministers.

(c) Ad-Hoc Committees and Permanent Committees of specialists and officials on specific subjects.

(d) A National Secretariat in each member country to carry out the work of the Association on behalf of that country and to service the Annual or Special Meetings of Foreign Ministers, the Standing Committee and such other committees as may hereafter be established.

FOURTH, that the Association is open for participation to all States in the South-East Asian Region subscribing to the aforementioned aims, principles and purposes.

FIFTH, that the Association represents the collective will of the nations of South-East Asia to bind themselves together in friendship and cooperation and, through joint efforts and sacrifices, secure for their peoples and for posterity the blessings of peace, freedom and prosperity.

DONE in Bangkok on the Eighth Day of August in the Year One Thousand Nine Hundred and Sixty-Seven.

Appendix 2: Treaty of Amity and Cooperation in Southeast Asia Indonesia, 24 February 1976

The High Contracting Parties :

CONSCIOUS of the existing ties of history, geography and culture, which have bound their peoples together;

ANXIOUS to promote regional peace and stability through abiding respect for justice and the rule or law and enhancing regional resilience in their relations;

DESIRING to enhance peace, friendship and mutual cooperation on matters affecting Southeast Asia consistent with the spirit and principles of the Charter of the United Nations, the Ten Principles adopted by the Asian-African Conference in Bandung on 25 April 1955, the Declaration of the Association of Southeast Asian Nations signed in Bangkok on 8 August 1967, and the Declaration signed in Kuala Lumpur on 27 November 1971;

CONVINCED that the settlement of differences or disputes between their countries should be regulated by rational, effective and sufficiently flexible procedures, avoiding negative attitudes which might endanger or hinder cooperation;

BELIEVING in the need for cooperation with all peace-loving nations, both within and outside Southeast Asia, in the furtherance of world peace, stability and harmony;

SOLEMNLY AGREE to enter into a Treaty of Amity and Cooperation as follows:

Chapter I : Purpose and Principles

Article 1

The purpose of this Treaty is to promote perpetual peace, everlasting amity and cooperation among their peoples which would contribute to their strength, solidarity and closer relationship,

Article 2

In their relations with one another, the High Contracting Parties shall be guided by the following fundamental principles:

a.   Mutual respect for the independence, sovereignty, equality, territorial integrity and national identity of all nations;
b.   The right of every State to lead its national existence free from external interference, subversion or coercion;
c.   Non-interference in the internal affairs of one another;
d.   Settlement of differences or disputes by peaceful means;
e.   Renunciation of the threat or use of force;
f.   Effective cooperation among themselves.

Chapter II : Amity

Article 3

In pursuance of the purpose of this Treaty the High Contracting Parties shall endeavour to develop and strengthen the traditional, cultural and historical ties of friendship, good neighbourliness and cooperation which bind them together and shall fulfill in good faith the obligations assumed under this Treaty. In order to promote closer understanding among them, the High Contracting Parties shall encourage and facilitate contact and intercourse among their peoples.

Chapter III : Cooperation
Article 4

The High Contracting Parties shall promote active cooperation in the economic, social, technical, scientific and administrative fields as well as in matters of common ideals and aspiration of international peace and stability in the region and all other matters of common interest.

Article 5

Pursuant to Article 4 the High Contracting Parties shall exert their maximum efforts multilaterally as well as bilaterally on the basis of equality, non-discrimination and mutual benefit.

Article 6

The High Contracting Parties shall collaborate for the acceleration of the economic growth in the region in order to strengthen the foundation for a prosperous and peaceful community of nations in Southeast Asia. To this end, they shall promote the greater utilization of their agriculture and industries, the expansion of their trade and the improvement of their economic infrastructure for the mutual benefit of their peoples. In this regard, they shall continue to explore all avenues for close and beneficial cooperation with other States as well as international and regional organisations outside the region.

Article 7

The High Contracting Parties, in order to achieve social justice and to raise the standards of living of the peoples of the region, shall intensify economic cooperation. For this purpose, they shall adopt appropriate regional strategies for economic development and mutual assistance.

Article 8

The High Contracting Parties shall strive to achieve the closest cooperation on the widest scale and shall seek to provide assistance to one another in the form of training and research facilities in the social, cultural, technical, scientific and administrative fields.

Article 9

The High Contracting Parties shall endeavour to foster cooperation in the furtherance of the cause of peace, harmony, and stability in the region. To this end, the High Contracting Parties shall maintain regular contacts and consultations with one another on international and regional matters with a view to coordinating their views actions and policies.

Article 10

Each High Contracting Parties shall not in any manner of form participate in any activity which shall constitute a threat to the political and economic stability, sovereignty, or territorial integrity of another High Contracting Party.

Article 11

The High Contracting Parties shall endeavour to strengthen their respective national resilience in their political, economic, sociocultural as well as security fields in conformity with their respective ideals and aspirations, free from external interference as well as internal subversive activities in order to preserve their respective national identities.

Article 12

The High Contracting Parties in their efforts to achieve regional prosperity and security, shall endeavour to cooperate in all fields for the promotion of regional resilience, based on the principles of self-confidence, self-reliance, mutual respect, cooperation of solidarity which will constitute the foundation for a strong and viable community of nations in Southeast Asia.

Chapter IV : Pacific Settlement of Disputes

Article 13

The High Contracting Parties shall have the determination and good faith to prevent disputes from arising. In case disputes on matters directly affecting them should arise, especially disputes likely to disturb regional peace and harmony, they shall refrain from the threat or use of force and shall at all times settle such disputes among themselves through friendly negotiations.

Article 14

To settle disputes through regional processes, the High Contracting Parties shall constitute, as a continuing body, a High Council comprising a Representative at ministerial level from each of the High Contracting Parties to take cognizance of the existence of disputes or situations likely to disturb regional peace and harmony.

Article 15

In the event no solution is reached through direct negotiations, the High Council shall take cognizance of the dispute or the situation and shall recommend to the parties in dispute appropriate means of settlement such as good offices, mediation, inquiry or conciliation. The High Council may however offer its good offices, or upon agreement of the parties in dispute, constitute itself into a committee of mediation, inquiry or conciliation. When deemed necessary, the High Council shall recommend appropriate measures for the prevention of a deterioration of the dispute or the situation.

Article 16

The foregoing provision of this Chapter shall not apply to a dispute unless all the parties to the dispute agree to their application to that dispute. However, this shall not preclude the other High Contracting Parties not party to the dispute from offering all possible assistance to settle the said dispute. Parties to the dispute should be well disposed towards such offers of assistance.

Article 17

Nothing in this Treaty shall preclude recourse to the modes of peaceful settlement contained in Article 33(1) of the Charter of the United Nations. The High Contracting Parties which are parties to a dispute should be encouraged to take initiatives to solve it by friendly negotiations before resorting to the other procedures provided for in the Charter of the United Nations.

Chapter V : General Provision

Article 18

This Treaty shall be signed by the Republic of Indonesia, Malaysia, the Republic of the Philippines, the Republic of Singapore and the Kingdom of Thailand. It shall be ratified in accordance with the constitutional procedures of each signatory State. It shall be open for accession by other States in Southeast Asia.

Article 19

This Treaty shall enter into force on the date of the deposit of the fifth instrument of ratification with the Governments of the signatory States which are designated Depositories of this Treaty and the instruments of ratification or accession.

Article 20

This Treaty is drawn up in the official languages of the High Contracting Parties, all of which are equally authoritative. There shall be an agreed common translation of the texts in the English language. Any divergent interpretation of the common text shall be settled by negotiation.

IN FAITH THEREOF the High Contracting Parties have signed the Treaty and have hereto affixed their Seals.

DONE at Denpasar, Bali, this twenty-fourth day of February in the year one thousand nine hundred and seventy-six.

APPENDIX 3: HANOI PLAN
OF ACTION

Introduction

The Second ASEAN Informal Summit, held in Kuala Lumpur on 15 December 1997, adopted the ASEAN Vision 2020 which sets out a broad vision for ASEAN in the year 2020: an ASEAN as a concert of Southeast Asian Nations, outward looking, living in peace, stability and prosperity, bonded together in partnership in dynamic development and in a community of caring societies.

In order to implement the long-term vision, action plans are being drawn up to realise this Vision. The Hanoi Plan of Action (HPA) is the first in a series of plans of action building up to the realisation of the goals of the Vision.

The HPA has a six-year timeframe covering the period from 1999 to 2004. The progress of its implementation shall be reviewed every three years to coincide with the ASEAN Summit Meetings.

In recognition of the need to address the current economic situation in the region, ASEAN shall implement initiatives to hasten economic recovery and address the social impact of the global economic and financial crisis. These measures reaffirm ASEAN commitments to closer regional integration and are directed at consolidating and strengthening the economic fundamentals of the Member Countries.

I. Strengthen Macroeconomic and Financial Cooperation

To restore confidence, regenerate economic growth and promote regional financial stability through maintaining sound macroeconomic and financial policies as well as strengthening financial systems and capital markets enhanced by closer consultations, so as to avoid future disturbances.

1.1   Maintain regional macroeconomic and financial stability.
      1.1.1   Strengthen the ASEAN Surveillance Process; and
      1.1.2   Structure orderly capital account liberalisation.

1.2   Strengthen financial systems.
      1.2.1   Adopt and implement sound international financial practices and standards, where appropriate by 2003;
      1.2.2   Coordinate supervision and efforts to strengthen financial systems;
      1.2.3   Develop deep and liquid financial markets to enable governments and private firms to raise long-term financing in local currency, thereby reducing the over dependence on bank finance and limiting the risks of financial crisis;
      1.2.4   Adopt and implement existing standards of disclosure and dissemination of economic and financial information; and
      1.2.5   Adopt prudential measures to mitigate the effects of sudden shifts in short-term capital flows.

1.3   Promote liberalization of the financial services sector.
      1.3.1   Intensify deregulation of the financial services sector; and
      1.3.2   Intensify negotiations of financial sector liberalization under the ASEAN Framework Agreement on Services (AFAS).

1.4   Intensify cooperation in money, tax and insurance matters.
      1.4.1   Study the feasibility of establishing an ASEAN currency and exchange rate system;

1.4.2   Establish an ASEAN Tax Training Institute by 2003;

1.4.3   Enhance the role of "ASEAN Re Corporation Limited" as a vehicle to further promote regional cooperation in reinsurance business; and

1.4.4   Establish an ASEAN Insurance Training and Research Institute by 2003.

1.5   Develop ASEAN Capital Markets.

1.5.1   Adopt and implement internationally accepted practices and standards by the year 2003, and where appropriate at a later date especially for the new Member Countries;

1.5.2   Establish a set of minimum standards for listing rules, procedures and requirements by 2003;

1.5.3   Coordinate supervision of and programmes to strengthen capital markets;

1.5.4   Improve corporate governance, transparency and disclosure;

1.5.5   Develop a mechanism for cross-listing of SMEs among ASEAN capital markets by 2003, and where appropriate at a later date for the new Member Countries;

1.5.6   Facilitate cross-border capital flows and investments;

1.5.7   Facilitate clearing and settlement systems within ASEAN;

1.5.8   Promote securitisation in ASEAN;

1.5.9   Foster collaborative and cooperative networks among capital market research and training centres in Member States;

1.5.10 Prepare the framework to develop bond markets in ASEAN by 2000; and

1.5.11 Promote networking among development banks in Member States for financing of productive projects.

II. Enhance Greater Economic Integraton

To create a stable, prosperous and highly competitive ASEAN Economic Region in which there is a free flow of goods, services and

investments, a freer flow of capital, equitable economic development
and reduced poverty and socio-economic disparities.

2.1   Accelerate the implementation of the ASEAN Free Trade Area
        (AFTA).
        2.1.1   Trade liberalization
                1.   Maximise the number of tariff lines whose CEPT
                        tariff rates shall be reduced to 0-5% by the year
                        2000 (2003 for Vietnam and 2005 for Laos and
                        Myanmar);
                2.   Maximise the number of tariff lines whose CEPT
                        tariff rates shall be reduced to 0% by the year 2003
                        (2006 for Vietnam and 2008 for Laos and
                        Myanmar); and
                3.   Expand the coverage of the CEPT Inclusion List
                        by shortening the Temporary Exclusion List,
                        Sensitive List and General Exception List.

        2.1.2   Customs harmonization
                1.   Enhance trade facilitation in customs by
                        simplifying customs procedures, expanding the
                        Green Lane to cover all ASEAN products and
                        implementing an ASEAN Harmonised Tariff
                        Nomenclature by the year 2000;
                2.   Promote transparency, consistency and
                        uniformity in the classification of goods traded
                        within ASEAN and enhance trade facilitation
                        through the provision of facilities for obtaining
                        pre-entry classification rulings/decisions at
                        national and regional levels by the year 2003;
                3.   Promote the use of transparent, consistent and
                        uniform valuation methods and rulings through
                        the implementation of the WTO Valuation
                        Agreement by the year 2000;
                4.   Operationalise and strengthen regional
                        guidelines on mutual assistance by the year
                        2003 to ensure the proper application of

customs laws, within the competence of the customs administrations and subject to their national laws;

5. Fully operationalize the ASEAN Customs Training Network by the year 2000; and

6. Undertake customs reform and modernization, in particular to implement risk management and post-importation audit by the year 2003.

2.1.3 Standards and conformity assessment

1. Harmonise product standards through alignment with international standards for products in priority sectors by the year 2000 and for regulated products by the year 2005;

2. Implement the ASEAN Framework Agreement on Mutual Recognition Arrangements (MRAs) by developing sectoral MRAs in priority areas beginning in 1999; and

3. Enhance the technical infrastructure and competency in laboratory testing, calibration, certification and accreditation by the year 2005, based on internationally-accepted procedures and guides; and

4. Strengthen information networking on standards and technical regulation through the use of, among others, the Internet, with the aim of meeting the requirements of the WTO Agreement on Technical Barriers to Trade and WTO Agreement on the Application of Sanitary and Phytosanitary Measures.

2.1.4 Other trade facilitation activities

1. Establish a mechanism of information exchange and disclosure requirements to promote transparency of government procurement regimes by the year 2003 to facilitate participation of ASEAN nationals and companies;

2. Establish contact points in 1999 to facilitate ongoing exchange of the above information;

3. Encourage the liberalization of government procurement;

4. Establish a mechanism of information exchange by 2003 to promote transparency of each domestic regulatory regime by publishing annual reports detailing actions taken by ASEAN Member States to deregulate their domestic regimes; and

5. Encourage the increased use of regional currencies for intra-ASEAN trade transactions.

2.2 Implement the Framework Agreement on ASEAN Investment Area (AIA).

The ASEAN Investment Area aims to enhance the competitiveness of the region for attracting higher and sustainable levels of direct investment flows into and within ASEAN. Three broad-based programmes of action shall form the thrust of the AIA arrangement. These are Cooperation and Facilitation, Promotion and Awareness, and Liberalization Programme. These programmes shall be implemented through individual and collective action plans, within the agreed schedules and timetable. The ASEAN Investment Area is to be realized through implementing, among others, the following key measures:

1. Immediately extend national treatment and open up all industries for investments. However, for some exceptions, as specified in the Temporary Exclusion List and the Sensitive List, these will be progressively liberalized to all ASEAN investors by 2010 or earlier and to all investors by 2020 in accordance with the provisions of the Framework Agreement on AIA;

2. Identify and progressively eliminate restrictive investment measures;

3. Liberalize rules, regulations and policies relating to investment; rules on licensing conditions; rules

relating to access to domestic finance; and rules to facilitate payment, receipts and repatriation of profits by investors;

4. Complete implementation of all the measures and activities identified in the Schedule 1 of "Cooperation and Facilitation Programme" under the AIA Agreement by 2010 or earlier;

5. Complete implementation of all the measures and activities identified in the Schedule II of "Promotion and Awareness Programme" under the AIA Agreement by 2010 or earlier;

6. Improve and enhance the measures and activities of the Cooperation and Facilitation, and Promotion and Awareness Programmes to further strengthen the implementation process of the AIA arrangement;

7. Undertake active and high profile joint investment promotion activities to promote greater awareness of investment opportunities in ASEAN to global and regional investors. This shall include, among others, joint publications of investment and business information as well as databases and statistics;

8. Promote freer flow of capital, skilled labour, professionals and technology among ASEAN Member States;

9. Work towards establishing a comparable approach of FDI data collection, measurement and reporting among the Member States;

10. Undertake activities to increase transparency of investment regimes of Member States; and

11. Identify areas for technical cooperation in human resource development, R&D, infrastructure development, SME and supporting industry development, information and industrial technology development.

2.3   Liberalize Trade in Services.
        The ASEAN Framework Agreement on Services will
        strengthen service suppliers and introduce more
        competition into this large and important sector of ASEAN
        Member's States and open new doors for service suppliers in
        the region.

  2.3.1   Liberalization
      1.   Progressively liberalize trade in services by
            initiating a new round of negotiations beginning
            1999 and ending 2001;
      2.   Expand the scope of negotiations in services
            beyond the seven priority sectors, identified at the
            Fifth ASEAN Summit, to cover all services sectors
            and all modes of supply;
      3.   Seek to accelerate the liberalization of trade in
            services through the adoption of alternative
            approaches to liberalization; and
      4.   Accelerate the free flow of professional and other
            services in the region.

  2.3.2   Facilitation
      1.   Encourage the free exchange of information and
            views among professional bodies in the region with
            the view to achieving mutual recognition
            arrangements;
      2.   Conduct an impact study by the year 2000 on
            the removal of transport, travel and
            telecommunication barriers in ASEAN; and
      3.   Develop standard classification and
            categorization of tourism products and services to
            facilitate the region's implementation of the
            General Agreement on Trade in Services
            (GATS) and the ASEAN Framework Agreement
            on Services (AFAS).

2.3.3   Cooperation
1. Strengthen and enhance existing cooperation efforts in service sectors through such means as establishing or improving infrastructure facilities, joint production, marketing and purchasing arrangements, research and development and exchange of information;
2. Develop cooperation activities in new sectors that are not covered by existing cooperation arrangements; and
3. Cooperate to harmonise entry regulations with regard to commercial presence.

2.4   Enhance food security and global competitiveness of ASEAN's food, agriculture and forestry products.
ASEAN would strive to provide adequate levels of food supply and food accessibility within ASEAN during instances of food shortages to ensure food security and at the same time, enhance the competitiveness of its food, agriculture and forestry sectors through developing appropriate technologies to increase productivity and by promoting intra- and extra-ASEAN trade and greater private sector investment in the food, agriculture and forestry sector.

2.4.1   Strengthen food security arrangements in the region.
1. Enhance ASEAN food security statistical database and information by establishing an ASEAN Food Security Information System (AFSIS) which would allow Member States to effectively forecast, plan and manage food supplies and utilisation of basic commodities;
2. Develop a Common Framework to analyse and review the regional food trade policies in the light of the AFTA, and to enhance intra-ASEAN food trade by undertaking a study on the long-term supply and demand prospects of major food

commodities (rice, corn, soybean, sugar, pulses and oilseeds) in ASEAN;

3. Strengthen the food marketing system of agricultural cooperatives for enhancing food security in ASEAN; and

4. Review the Agreement on the ASEAN Emergency Rice Reserve (AERR) to realise effective cross-supply arrangements of food during times of emergency.

2.4.2 Develop and Adopt Existing and New Technologies.

1. Conduct collaborative research to develop new/improved technologies in food, agriculture and forestry production, post-harvest and processing activities and sharing of research results and available technology;

2. Conduct R&D in critical areas to reduce the cost of inputs for food, agriculture and forestry production; and

3. Strengthen programmes in food, agriculture and agro-forestry technology transfer, training and extension to increase productivity.

2.4.3 Enhance the Marketability of ASEAN Food, Agriculture and Forestry Products/Commodities.

1. Develop, harmonize and adopt quality standards and regulations for food, agriculture and forestry products;

2. Promote diversification of forest products; and

3. Promote and implement training programmes and share and exchange expertize in the field of food, agriculture and forestry.

2.4.4 Enhance Private Sector Involvement.

1. Conduct a study to identify high-impact investment opportunities in key areas under the food, agriculture and forestry sectors in ASEAN

and to provide essential information for investment decisions on these opportunities; and

2. Establish networking and strategic alliances with the private sector to promote investment and joint venture opportunities in ASEAN.

2.4.5 Enhance ASEAN Cooperation and Joint Approaches in International and Regional Issues.

1. Strengthen ASEAN's cooperation and joint approaches in addressing issues and problems affecting trade in the region's food, agriculture and forestry products including environment and labour issues; and

2. Seek closer cooperation and negotiate, through relevant ASEAN bodies, with trading partners on market access for ASEAN products.

2.4.6 Promote Capacity Building and Human Resources Development.

1. Promote and implement training programmes in the field of food, agriculture and forestry, including the exchange of experts; and

2. Develop and strengthen agricultural rural communities through enhanced human resource development.

2.5 Intensify industrial cooperation.

1. Expedite the implementation of AICO.

2. Establish a Directory of Major ASEAN Manufacturing Companies;

3. Explore the merits of common competition policy;

4. Increase value-added contribution of ASEAN Manufacturing Sector;

5. Explore/develop other areas of cooperation that has not been covered under the existing arrangement; and

6. Establish R&D/Skill Development Centres.

2.6   Foster small and medium enterprizes (SMEs).

Recognizing that small and medium scale enterprizes constitute
the majority of industrial enterprises in ASEAN and that they
play a significant role in the overall economic development of
Member States, ASEAN needs to cooperate in order to develop
a modern, dynamic, competitive and efficient SME sector. The
SME cooperation will address priority areas of human resource
development, information dissemination, access to technology
and technology sharing, finance and market. The SME
cooperation will also ensure the development and
implementation of non-discriminatory market-oriented policies
in ASEAN that will provide a more favourable environment for
SME development.

2.6.1   Facilitation
1.   Encourage Member States to establish national
        export financing/credit guarantee schemes for SMEs;
2.   Explore the possibility of establishing regional
        export financing/credit guarantee scheme;
3.   Explore the possibility of establishing an ASEAN
        Investment Fund for SME; and
4.   Explore the possibility of establishing a trade or
        industrial cooperation scheme to promote
        intra-ASEAN cooperation for SMEs.

2.6.2   Cooperation
1.   Compile Member States' SME policies and best
        practices in selected sectors to enhance mutual
        understanding and possible adoption;
2.   Compile and provide information to SMEs on
        policies and opportunities including electronic
        media such as the Internet websites;
3.   Promote information networking between existing
        SME-related organizations in ASEAN;
4.   Promote awareness among SMEs on benefits and
        availability of other sources of finance such as
        venture-capital and equity;

5. Enhance interactions between Government Sector Institutions (GSI) and Private Sector Institutions (PSI) on SME development by convening biennial GSI/PSI conference;

6. Undertake selected sectoral regional study on the potential areas of finance, market, production technology and management for possible trade and industrial cooperation between/among SMEs in the region;

7. Organise annual ASEAN match-making workshops to promote SME joint-ventures and linkages between SMEs and LSEs;

8. Organise annual joint ASEAN trade promotion activities/trade exposition;

9. Encourage national venture-capital company to go regional;

10. Organise annual meetings of all national Credit Guarantee Corporations (CGC) in ASEAN;

11. Harness the capacity of non-ASEAN SMEs as a source of technology to ASEAN SMEs;

12. Organise biennial ASEAN technology exposition;

13. Organise regular joint training programmes, seminars and workshops for SMEs;

14. Compile and publish a directory of resource persons in ASEAN in the area of production technology and management;

15. Develop programmes on entrepreneurship development and innovation in all Member States; and

16. Assist new members of ASEAN on SME development through specialized training programmes and technical assistance.

2.7   Further intellectual property cooperation.

To ensure adequate and effective protection, including legislation, administration and enforcement, of intellectual property rights in the region based on the principles of Most

Favoured Nation (MFN) treatment, national treatment and transparency as set out in the TRIPS Agreement.

2.7.1   Protection
1.   Strengthen civil and administrative procedures and remedies against infringement of intellectual property rights and relevant legislation; and
2.   Provide and expand technical cooperation in relation to areas such as patent search and examination, computerization and human resource development for the implementation of the TRIPS Agreement.

2.7.2   Facilitation
1.   Deepen Intellectual Property policy exchange among ASEAN Member States;
2.   Survey the current status of intellectual property rights protection in each ASEAN Member State with a view to studying measures, including development principles, for the effective enforcement of intellectual property rights;
3.   Develop a contact point list of public and business/private sector experts on intellectual property rights and a list of law enforcement officers, the latter list for the purpose of establishing a network to prevent cross-border flow of counterfeits;
4.   Exchange information on well-known marks as a first step in examining the possibility of establishing a region-wide trademark system;
5.   Exchange information on current intellectual property rights administrative systems with a view to simplifying and standardising administrative systems throughout the region;
6.   Ensure that intellectual property legislation conform to the TRIPS Agreement of the World Trade Organization through the review of intellectual property laws and introduction of

TRIPS-consistent laws. This would begin with a comprehensive review of existing legislation to be completed by the year 2000; and

7. Strengthen intellectual property administration by setting up an ASEAN electronic database by the year 2004 on patents, designs, geographical indications, trademarks and information on copyright and layout design of integrated circuits.

2.7.3 Cooperation

1. Implement an ASEAN Regional Trademark and Patent Filing System by the year 2000;
2. Establish an ASEAN Regional Fund for Trademark and Patent by the year 2000;
3. Finalise and implement an ASEAN Common Form for Trade Mark and Patent Applications;
4. Establish a regional trademark and patent registration system; or establish a regional trademark or patent office (on voluntary basis);
5. Promote accession of Member States to international treaties;
6. Promote Intellectual Property public and private sector awareness;
7. Introduce Intellectual Property as a subject in the curriculum of higher learning institutions;
8. Develop training programmes for Intellectual Property officials; and
9. Enhance intellectual property enforcement and protection through establishing mechanisms for the dissemination of information on ASEAN intellectual property administration, registration and infringement; facilitating interaction among legal and judicial bodies through seminars, etc.; facilitating networking among intellectual enforcement agencies; encouraging bilateral/ plurilateral arrangements on mutual protection

and joint cooperation in enforcement of Intellectual Property Rights.

2.8   Encourage electronic commerce.

    2.8.1   Create policy and legislative environment to facilitate cross-border Electronic Commerce;

    2.8.2   Ensure the coordination and adoption of framework and standards for cross-border Electronic Commerce, which is in line with international standards and practices; and

    2.8.3   Encourage technical cooperation and technology transfer among Member States in the development of Electronic Commerce infrastructure, applications and services.

2.9   Promote ASEAN tourism.

    2.9.1   Launch the Visit ASEAN Millennium Year as the catalytic focus for the first plan of action;

    2.9.2   Conduct Strategic Studies for Joint Marketing of the ASEAN Region in the 21st Century, and the convening of Top-level Tourism Marketing Missions to promote the region;

    2.9.3   Develop a Website/Information Database on relevant tourism statistical data and other related information within the ASEAN Secretariat by the beginning of the year 2000;

    2.9.4   Establish a Network among ASEAN Tourism Training Centres with emphazis on new job skills and new technologies by 2001 in tourism policy and planning;

    2.9.5   Develop trainer and training material database for ASEAN to be completed by 2001;

    2.9.6   Conduct Eco-Tourism Promotion Programmes for Travel Trade and Consumers;

    2.9.7   Complete cruise tourism development study in ASEAN by the year 2000.

    2.9.8   Encourage the establishment of the ASEAN Lane for facilitating intra-ASEAN travel;

2.9.9 Increase the use of the Internet or other electronic global distribution systems in the ASEAN travel industry; and

2.9.10 Launch the ASEAN Tourism Investment Guide in 1999.

2.10 Develop regional infrastructure.

To intensify cooperation in the development of highly efficient and quality infrastructure, and in the promotion and progressive liberalization of these services sectors:

2.10.1 Transport

1. Develop the Trans-ASEAN transportation network by the year 2000 as the trunkline or main corridor for the movement of goods and people in ASEAN, consisting of major road (interstate highway) and railway networks, principal ports and sea lanes for maritime traffic, inland waterway transport and major civil aviation links;

2. Operationalise the ASEAN Framework Agreement on the Facilitation of Goods in Transit by year 2000. For this purpose, its implementing Protocols will be finalised and concluded by December 1999;

3. Target the conclusion and operationalization of the ASEAN Framework Agreement on the Facilitation of Inter-State Transport by the year 2000;

4. Implement the ASEAN Framework Agreement on Multimodal Transport;

5. Develop a Maritime/Shipping Policy for ASEAN to cover, among others, transhipment, enhancing the competitiveness of ASEAN ports, further liberalization of maritime transport services, and the integration of maritime transport in the intermodal and logistics chain;

6. Adopt harmonized standards and regulations with regard to vehicle specifications (e.g. width, length,

height and weight), axle load limits, maximum weights and pollution or emission standards;

7. Institute the policy framework and modalities by the year 2000 for the development of a Competitive Air Services Policy which may be a gradual step towards an Open Sky Policy in ASEAN; and

8. Develop and implement the Singapore-Kunming Rail Link and the ASEAN Highway Network Projects.

2.10.2 Telecommunications

1. Achieve the interoperability and interconnectivity of the National Information Infrastructures (NIIs) of Member States by the year 2010;

2. Develop and implement an ASEAN Plan of Action on Regional Broadband Interconnectivity by the year 2000; and

3. Intensify cooperation in ensuring seamless roaming of telecommunications services (i.e., wireless communications) within the region, as well as in facilitating intra-ASEAN trade in telecommunications equipment and services.

2.10.3 Energy

1. Ensure security and sustainability of energy supply, efficient utilisation of natural energy resource in the region and the rational management of energy demand, with due consideration of the environment; and

2. Institute the policy framework and implementation modalities by 2004 for the early realization of the trans-ASEAN energy networks covering the ASEAN Power Grid and the Trans-ASEAN Gas Pipeline Projects as a more focused continuation of the Medium-Term Programme of Action (1995-1999).

2.10.4 Water utility

1. Cooperate on a regular basis, exchange of information, knowledge, and experiences among Member States as means to improve water resources management and water supply system within the region; and

2. Support the development of Trans-ASEAN land and submarine pipeline for conveyance of raw water between ASEAN Member States.

2.11   Further development of growth areas.

To narrow the gap in the level of development among Member States and to reduce poverty and socio-economic disparities in the region.

2.11.1 Actively expedite the implementation and further development of growth areas such as the Brunei-Indonesia-Malaysia-Philippines East ASEAN Growth Area (BIMP-EAGA), Indonesia-Malaysia-Singapore Growth Triangle (IMS-GT), Indonesia-Malaysia-Thailand Growth Triangle (IMT-GT), and the inter-state areas along the West-East Corridor (WEC) of Mekong Basin in Vietnam, Laos, Cambodia and North-eastern Thailand within the ASEAN-Mekong Basin Development Cooperation Scheme.

2.11.2 Facilitate the economic integration of the new Members into ASEAN.

III. Promote Science & Technology Development and Develop Information Technology Infrastructure

3.1   Establish the ASEAN Information Infrastructure (AII).

3.1.1 Forge agreements among Member Countries on the design, standardization, inter-connection and inter-operability of Information Technology systems by 2001.

3.1.2 Ensure the protection of intellectual property rights and consumer rights.

3.2   Develop the information content of the AII by 2004.

3.3   Establish networks of science & techonology centres of excellence and academic institutions by 2001.

3.4   Intensify research & development (R&D) in applications of strategic and enabling technologies.

3.5   Establish a technology scan mechanism and institutionalize a system of science & technology indicators by 2001.

3.6   Develop innovative systems for programme management and revenue generation to support ASEAN science and technology.

3.7   Promote greater public and private sector collaboration in science and technology, particularly in information technology.

3.8   Undertake studies on the evolution of new working conditions and living environments resulting from widespread use of information technology by 2001.

IV. Promote Social Development and Address the Social Impact of the Financial and Economic Crisis

4.1   Strive to mitigate the social impact of the regional financial and economic crisis.

4.2   Implement the Plan of Action on ASEAN Rural Development and Poverty Eradication and, in view of the financial and economic crisis, implement the ASEAN Plan of Action on Social Safety Nets to ensure that measures are taken to protect the most vulnerable sectors of our societies.

4.3   Use the ASEAN Foundation to support activities and social development programmes aimed at addressing issues of unequal economic development, poverty and socio-economic disparities.

4.4   Implement the ASEAN Plan of Action for Children which provides for the framework for ensuring the survival, protection and development of children.

4.5   Strengthen ASEAN collaboration in combating the trafficking in, and crimes of violence against, women and children.

4.6   Enhance the capacity of the family and community to care for the elderly and the disabled.

4.7   Strengthen the ASEAN Regional Aids Information and Reference Network.

4.8   Enhance exchange of information in the field of human rights among ASEAN Countries in order to promote and protect all human rights and fundamental freedoms of all peoples in accordance with the Charter of the United Nations, the Universal Declaration of Human Rights and the Vienna Declaration and Programme of Action.

4.9   Work towards the full implementation of the Convention on the Rights of the Child and the Convention on the Elimination of all Forms of Discrimination against Women and other international instruments concerning women and children.

4.10   Strengthen regional capacity to address transnational crime.

4.11   Implement the ASEAN Work Programme to Operationalize the ASEAN Plan of Action on Drug Abuse Control by 2004, and continue developing and implementing high-profile flagship programmes on drug abuse control, particularly those related to prevention education for youth, and treatment and rehabilitation.

V. *Promote Human Resource Development*

5.1   Strengthen the ASEAN University Network and move forward the process of transforming it into the ASEAN University.

5.2   Strengthen the education systems in Member Countries by 2001 so that all groups of people, including the disadvantaged, can have equal access to basic, general and higher education.

5.3   Implement the ASEAN Work Programme on Informal Sector Development to provide opportunities for self-employment and entrepreneurship.

5.4   Implement the ASEAN Work Programme on Skills Training for Out-of-School Youth by 2004, to strengthen their capacity to obtain gainful employment.

5.5   Strengthen regional networking of HRD centres of excellence and develop the regional capacity for HRD planning and labour market monitoring.

5.6   Establish and strengthen networks in education and training, particularly those promoting occupational safety and health, skills training for out-of-school youth, distance education by 2004.

5.7   Intensify efforts of the ASEAN Network for Women in Skills
       Training to enhance the capacity of disadvantaged women to
       enter the work force.

5.8   Begin to implement the ASEAN Science and Technology
       Human Resource Programme addressing the needs of industry
       and business by 2000.

5.9   Implement regional training programmes for ASEAN Civil
       Service Officers and strengthen networks among ASEAN Civil
       Service Commissions.

5.10   Establish networks of professional accreditation bodies to
       promote regional mobility and mutual recognition of
       technical and professional credentials and skills standards,
       beginning in 1999.

VI. Protect the Environment and Promote Sustainable Development

6.1   Fully implement the ASEAN Cooperation Plan on
       Transboundary Pollution with particular emphazis on the
       Regional Haze Action Plan by the year 2001.

6.2   Strengthen the ASEAN Specialized Meteorological Centre
       with emphazis on the ability to monitor forest and land fires and
       provide early warning on transboundary haze by the year 2001.

6.3   Establish the ASEAN Regional Research and Training Centre
       for Land and Forest Fire Management by the year 2004.

6.4   Strengthen the ASEAN Regional Centre for Biodiversity
       Conservation by establishing networks of relevant institutions
       and implement collaborative training and research activities by
       the year 2001.

6.5   Promote regional coordination for the protection of the
       ASEAN Heritage Parks and Reserves.

6.6   Develop a framework and improve regional coordination for the
       integrated protection and management of coastal zones by the
       year 2001.

6.7   Strengthen institutional and legal capacities to implement
       Agenda 21 and other international environmental agreements
       by the year 2001.

6.8   Harmonize the environmental databases of Member Countries by the year 2001.

6.9   Implement an ASEAN regional water conservation programme by the year 2001.

6.10   Establish a regional centre or network for the promotion of environmentally sound technologies by the year 2004.

6.11   Formulate and adopt an ASEAN Protocol on access to genetic resources by the year 2004.

6.12   Develop a Regional Action Plan for the Protection of the Marine Environment from Land-based and Sea-based Activities by the year 2004.

6.13   Implement the Framework to Achieve Long-Term Environmental Goals for Ambient Air and River Water Qualities for ASEAN Countries.

6.14   Enhance regional efforts in addressing climatic change.

6.15   Enhance public information and education in awareness of and participation in environmental and sustainable development issues.

VII. Strengthen Regional Peace and Security

7.1   Consolidate and strengthen ASEAN's solidarity, cohesiveness and harmony by strengthening national and regional resilience through enhanced cooperation and mutual assistance to further promote Southeast Asia as a Zone of Peace, Freedom and Neutrality.

7.2.   Promote coherent and comprehensive programmes of bilateral and regional cooperation and technical assistance to ASEAN member states to strengthen their integration into the community of Southeast Asian nations.

7.3   Ratify the Second Protocol of the Treaty of Amity and Cooperation in Southeast Asia (TAC) as soon as possible.

7.4   Encourage and facilitate the accession by ASEAN's Dialogue Partners and other interested countries to the Treaty of Amity and Cooperation with a view to developing the TAC into a code of conduct governing relations between Southeast Asian States and those outside the region.

7.5   Formulate draft rules of procedure for the operations of the High Council as envisioned in TAC.

7.6   Encourage greater efforts towards the resolution of outstanding problems of boundaries delimitation between ASEAN member states.

7.7   Ensure border security and facilitate safe and convenient border crossings.

7.8   Encourage Member Countries to cooperate in resolving border-related problems and other matters with security implications between ASEAN member countries.

7.9   Promote efforts to secure acceptance by Nuclear Weapon States of the Treaty on Southeast Asia Nuclear Weapon-Free Zone (SEANWFZ), including their early accession to the Protocol to the SEANWFZ Treaty.

7.10   Convene the Commission for SEANWFZ Treaty to oversee the implementation of the Treaty and ensure compliance with its provisions.

7.11   Support and participate actively in all efforts to achieve the objectives of general and complete disarmament, especially the non-proliferation of nuclear weapons and other weapons of mass destruction.

7.12   Encourage ASEAN Member Countries parties to a dispute to engage in friendly negotiation and use the bilateral and regional processes of peaceful settlement of dispute or other procedures provided for in the U.N. Charter.

7.13   Enhance efforts to settle disputes in the South China Sea through peaceful means among the parties concerned in accordance with universally recognized international law, including the 1982 U.N. Convention on the Law of the Sea.

7.14   Continue efforts to promote confidence-building measures in the South China Sea between and among parties concerned.

7.15   Encourage all other parties concerned to subscribe to the ASEAN Declaration on the South China Sea.

7.16   Promote efforts to establish a regional code of conduct in the South China Sea among the parties directly concerned.

7.17   Intensify intra-ASEAN security cooperation through existing mechanisms among foreign affairs and defense officials.

VIII. Enhance ASEAN's Role as an Effective Force for Peace, Justice, and Moderation in the Asia-Pacific and in the World

8.1   Maintain ASEAN's chairmanship in the ASEAN Regional Forum (ARF) process.

8.2   Undertake, actively and energetically, measures to strengthen ASEAN's role as the primary driving force in the ARF, including directing the ASEAN Secretary-General to provide the necessary support and services to the ASC Chairman in coordinating ARF activities.

8.3   Formulate initiatives to advance, on a consensus basis and at a pace comfortable to all, the ARF process from its current emphasis on confidence-building to promoting preventive diplomacy.

8.4   Promote public awareness of the ARF process and the need for ASEAN's role as the primary driving force in respective ASEAN Member Countries.

8.5   Continue the involvement of ASEAN defense and security officials together with foreign affairs officials in ARF activities.

8.6   Develop a set of basic principles based on TAC as an instrument for promoting cooperative peace in the Asia-Pacific region.

8.7   Enhance consultation and coordination of ASEAN positions at the United Nations and other international fora.

8.8   Revitalize ASEAN's relations with Dialogue Partners on the basis of equality, non-discrimination and mutual benefit.

IX. Promote ASEAN Awareness and Its Standing in the International Community

9.1   Support the activities of the ASEAN Foundation and other available resources and mechanisms to promote ASEAN awareness among its people.

9.2   Launch, within ASEAN's existing resources, a concerted communications programme to promote ASEAN's standing in the international community and strengthen confidence in ASEAN as an ideal place for investment, trade and tourism.

9.3   Establish and operate an ASEAN satellite channel by year 2000.

9.4   Provide and disseminate materials on ASEAN's efforts to cope with the financial and economic crisis.

9.5   Publicise ASEAN's HPA priorities through ASEAN's external mechanisms with its Dialogue Partners.

9.6   Develop linkages with mass media networks and websites on key areas of ASEAN cooperation to disseminate regular and timely information on ASEAN.

9.7   Prepare and adopt an ASEAN Declaration on Cultural Heritage by year 2000.

9.8   Mount professional productions of ASEAN performances and exhibitions within and outside ASEAN and provide adequate mass media coverage on such activities.

9.9   Organize art and cultural immersion camps and exchange programmes for the youth and encourage their travel to other ASEAN Member Countries.

9.10   Establish an ASEAN Multi-Media Centre by the year 2001 to conduct professional training programmes and provide production facilities and services for mass media and communication practitioners.

X.   Improve ASEAN's Structures and Mechanisms

10.1   Review ASEAN's overall organizational structure in order to further improve its efficiency and effectiveness, taking into account the expansion of ASEAN activities, the enlargement of ASEAN membership, and the regional situation.

10.2   Review and streamline ASEAN external relations mechanisms with its Dialogue Partners, regional organisations and other economic groupings.

10.3   Review the role, functions and capacity of the ASEAN Secretariat to meet the increasing demands of ASEAN and to support the implementation of the Hanoi Plan of Action.

APPENDIX 4: FRAMEWORK AGREEMENT ON ENHANCING ECONOMIC COOPERATION SINGAPORE, 28 JANUARY 1992

The Sultan of Brunei Darussalam, the President of the Republic of Indonesia, the Prime Minister of Malaysia, the President of the Republic of the Philippines, the Prime Minister of the Republic of Singapore and the Prime Minister of the Kingdom of Thailand:

REAFFIRMING their commitment to the ASEAN Declaration of 8 August 1967, the Declaration of ASEAN Concord of 24 February 1976, the Treaty of Amity and Cooperation in Southeast Asia of 24 February 1976, the 1977 Accord of Kuala Lumpur and the Manila Declaration of 15 December 1987;

DESIRING to enhance intra-ASEAN economic cooperation to sustain the economic growth and development of all Member States which are essential to the stability and prosperity of the region;

REITERATING their commitment to the principles of the General Agreement on Tariffs and Trade (hereinafter referred to as "GATT");

RECOGNIZING that tariff and non-tariff barriers are impediments to intra-ASEAN trade and investment flows, and that existing commitments to remove these trade barriers could be extensively improved upon;

NOTING the significant unilateral efforts made by Member States in recent years to liberalize trade and promote investments, and the importance of extending such policies to further open up their economies, given the comparative advantages and complementarity of their economies;

RECOGNIZING that Member States, having different economic interests, could benefit from subregional arrangements;

CONSCIOUS of the rapid and pervasive changes in the international political and economic landscape, as well as both challenges and opportunities yielded thereof, which need more cohesive and effective performance of intra-ASEAN economic cooperation;

MINDFUL of the need to extend the spirit of friendship and cooperation among Member States to other regional economies, as well as those outside the region which contribute to the overall economic development of Member States;

RECOGNIZING further the importance of enhancing other fields of economic cooperation such as in science and technology, agriculture, financial services and tourism;

Have Agreed as Follows:

Article 1:

1. Member States shall endeavour to strengthen their economic cooperation through an outward-looking attitude so that their cooperation contributes to the promotion of global trade liberalization.

2. Member States shall abide by the principle of mutual benefit in the implementation of measures or initiatives aimed at enhancing ASEAN economic cooperation.

3. All Member States shall participate in intra ASEAN economic arrangements. However, in the implementation of these economic arrangements, two or more Member States may proceed first if other Member States are not ready to implement these arrangements.

Article 2: Areas of Cooperation

A.   *Cooperation in Trade*

1.   All Member States agree to participate in the ASEAN Free Trade Area (AFTA) within 15 years. A ministerial-level Council will be set up to supervise, coordinate and review the implementation of the AFTA.
2.   The Common Effective Preferential Tariff (CEPT) Scheme shall be the main mechanism for the AFTA. For products not covered by the CEPT Scheme, the ASEAN Preferential Trading Arrangements (PTA) or any other mechanism to be agreed upon, may be used.
3.   Member States shall reduce or eliminate non tariff barriers between and among each other on the import and export of products as specifically agreed upon under existing arrangements or any other arrangements arising out of this Agreement.
4.   Member States shall explore further measure on border and non-border areas of cooperation to supplement and complement the liberalization of trade.

B.   *Cooperation in Industry, Minerals and Energy*

1.   Member States agree to increase investment industrial linkages and complementarity by adopting new and innovative measures, as well as strengthening existing arrangements in ASEAN.
2.   Member States shall provide flexibility for new forms of industrial cooperation. ASEAN shall strengthen cooperation in the development of the minerals sector.
3.   Member States shall enhance cooperation in the field of energy, including energy planning, exchange of information, transfer of technology, research and development, manpower training, conservation and efficiency, and the exploration, production and supply of energy resources.

C.   *Cooperation in Finance and Banking*

1.   Member States shall strengthen and develop further ASEAN economic cooperation in the field of capital

markets, as well as find new measures to increase cooperation in this area.

2.   Member States shall encourage and facilitate free movement of capital and other financial resources including further liberalization of the use of ASEAN currencies in trade and investments, taking into account their respective national laws, monetary controls and development objectives.

D.   *Cooperation in Food, Agriculture and Forestry*

1.   Member States agree to strengthen regional cooperation in the areas of development, production and promotion of agricultural products for ensuring food security and upgrading information exchanges in ASEAN.

2.   Member States agree to enhance technical joint cooperation to better manage, conserve, develop and market forest resources.

E.   *Cooperation in Transportation and Communications*

1.   Member States agree to further enhance regional cooperation for providing safe, efficient and innovative transportation and communications infrastructure network.

2.   Member States shall also continue to improve and develop the intra-country postal and telecommunications system to provide cost-effective, high quality, and customer-oriented services.

Article 3: Other Areas of Cooperation

1.   Member States agree to increase cooperation in research and development, technology transfer, tourism promotion, human resource development and other economic related areas. Full account shall also be taken of existing ASEAN arrangements in these areas.

2.   Member States, through the appropriate ASEAN bodies, shall regularly consult and exchange views on regional and international developments and trends, and identify ASEAN priorities and challenges.

Article 4: Sub-Regional Economic Arrangements

Member States acknowledge that sub-regional arrangements among themselves, or between ASEAN Member States and non-ASEAN economies, could complement overall ASEAN economic cooperation.

Article 5: Extra-Asean Economic Cooperation

To complement and enhance economic cooperation among Member States, and to respond to the rapidly changing external conditions and trends in both the economic and political fields, Member States agree to establish and/or strengthen cooperation with other countries, as well as regional and international organizations and arrangements.

Article 6: Private Sector Participation

Member States recognise the complementarity of trade and investment opportunities, and therefore encourage, among others, cooperation and exchanges among the ASEAN private sectors and between ASEAN and non-ASEAN private sectors, and the consideration of appropriate policies aimed at promoting greater intra-ASEAN and extra-ASEAN investments and other economic activities.

Article 7: Monitoring Body

The ASEAN Secretariat shall function as the body responsible for monitoring the progress of any arrangements arising from this Agreement. Member States shall cooperate with the ASEAN Secretariat in the performance of its duties.

Article 8: Review of Progress

The ASEAN Economic Ministers' Meeting and its subsidiary bodies shall review the progress of implementation and coordination of the elements contained in this Agreement.

Article 9: Settlement of Disputes

Any differences between the Member States concerning the interpretation or application of this Agreement or any arrangements arising therefrom shall, as far as possible, be settled amicably between the parties. Whenever necessary, an appropriate body shall be designated for the settlement of disputes.

Article 10: Supplementary Agreements or Arrangements

Appropriate ASEAN economic agreements or arrangements, arising from this Agreement, shall form an integral part of this Agreement.

Article 11: Other Arrangements

1. This Agreement or any action taken under it shall not affect the rights and obligations of the Member States under any existing agreements to which they are parties.
2. Nothing in this Agreement shall affect the power of Member States to enter into other agreements not contrary to the terms and objectives of this Agreement.

Article 12: General Exceptions

Nothing in this Agreement shall prevent any Member State from taking action and adopting measures which it considers necessary for the protection of its national security, the protection of public morals, the protection of human, animal or plant life and health, and the protection of articles of artistic, historic and archaeological value.

Article 13: Amendments

All Articles of this Agreement may be modified through amendments to this Agreement agreed upon by all the Member States. All amendments shall become effective upon acceptance by all Member States.

Article 14: Entry into Force

This Agreement shall be effective upon signing.

Article 15: Final Provision

This Agreement shall be deposited with the Secretary General of the ASEAN Secretariat who shall promptly furnish a certified copy thereof to each Member State.

IN WITNESS WHEREOF, the undersigned have signed this Framework Agreement on Enhancing ASEAN Economic Cooperation.

DONE at Singapore, this 28th day of January, 1992 in a single copy in the English Language.

APPENDIX 5: SINGAPORE DECLARATION 28 JANUARY 1992

1. We, the Heads of State and Government of ASEAN, are encouraged by the achievements of ASEAN in the last twenty-five years, and are convinced that ASEAN cooperation remains vital to the well-being of our peoples.

2. Having reviewed the profound international political and economic changes that have occurred since the end of the Cold War and considered their implications for ASEAN, we declare that:

ASEAN shall move towards a higher plane of political and economic cooperation to secure regional peace and prosperity;

ASEAN shall constantly seek to safeguard its collective interests in response to the formation of large and powerful economic groupings among the developed countries, in particular through the promotion of an open international economic regime and by stimulating economic cooperation in the region;

ASEAN shall seek avenues to engage[sic] member states in new areas of cooperation in security matters; and

ASEAN shall forge a closer relationship based on friendship and cooperation with the Indochinese countries, following the settlement on Cambodia.

Political and Security Cooperation

3.　　In the field of political and security cooperation, we have agreed that:

ASEAN welcomes accession by all countries in Southeast Asia to the Treaty of Amity and Cooperation in Southeast Asia, which will provide a common framework for wider regional cooperation embracing the whole of Southeast Asia;

　　ASEAN will also seek the cognizance of the United Nations for the Treaty through such means as an appropriate Resolution. This will signify ASEAN's commitment to the centrality of the UN role in the maintenance of international peace and security as well as promoting cooperation for socio-economic development;

　　ASEAN could use established fora to promote external dialogues on enhancing security in the region as well as intra-ASEAN dialogues on ASEAN security cooperation (such as the regional security seminars held in Manila and Bangkok in 1991, and the workshops on the South China Sea held in Bali in 1990 and Bandung in 1991), taking full cognizance of the Declaration of ASEAN Concord. To enhance this effort, ASEAN should intensify its external dialogues in political and security matters by using the ASEAN Post Ministerial Conferences (PMC);

　　ASEAN has made major strides in building cooperative ties with states of the Asia-Pacific region and shall continue to accord them a high priority;

　　ASEAN will seek to realise the Zone of Peace, Freedom and Neutrality (ZOPFAN) and a South East Asian Nuclear Weapon Free Zone (SEANWFZ) in consultation with friendly countries, taking into account changing circumstances;

　　ASEAN will closely cooperate with the United Nations and the international community in ensuring the full implementation of the Peace Agreements signed in Paris in October 1991;

　　ASEAN supports the Cambodian Supreme National Council in calling on the UN Secretary General to despatch UNTAC as early as possible in order to preserve the momentum of the peace process and to implement the gains realized by the signing of the Paris Peace Agreements. ASEAN calls on all parties in Cambodia to implement seriously the process of national reconciliation which is essential to a genuine and lasting peace in Cambodia; and

ASEAN will play an active part in international programmes for the reconstruction of Vietnam, Laos and Cambodia.

4.   Conscious of the central role of the United Nations in the post-Cold War, we agree that:

The proposed Summit of members of the United Nations Security Council should help shape the United Nations' role for the promotion of a more equitable international political and economic order, and for the democratisation of the United Nations' decision-making processes in order to make the organization truly effective in meeting its obligations;

ASEAN will participate actively in efforts to ensure that the United Nations is a key instrument for maintaining international peace and security; and

ASEAN will encourage all efforts to strengthen the United Nations, including its role and capabilities in peacekeeping and peacemaking, in accordance with the United Nations Charter.

Directions in ASEAN Economic Cooperation

5.   In the field of economic cooperation, we have agreed that:

To further accelerate joint efforts in enhancing intra-ASEAN economic cooperation, ASEAN shall adopt appropriate new economic measures as contained in the Framework Agreement on Enhancing ASEAN Economic Cooperation directed towards sustaining ASEAN economic growth and development which are essential to the stability and prosperity of the region;

ASEAN shall establish the ASEAN Free Trade Area using the Common Effective Preferential Tariff (CEPT) Scheme as the main mechanism within a time frame of 15 years beginning 1 January 1993 with the ultimate effective tariffs ranging from 0% to 5%.

ASEAN member states have identified the following fifteen groups of products to be included in the CEPT Scheme for accelerated tariff reductions:

vegetable oils
cement
chemicals
pharmaceuticals
fertiliser
plastics
rubber products
leather products
pulp
textiles
ceramic and glass products
gems and jewellery
copper cathodes
electronics
wooden and rattan furniture

ASEAN shall increase investments, industrial linkages and complementarity by adopting new and innovative measures, as well as strengthening existing arrangements in ASEAN and providing flexibility for new forms of industrial cooperation;

ASEAN shall strengthen and develop further cooperation in the field of capital markets, and shall encourage and facilitate free movement of capital and other financial resources;

ASEAN shall further enhance regional cooperation to provide safe, efficient and innovative transportation and communications infrastructure network;

ASEAN shall also continue to improve and develop the intra-country postal and telecommunications system to provide cost-effective, high quality and customer-oriented services;

ASEAN shall adopt joint efforts to strengthen trade promotion and negotiations on ASEAN agricultural products in order to enhance ASEAN's competitive posture, and to sustain the expansion of ASEAN agricultural exports in the international markets;

ASEAN acknowledges that sub-regional arrangements among themselves, or between ASEAN member states and non-ASEAN economies could complement overall ASEAN economic cooperation;

ASEAN recognises the importance of strengthening and/or establishing cooperation with other countries, regional/multilateral economic organizations, as well as Asia-Pacific Economic Cooperation (APEC) and an East Asia Economic Caucus (EAEC). With regard to APEC, ASEAN attaches importance to APEC's fundamental objective of sustaining the growth and dynamism of the Asia-Pacific region. With respect to an EAEC, ASEAN recognizes that consultations on issues of common concern among East Asian economies, as and when the need arises, could contribute to expanding cooperation among the region's economies, and the promotion of an open and free global trading system;

Further, recognising the importance of non-tariff and non-border areas of cooperation to complement tariff liberalisation in increasing regional trade and investment, ASEAN shall further explore cooperation in these areas with a view to making recommendations to the Fifth ASEAN Summit;

ASEAN shall continue with its concerted efforts in the promotion of tourism, particularly in making the Visit ASEAN Year 1992 a success;

ASEAN shall continue to step up cooperation in other economic-related areas, such as science and technology transfer and human resource development;

ASEAN shall enhance cooperation and collective action in international and inter-regional fora as well as in international organisations and regional groupings. ASEAN shall also continue to enhance relations with its dialogue partners and other producing/consuming countries towards the advancement of the commodity sector in the region and in addressing international commodity issues;

ASEAN recognizes that sustained economic growth requires considerable inputs of energy. As member states continue to industrialize and strengthen their industrial base, ASEAN shall focus and strengthen cooperation in energy security, conservation and the search for alternative fuels;

ASEAN recognizes the complementarity of trade and investment opportunities and therefore encourages, among others, increased cooperation and exchanges among the ASEAN private sectors, and the consideration of appropriate policies for greater intra-ASEAN investments;

ASEAN shall continue to uphold the principles of free and open trade embodied in the General Agreement on Tariffs and Trade (GATT), and work towards maintaining and strengthening an open multilateral trading system;

ASEAN shall work collectively to ensure that the Uruguay Round addresses the key concerns and interests of the ASEAN economies, and adopt a pragmatic and realistic approach, in using the Draft Final Text as at 20 December 1991 as a reasonable basis for completing negotiations; and

ASEAN strongly urges major trading countries to settle their differences on agriculture and other areas, and likewise use the Draft Final Text to work towards an early and successful conclusion of the Uruguay Round.

Review of ASEAN's External Relation

6.   In reviewing ASEAN's external relations, we have agreed that:

ASEAN, as part of an increasingly interdependent world, should intensify cooperative relationships with its Dialogue partners, namely Australia, Canada, the European Community, Japan, the Republic of Korea, New Zealand and the United States, and engage[sic] in consultative relationships with interested non-Dialogue countries and international organizations; and

While ASEAN's cooperative relationships with the Dialogue partners have made significant progress, ASEAN should strengthen existing dialogue mechanisms and develop new ones where necessary for the enhancement of economic relations with these countries, especially ASEAN's major economic partners.

ASEAN Functional Cooperation

7.   In the field of functional cooperation, we have agreed that:

The ASEAN member countries shall continue to enhance awareness of ASEAN among the people in the region through the expansion of ASEAN Studies as part of Southeast Asian Studies in the school and university curricula and the introduction of ASEAN student exchange programmes at the secondary and tertiary levels of education;

ASEAN should help hasten the development of a regional identity and solidarity, and promote human resource development by considering ways to further strengthen the existing network of the leading universities and institutions, of higher learning in the ASEAN region with a view to ultimately establishing an ASEAN University based on this expanded network;

ASEAN functional [cooperation] shall be designed for a wider involvement and increased participation by women in the development of ASEAN countries in order to meet their needs and aspirations. This cooperation shall also extend to the development of children to realise their full potential;

The ASEAN member countries shall continue to play an active part in protecting the environment by continuing to cooperate in promoting the principle of sustainable development and integrating it into all aspects of development;

ASEAN member countries should continue to enhance environmental cooperation, particularly in issues of transboundary pollution, natural disasters, forest fires and in addressing the antitropical timber campaign;

The developed countries should commit themselves to assist developing countries by providing them new and additional financial resources as well as the transfer of, and access to environmentally sound technology on concessional and preferential terms;

The developed countries should also help to maintain an international environment supportive of economic growth and development;

ASEAN looks forward to seeing these commitments reflected in the outcome of the United Nations Conference on Environment and Development in 1992 at Rio de Janeiro;

As Non-governmental Organizations (NGOS) play an important role in social development, ASEAN shall encourage the exchange of information among NGOs in the region and help expand their participation in intra-ASEAN functional cooperation;

ASEAN shall intensify its cooperation in overcoming the serious problem of drug abuse and illicit drug trafficking at the national, regional and international levels; and

ASEAN shall make a coordinated effort in curbing the spread of AIDS by exchanging information on AIDS, particularly in the formulation and implementation of policies and programmes against the deadly disease.

Restructuring of ASEAN Institutions

8.   To strengthen ASEAN, we have agreed that:

ASEAN Heads of Government shall meet formally every three years with informal meetings in between;

The ASEAN organizational structure, especially the ASEAN Secretariat, shall be streamlined and strengthened with more resources;

The Secretary-General of the ASEAN Secretariat shall be redesignated as the Secretary-General of ASEAN with an enlarged mandate to initiate, advise, coordinate and implement ASEAN activities;

The Secretary-General of ASEAN shall be appointed on merit and accorded ministerial status;

The professional staff of the ASEAN Secretariat be appointed on the principle of open recruitment and based on a quota system to ensure representation of all ASEAN countries in the Secretariat;

The five present ASEAN Economic Committees be dissolved and the Senior Economic Officials Meeting (SEOM) be tasked to handle all aspects of ASEAN economic cooperation; and

A ministerial-level Council be established to supervise, coordinate and review the implementation of the Agreement on the Common Effective Preferential Tariff (CEPT) Scheme for the ASEAN Free Trade Area (AFTA).

DONE at Singapore on the 28th of January 1992.

APPENDIX 6: AGREEMENT ON THE COMMON EFFECTIVE PREFERENTIAL TARIFF SCHEME FOR THE ASEAN FREE TRADE AREA

The Governments of Brunei Darussalam, the Republic of Indonesia, Malaysia, the Republic of the Philippines, the Republic of Singapore and the Kingdom of Thailand, Member States of the Association of South East Asian Nations (ASEAN):

MINDFUL of the Declaration of ASEAN Concord signed in Bali, Indonesia on 24 February 1976 which provides that Member States shall cooperate in the field of trade in order to promote development and growth of new production and trade;

RECALLING that the ASEAN Heads of Government, at their Third Summit Meeting held in Manila on 13-15 December 1987, declared that Member States shall strengthen intra-ASEAN economic cooperation to maximise the realization of the region's potential in trade and development;

NOTING that the Agreement on ASEAN Preferential Trading Arrangements (PTA) signed in Manila on 24 February 1977 provides for the adoption of various instruments on trade liberalization on a preferential basis;

ADHERING to the principles, concepts and ideals of the Framework Agreement on Enhancing ASEAN Economic Cooperation signed in Singapore on 28 January 1992;

CONVINCED that preferential trading arrangements among ASEAN Member States will act as a stimulus to the strengthening of national and ASEAN Economic resilience, and the development of the national economies of Member States by expanding investment and production opportunities, trade, and foreign exchange earnings;

DETERMINED to further cooperate in the economic growth of the region by accelerating the liberalisation of intra-ASEAN trade and investment with the objective of creating the ASEAN Free Trade Area using the Common Effective Preferential Tariff (CEPT) Scheme;

DESIRING to effect improvements on the ASEAN PTA in consonance with ASEAN's international commitments;

Have Agreed as Follows:

Article 1 : Definitions

For the purposes of this Agreement :

1. "CEPT" means the Common Effective Preferential Tariff, and it is an agreed effective tariff, preferential to ASEAN, to be applied to goods originating from ASEAN Member States, and which have been identified for inclusion in the CEPT Scheme in accordance with Articles 2(5) and 3.

2. "Non-Tariff Barriers" mean measures other than tariffs which effectively prohibit or restrict import or export of products within Member States.

3. "Quantitative restrictions" mean prohibitions or restrictions on trade with other Member States, whether made effective through quotas, licenses or other measures with equivalent effect, including administrative measures and requirements which restrict trade.

4. "Foreign exchange restrictions" mean measures taken by Member States in the form of restrictions and other administrative procedures in foreign exchange which have the effect of restricting trade.

5. "PTA" means ASEAN Preferential Trading Arrangements stipulated in the Agreement on ASEAN Preferential Trading Arrangements, signed in Manila on 24 February 1977, and in the Protocol on Improvements on Extension of Tariff Preferences under the ASEAN Preferential

Trading Arrangements (PTA), signed in Manila on 15
December 1987.

6. "Exclusion List" means a list containing products that are
excluded from the extension of tariff preferences under the
CEPT Scheme.

7. "Agricultural products" mean :

    (a) agricultural raw materials/unprocessed products covered
under Chapters 1-24 of the Harmonized System (HS),
and similar agricultural raw materials/unprocessed
products in other related HS Headings; and

    (b) products which have undergone simple processing with
minimal change in form from the original products.

Article 2 : General Provisions

1. All Member States shall participate in the CEPT Scheme.

2. Identification of products to be included in the CEPT Scheme
shall be on a sectoral basis, i.e., at HS 6-digit level.

3. Exclusions at the HS 8/9 digit level for specific products are
permitted for those Member States, which are temporarily not
ready to include such products in the CEPT Scheme. For
specific products, which are sensitive to a Member State
pursuant to Article 1(3) of the Framework Agreement on
Enhancing ASEAN Economic Cooperation, a Member State
may exclude products from the CEPT Scheme, subject to a
waiver of any concession herein provided for such products. A
review of this Agreement shall be carried out in the eighth year
to decide on the final Exclusion List or any amendment to this
Agreement.

4. A product shall be deemed to be originating from ASEAN
Member States, if at least 40% of its content originates from any
Member State.

5. All manufactured products, including capital goods, processed
agricultural products and those products falling outside the
definition of agricultural products, as set out in this Agreement,
shall be in the CEPT Scheme. These products shall

automatically be subject to the schedule of tariff reduction, as set out in Article 4 of this Agreement. In respect of PTA items, the schedule of tariff reduction provided for in Article 4 of this Agreement shall be applied, taking into account the tariff rate after the application of the existing margin of preference (MOP) as at 31 December 1992.

6.   All products under the PTA which are not transferred to the CEPT Scheme shall continue to enjoy the MOP existing as at 31 December 1992.

7.   Member States, whose tariffs for the agreed products are reduced from 20% and below to 0%-5%, even though granted on an MFN basis, shall still enjoy concessions. Member States with tariff rates at MFN rates of 0%-5% shall be deemed to have satisfied the obligations under this Agreement and shall also enjoy the concessions.

Article 3 : Product Coverage

This Agreement shall apply to all manufactured products, — including capital goods, processed agricultural products, and those products failing outside the definition of agricultural products as set out in this Agreement. Agricultural products shall be excluded from the CEPT Scheme.

Article 4 : Schedule of Tariff Reduction

1.   Member States agree to the following schedule of effective preferential tariff reductions:

   (a)   The reduction from existing tariff rates to 20% shall be done within a time frame of 5 years to 8 years, from 1 January 1993, subject to a programme of reduction to be decided by each Member State, which shall be announced at the start of the programme. Member States are encouraged to adopt an annual rate of reduction, which shall be (X-20)%/5 or 8, where X equals the existing tariff rates of individual Member States.

(b)   The subsequent reduction of tariff rates from 20% or
        below shall be done within a time frame of 7 years. The
        rate of reduction shall be at a minimum of 5% quantum
        per reduction. A programme of reduction to be decided
        by each Member State shall be announced at the start
        of the programme.

(c)   For products with existing tariff rates of 20% or
        below as at 1 January 1993, Member States shall
        decide upon a programme of tariff reductions, and
        announce at the start, the schedule of tariff
        reductions. Two or more Member States may enter
        into arrangements for tariff reduction to 0%-5% on
        specific products at an accelerated pace to be
        announced at the start of the programme.

2. Subject to Articles 4(1)(b) and 4(1)(c) of this Agreement,
    products which reach, or are at tariff rates of 20% or below, shall
    automatically enjoy the concessions.

3. The above schedules of tariff reduction shall not prevent
    Member States from immediately reducing their tariffs to
    0%-5% or following an accelerated schedule of tariff reduction.

Article 5 : Other Provisions

A. Quantitative Restrictions and Non-Tariff Barriers

1. Member States shall eliminate all quantitative restrictions in
    respect of products under the CEPT Scheme upon enjoyment of
    the concessions applicable to those products.

2. Member States shall eliminate other non-tariff barriers on a
    gradual basis within a period of five years after the enjoyment of
    concessions applicable to those products.

B. Foreign Exchange Restrictions

Member States shall make exceptions to their foreign exchange
restrictions relating to payments for the products under the CEPT
Scheme, as well as repatriation of such payments without prejudice to

their rights under Article XVIII of the General Agreement on Tariff and Trade (GATT) and relevant provisions of the Articles of Agreement of the International Monetary Fund (IMF).

C.   *Other Areas of Cooperation*

Member States shall explore further measures on border and non-border areas of cooperation to supplement and complement the liberalization of trade. These may include, among others, the harmonization of standards, reciprocal recognition of tests and certification of products, removal of barriers to foreign investments, macroeconomic consultations, rules for fair competition, and promotion of venture capital.

D.   *Maintenance of Concessions*

Member States shall not nullify or impair any of the concessions as agreed upon through the application of methods of customs valuation, any new charges or measures restricting trade, except in cases provided for in this Agreement.

Article 6 : Emergency Measures

1.   If, as a result of the implementation of this Agreement, import of a particular product eligible under the CEPT Scheme is increasing in such a manner as to cause or threaten to cause serious injury to sectors producing like or directly competitive products in the importing Member States, the importing Member States may, to the extent and for such time as may be necessary to prevent or to remedy such injury, suspend preferences provisionally and without discrimination, subject to Article 6(3) of this Agreement. Such suspension of preferences shall be consistent with the GATT.

2.   Without prejudice to existing international obligations, a Member State, which finds it necessary to create or intensify quantitative restrictions or other measures limiting imports with a view to forestalling the threat of or stopping a serious decline of its monetary reserves, shall endeavour to do so in a manner, which safeguards the value of the concessions agreed upon.

3. Where emergency measures are taken pursuant to this Article, immediate notice of such action shall be given to the Council referred to in Article 7 of this Agreement, and such action may be the subject of consultation as provided for in Article 8 of this Agreement.

Article 7 : Institutional Arrangements

1. The ASEAN Economic Ministers (AEM) shall, for the purposes of this Agreement, establish a ministerial-level Council comprising one nominee from each Member State and the Secretary-General of the ASEAN Secretariat. The ASEAN Secretariat shall provide the support to the ministerial-level Council for supervising, coordinating and reviewing the implementation of this Agreement, and assisting the AEM in all matters relating thereto. In the performance of its functions, the ministerial-level Council shall also be supported by the Senior Economic Officials' Meeting (SEOM).

2. Member States which enter into bilateral arrangements on tariff reductions pursuant to Article 4 of this Agreement shall notify all other Member States and the ASEAN Secretariat of such arrangements.

3. The ASEAN Secretariat shall monitor and report to the SEOM on the implementation of the Agreement pursuant to the Article III(2)(8) of the Agreement on the Establishment of the ASEAN Secretariat. Member States shall cooperate with the ASEAN Secretariat in the performance of its duties.

Article 8 : Consultations

1. Member States shall accord adequate opportunity for consultations regarding any representations made by other Member States with respect to any matter affecting the implementation of this Agreement. The Council referred to in Article 7 of this Agreement, may seek guidance from the AEM in respect of any matter for which it has not been possible to find a satisfactory solution during previous consultations.

2. Member States, which consider that any other Member State has not carried out its obligations under this Agreement, resulting in the nullifications or impairment of any benefit accruing to them, may, with a view to achieving satisfactory adjustment of the matter, make representations or proposal to the other Member States concerned, which shall give due consideration to the representations or proposal made to it.

3. Any differences between the Member States concerning the interpretation or application of this Agreement shall, as far as possible, be settled amicably between the parties. If such differences cannot be settled amicably, it shall be submitted to the Council referred to in Article 7 of this Agreement, and if necessary, to the AEM.

Article 9 : General Exceptions

Nothing in this Agreement shall prevent any Member State from taking action and adopting measures, which it considers necessary for the protection of its national security, the protection of public morals, the protection of human, animal or plant life and health, and the protection of articles of artistic, historic and archaeological value.

Article 10 : Final Provisions

1. The respective Governments of Member States shall undertake the appropriate measures to fulfill the agreed obligations arising from this Agreement.

2. Any amendment to this Agreement shall be made by consensus and shall become effective upon acceptance by all Member States.

3. This Agreement shall be effective upon signing.

4. This Agreement shall be deposited with the Secretary-General of the ASEAN Secretariat, who shall likewise promptly furnish a certified copy thereof to each Member State.

5. No reservation shall be made with respect to any of the provisions of this Agreement. In witness Whereof, the undersigned, being duly authorised thereto by their respective Governments, have signed this Agreement on Common

Effective Preferential Tariff (CEPT) Scheme for the Free Trade Area (AFTA).

Done at Singapore, this 28th day of January, 1992 in a single copy in the English Language.

APPENDIX 7: PROTOCOL TO AMEND THE AGREEMENT ON THE COMMON EFFECTIVE PREFERENTIAL TARIFF SCHEME FOR THE ASEAN FREE TRADE AREA

The Governments of Brunei Darussalam, the Republic of Indonesia, Malaysia, the Republic of the Philippines, the Republic of Singapore and the Kingdom of Thailand, Member States of the Association of South East Asian Nations (ASEAN);

NOTING the Agreement on the Common Effective Preferential Tariff (CEPT) Scheme for the ASEAN Free Trade Area (AFTA) ("the Agreement") signed in Singapore on 28 January 1992;

RECALLING the Protocol to Amend the Framework Agreement on Enhancing ASEAN Economic Cooperation (1992) signed on 15 December 1995 in Bangkok by the Heads of Government reflecting the acceleration of the CEPT Scheme for AFTA from the year 2008 to the year 2003;

RECOGNIZING the need to amend the Agreement to reflect the latest developments in ASEAN;

Have Agreed as Follows:

Article 1

Article 2, paragraphs 3, 5 and 6 of the Agreement be amended to read as follows:

"3.   Exclusions at the HS 8/9 digit level for specific products are permitted for those Member States, which are temporarily not ready to include such products in the CEPT Scheme. For specific products, which are sensitive to a Member State, pursuant to Article 1 (3) of the Framework Agreement on Enhancing ASEAN Economic Cooperation, a Member State may exclude products from the CEPT Scheme, subject to a waiver of any concession herein provided for such products. These temporarily excluded products are to be gradually included into the CEPT by 1 January 2000.

5.   All manufactured products, including capital goods, and agricultural products shall be in the CEPT Scheme. These products shall automatically be subject to the schedule of tariff reduction set out in Article 4 of the Agreement as revised in Article 3 of this Protocol. In respect of PTA items, the schedule of tariff reduction provided for in the revised Article 4(A) set out in Article 3 of this Protocol shall be applied, taking into account the tariff rate after the application of tile[sic] existing margin of preference (MOP) as at 31 December 1992.

6.   All products under the PTA which are not in the list for tariff reductions of the CEPT Scheme shall continue to enjoy the MOPs existing as at 31 December 1992.

Article 2

Article 3 of the Agreement be amended to read as follows:

"This Agreement shall apply to all manufactured products including capital goods, and agricultural products.".

Article 3

Article 4 of the Agreement be substituted with the following:

"Schedule of Tariff Reduction and Enjoyment of concessions
Schedule of Tariff Reduction

1.   Member States agree to the following schedule of effective preferential tariff reductions:

a.　The reduction from existing tariff rates to 20% shall be completed within a time frame of 5 years, from 1 January 1993, subject to a programme of reduction to be decided by each Member State, which shall be announced at the start of the programme. Member States are encouraged to adopt an annual rate of reduction, which shall be $(X\text{-}20)\%/5$, where X equals the existing tariff rates of individual Member States.

b.　The subsequent reduction of tariff rates from 20% or below shall be completed within a time frame of 5 years. The rate of reduction shall be at a minimum of 5% quantum per reduction. A programme of reduction to be decided by each Member State shall be announced at the start of the programme.

c.　For products with existing tariff rates of 20% or below as at 1 January 1993, Member States shall decide upon a programme of tariff reductions, and announce at the start, the schedule of tariff reductions.

2.　The above schedules of tariff reduction shall not prevent Member States from immediately reducing their tariffs to 0%-5% or following an accelerated schedule of tariff reduction.

B.　*Enjoyment of Concessions*

Subject to Articles 4(A)(1 b) and 4(A)(1 c) of the Agreement, products which reach, or are at tariff rates of 20% or below, shall automatically enjoy the concessions.".

Article 4

The following be inserted after Article 9 as a new Article 9A to the Agreement:
"Accession of New Members

New Members of ASEAN shall accede to this Agreement on terms and conditions, which are consistent with the Framework Agreement on Enhancing ASEAN Economic Cooperation (1992) and the Agreement, and which have been agreed between them and the existing Members of ASEAN.".

Article 5

This Protocol shall enter into force upon the deposit of instruments of ratification or acceptance by all signatory governments with the Secretary-General of ASEAN which shall be done not later than 1 January 1996.

This Protocol shall be deposited with the Secretary-General of ASEAN, who shall promptly furnish a certified copy thereof to each Member Country.

IN WITNESS WHEREOF, the undersigned, being duly authorised thereto by their respective Governments, have signed the Protocol to Amend the Common Effective Preferential Tariff (CEPT) Scheme for the ASEAN Free Trade Area (AFTA).

DONE at Bangkok, this 15th day of December 1995 in a single copy in the English Language.

APPENDIX 8: PROTOCOL TO AMEND THE FRAMEWORK AGREEMENT ON ENHANCING ASEAN ECONOMIC COOPERATION

The Sultan of Brunei Darussalam, the President of the Republic of Indonesia, the Prime Minister of Malaysia, the President of the Republic of the Philippines, the Prime Minister of the Republic of Singapore and the Prime Minister of the Kingdom of Thailand;

RECALLING the Framework Agreement on Enhancing ASEAN Economic Cooperation ("the Agreement") signed on 28 January 1992 at the Fourth Summit Meeting held in Singapore;

DESIRING to expedite the implementation of the Common Effective Preferential Tariff (CEPT) Scheme for the ASEAN Free Trade Area (AFTA);

NOTING that Article 12A of the Agreement provides for amendments to it;

Have Agreed as Follows:

Article 1

Article 2, section A, paragraph 1 of the Agreement shall be amended by deleting the expression "15 years" and substituting it with the expression "10 years (beginning 1 January 1993)".

Article 2

The following shall be inserted after Article 12 as a new Article 12A to the Agreement:

"Accession of New Members New Members of ASEAN shall accede to the Agreement on terms and conditions consistent with it and which have been agreed between them and the existing Members of ASEAN.".

Article 3

This Protocol shall enter into force upon the deposit of instruments of ratification or acceptance by all signatory governments with the Secretary-General of ASEAN which shall be done not later than 1 January 1996.

This Protocol shall be deposited with the Secretary-General of ASEAN, who shall promptly furnish a certified copy thereof to each Member Country.

IN WITNESS WHEREOF, the undersigned have signed the Protocol to Amend the Framework Agreement on Enhancing ASEAN Economic Cooperation.

DONE at Bangkok, this 15th day of December 1995 in a single copy in the English Language.

APPENDIX 9: BASIC AGREEMENT ON THE ASEAN INDUSTRIAL COOPERATION SCHEME

The Governments of Brunei Darussalam, the Republic of Indonesia, Malaysia, the Republic of the Philippines, the Republic of Singapore, the Kingdom of Thailand and the Socialist Republic of Vietnam, Member States of the Association of South East Asian Nations (ASEAN);

REAFFIRMING their desire to collaborate for the acceleration of economic growth in the region to promote greater industrialization of their economies, to expand their trade and investment and to improve the economic infrastructure for the mutual benefit of their people;

MINDFUL of the rapid development in the international economic environment and the need to maintain ASEAN's attractiveness and competitiveness as an investment region;

RECOGNIZING that the liberalization of trade and investment in ASEAN Countries can support meaningful industrial cooperation which can greatly contribute to strengthening and broadening the base of their industrial sector;

CONVINCED that ASEAN industrial cooperation will increase intra-ASEAN investment and investment from non-ASEAN sources;

CONVINCED ALSO that the sharing of resources will foster closer ASEAN economic integration as well as enhance the technology base, economies of scale and scope, and the competitiveness of ASEAN industries;

NOTING the proposal by the ASEAN Chambers of Commerce and Industry (ASEAN-CCI) on the ASEAN industrial cooperation scheme and the confidence expressed by the ASEAN-CCI in the viability of the scheme;

DESIRING to provide the guidelines and institutional framework within which the ASEAN private sector may collaborate on the basis of mutual and equitable benefits for the ASEAN Member Countries and increased industrial production for the region as a whole;

MINDFUL of the need to develop the growth of Small and Medium Scale Enterprises (SMEs) taking into consideration the stages of development among ASEAN Member Countries;

ADHERING to the principles, concepts and ideals of the Framework Agreement on Enhancing ASEAN Economic Cooperation and the Agreement on the Common Effective Preferential Tariff (CEPT) Scheme for the ASEAN Free Trade Area;

DO HEREBY AGREE to pursue the ASEAN Industrial Cooperation Scheme as stipulated by the following provisions:

Article 1

Definitions

For the purposes of this Agreement :

1. "AICO Scheme" shall mean the ASEAN Industrial Cooperation Scheme established by this Agreement.

2. "AICO Arrangement" shall mean a cooperative arrangement consisting of a minimum of two Participating Countries and one Participating Company in each Participating Country.

3. "Participating Countries" shall mean ASEAN Member Countries which agree to participate in an AICO Arrangement by granting the specified privileges to the Participating Companies.

4. "Participating Companies" shall mean companies incorporated and operating in ASEAN Member Countries meeting the criteria under Article 2(1) and Article 3 of this Agreement.

5. "AICO Products" refer to the following:

   a. AICO Final Products shall be the final output which does not undergo any further processing within the specific AICO arrangement; or

b.   AICO Intermediate Products shall be products used within the AICO arrangement as an input to the AICO Final Product; or

c.   AICO Raw Materials shall be used as input to an intermediate product or as direct input to the AICO Final Product; which shall be reflected in the Certificate of Eligibility (COE) issued to the Participating Companies.

6.   "Preferential Tariff Rates" shall mean the advanced CEPT rates fixed by Participating Countries within the range of 0% to 5%.

7.   "National Authorities" shall mean the relevant authorities of ASEAN Member Countries responsible for the approval of an AICO application and the granting of privileges.

Article 2

General Provisions

1.   The AICO Arrangement shall be made up of Participating Companies incorporated and operating in different ASEAN Member Countries which seek to cooperate in the manufacture of AICO Products.

2.   The number of Participating Companies in an AICO Arrangement may change subject to the defined minimum level.

3.   An AICO Arrangement may have more than one Participating Company in each of the Participating Countries and may cover multiple products.

Article 3

Eligibility Criteria

1.   Companies wishing to benefit from the privileges of the AICO Scheme shall fulfill the following criteria:

a.   be incorporated and operating in an ASEAN Member Country;

b.   have a minimum of 30% national equity. The equity condition may be waived after consultation by the Participating Countries in cases where the proposing companies meet the other criteria of this Article; and

c.   undertake resource sharing, industrial complementation or industrial cooperation activities.

2.   Each Participating Company of an AICO Arrangement must submit documentary evidence on resource sharing, industrial complementation or industrial cooperation activities such as joint ventures, joint manufacturing, technology transfer, training, licensing, consolidated purchasing and procurement, management service, sales and marketing agreement or other areas of cooperation.

Article 4

Product Coverage and Eligibility

1.   All products, other than products listed in Article 9 (General Exception) of the Agreement of the CEPT Scheme, shall be eligible for the AICO Scheme.

2.   Product approval shall be at HS 8-digit level and above.

3.   An AICO Product shall meet the Rules of Origin of the CEPT Scheme.

Article 5

Privileges

1.   A Participating Company shall be entitled to the following privileges under the AICO Scheme:

a.   approved AICO Products traded between Participating Companies shall enjoy preferential tariff rates of 0%-5%, the actual rate of which shall be determined by each Participating Country. The preferential tariff shall cease when the tariff rate of the product reaches the final CEPT rate;

b. local content accreditation shall be accorded, where applicable, to products manufactured by Participating Companies; and

c. non-tariff incentives offered by the respective National Authorities.

The granting of these incentives shall be based on the fulfillment of the requirements of the respective Participating Country.

2. ASEAN Member Countries may subsequently introduce additional tariff and non-tariff incentives under this Agreement.

Article 6

Operating Guidelines and Award Principles

1. An AICO Arrangement shall only require the approval of the Participating Countries.

2. A Participating Company shall be accorded the privileges under this Agreement upon the approval of its application in accordance with the provisions of Article 7.

3. The approval of an AICO Arrangement shall not be limited to the initial applicants manufacturing a particular AICO Product. Subsequent applications from companies manufacturing the same AICO Products shall also be approved once the companies meet the eligibility criteria.

4. A prospective company in a non-participating Member Country could participate in an on-going AICO Arrangement if the non-participating country agrees to extend the preferential tariff rates to the AICO Products and upon the agreement of the existing Participating Countries.

5. A Participating Company shall use the intermediate parts and raw materials only in the manufacture of AICO Products. A Participating Country may withdraw the privileges under this Agreement if a Participating Company violates this obligation.

Article 7

Application Procedures

1. Interested companies wishing to participate in an AICO Arrangement shall apply directly to the National Authorities for approval.
2. ASEAN Member Countries shall inform the ASEAN Secretariat of their participation in an AICO Arrangement and the tariff rate to be applied within the 0%-5% band, within 60 days of receipt of the application. ASEAN Member Countries which are unable to indicate a decision on the tariff rate within this period shall nevertheless indicate their decision on acceptance or otherwise, of the arrangement and the product as an AICO Product.
3. The ASEAN Secretariat shall issue the COE within 14 days of the receipt of approval from Participating Countries.
4. The Participating Company shall use the COE to claim preferential tariff rates and to apply for non-tariff incentives from the relevant National Authorities.
5. Participating Countries shall grant the Preferential Tariff Rates within 60 days from the date of the issuance of the COE by the ASEAN Secretariat.

Article 8

Monitoring Body

1. National Authorities shall monitor the implementation of their respective AICO Arrangements. The ASEAN Secretariat shall be responsible for the overall monitoring of the AICO Scheme. For this purpose, Participating Countries shall submit regular reports on the AICO Arrangements in their respective countries to the ASEAN Secretariat.
2. The ASEAN Economic Ministers (AEM) Meeting and its subsidiary bodies shall review the progress and implementation of the AICO Scheme.

Article 9

Settlement of Dispute

Any differences between the ASEAN Member Countries concerning the interpretation or application of this Agreement shall, as far as possible, be settled amicably between the parties. If such differences cannot be settled amicably, it shall be submitted to the Dispute Settlement Mechanism.

Article 10

Accession of New Members

New Members of ASEAN shall accede to this Agreement by signing and depositing the instrument of ratification with the Secretary-General of ASEAN.

Article 11

Other Provisions

1.   The scope of coverage of this Agreement shall subsequently be expanded to include additional sectors.
2.   Participating Countries shall eliminate all quantitative restrictions and non-tariff barriers applicable to an approved AICO product.

Article 12

Repealing Provisions

Upon the entry into force, this Agreement shall supersede the Basic Agreement on ASEAN Industrial Joint Ventures (AIJVs) dated 15 December 1987 and the Memorandum of Understanding on the Brand-to-Brand Complementation (BBC) Scheme dated 18 October 1988 subject to the following conditions:

a.   that BBC and AIJV applications shall not be accepted upon entry into force of this Agreement;
b.   only amendments to approved models in the BBC Scheme shall be allowed;

c.   that existing BBC companies shall continue to enjoy the margin
of preference and the local content accreditation for products
approved to this date until the expiry of the current car model
previously approved; and

d.   for existing AIJVs, the privileges shall cease on 31 December
2002. With effect from 1 January 2003 the final CEPT rate
shall apply.

Article 13

Final Provisions

1.   The respective Governments of ASEAN Member Countries
shall undertake the appropriate measures to fulfill the
obligations arising from this Agreement;

2.   Any amendment to this Agreement shall be made by consensus
and shall become effective upon acceptance by all ASEAN
Member Countries;

3.   No reservation shall be made with respect to any of the
provisions of this Agreement;

4.   This Agreement shall be deposited with the Secretary-General
of ASEAN who shall promptly furnish a certified copy thereof
to each ASEAN Member Country; and

5.   This Agreement shall enter into force upon the deposit of
instruments of ratification or acceptance by all signatory
Governments with the Secretary-General of ASEAN.

IN WITNESS HEREOF, the undersigned have signed this Agreement
on ASEAN Industrial Cooperation Scheme.

DONE at Singapore, this27th day of April 1996 in a single copy in
the English Language.

APPENDIX 10: FRAMEWORK AGREEMENT ON THE ASEAN INVESTMENT AREA

The Governments of Brunei Darussalam, the Republic of Indonesia, the Lao People's Democratic Republic, Malaysia, the Union of Myanmar, the Republic of the Philippines, the Republic of Singapore, the Kingdom of Thailand and the Socialist Republic of Vietnam, Member States of the Association of South-East Asian Nations (ASEAN);

REAFFIRMING the importance of sustaining economic growth and development in all Member States through joint efforts in liberalising trade and promoting intra-ASEAN trade and investment flows enshrined in the Framework Agreement on Enhancing ASEAN Economic Co-operation signed in Singapore on 28 January 1992;

RECALLING the decision of the Fifth ASEAN Summit held on 15 December 1995 to establish an ASEAN Investment Area (hereinafter referred to as "AIA"), in order to enhance ASEAN's attractiveness and competitiveness for promoting direct investments;

AFFIRMING their commitment to the 1987 ASEAN Agreement for the Promotion and Protection of Investments and its 1996 Protocol to enhance investor confidence for investing in ASEAN;

MINDFUL of the decision to establish an ASEAN Free Trade Area (AFTA) and the implementation of the ASEAN Industrial Co-operation (AICO) Scheme, to encourage greater investment flows into the region;

RECOGNIZING that direct investment is an important source of finance for sustaining the pace of economic, industrial, infrastructure and technology development; hence, the need to attract higher and sustainable level of direct investment flows in ASEAN;

DETERMINED to realise the vision of ASEAN to establish a competitive ASEAN Investment Area through a more liberal and transparent investment environment by 1st January 2010; and

BEARING IN MIND that the measures agreed upon to establish a competitive ASEAN Investment Area by 2010 shall contribute towards ASEAN Vision 2020.

Have Agreed as Follows:

Article 1

Definition

For the purpose of this Agreement:

"ASEAN investor" means —
- a national of a Member State; or
- any juridical person of a Member State,

making an investment in another Member State, the effective ASEAN equity of which taken cumulatively with all other ASEAN equities fulfills at least the minimum percentage required to meet the national equity requirement and other equity requirements of domestic laws and published national policies, if any, of the host country in respect of that investment.

For the purpose of this definition, equity of nationals or juridical persons of any Member State shall be deemed to be the equity of nationals or juridical persons of the host country.

"effective ASEAN equity" in respect of an investment in an ASEAN Member State means ultimate holdings by nationals or juridical persons of ASEAN Member States in that investment.

Where the shareholding/equity structure of an ASEAN investor makes it difficult to establish the ultimate holding structure, the rules and procedures for determining effective equity used by the Member State in which the ASEAN investor is investing may be applied. If necessary, the Co-ordinating Committee on Investment shall prepare guidelines for this purpose.

"juridical person" means any legal entity duly constituted or otherwise organized under applicable law of a Member State, whether for profit or otherwise, and whether privately-owned or governmentally-owned, including any corporation, trust, partnership, joint venture, sole proprietorship or association.

"measures" means laws, regulations, rules, procedures, decisions, administrative actions, or any other actions affecting investments taken by Member States.

"national" means a natural person having the citizenship of a Member State in accordance with its applicable laws.

Article 2

Coverage

This Agreement shall cover all direct investments other than –
1. portfolio investments; and
2. matters relating to investments covered by other ASEAN Agreements, such as the ASEAN Framework Agreement on Services.

Article 3

Objectives

The objectives of this Agreement are:

1. to establish a competitive ASEAN Investment Area with a more liberal and transparent investment environment amongst Member States in order to -
    1. substantially increase the flow of investments into ASEAN from both ASEAN and non-ASEAN sources;
    2. jointly promote ASEAN as the most attractive investment area;
    3. strengthen and increase the competitiveness of ASEAN's economic sectors;

4.   progressively reduce or eliminate investment
       regulations and conditions which may impede
       investment flows and the operation of investment
       projects in ASEAN; and

2.   to ensure that the realization of the above objectives would
       contribute towards free flow of investments by 2020.

Article 4

Features

The AIA shall be an area where:

1.   there is a co-ordinated ASEAN investment co-operation
       programme that will generate increased investments from
       ASEAN and non-ASEAN sources;
2.   national treatment is extended to ASEAN investors by 2010,
       and to all investors by 2020, subject to the exceptions provided
       for under this Agreement;
3.   all industries are opened for investment to ASEAN investors by
       2010 and to all investors by 2020, subject to the exceptions
       provided for under this Agreement;
4.   the business sector has a larger role in the co-operation efforts
       in relation to investments and related activities in ASEAN; and
5.   there is freer flow of capital, skilled labour and professionals,
       and technology amongst Member States.

Article 5

General Obligations

To realize the objectives referred to in Article 3, the Member
States shall:

1.   ensure that measures and programmes are undertaken on a fair
       and mutually beneficial basis;
2.   undertake appropriate measures to ensure transparency and
       consistency in the application and interpretation of their

investment laws, regulations and administrative procedures in order to create and maintain a predictable investment regime in ASEAN;

3. begin the process of facilitation, promotion and liberalization which would contribute continuously and significantly to achieving the objective of a more liberal and transparent investment environment;

4. take appropriate measures to enhance the attractiveness of the investment environment of Member States for direct investment flows; and

5. take such reasonable actions as may be available to them to ensure observance of the provisions of this Agreement by the regional and local governments and authorities within their territories.

Article 6

Programme and Action Plans

1. Member States shall, for the implementation of the obligations under this Agreement, undertake the joint development and implementation of the following programmes:

   1. co-operation and facilitation programme as specified in Schedule I;
   2. promotion and awareness programme as specified in Schedule II; and
   3. liberalization programme as specified in Schedule III.

2. Member States shall submit Action Plans for the implementation of the programmes in paragraph 1 to the AIA Council established under Article 16 of this Agreement.

3. The Action Plans shall be reviewed every 2 years to ensure that the objectives of this Agreement are achieved.

Article 7

Opening Up of Industries and National Treatment

1. Subject to the provisions of this Article, each Member State shall:

    1. open immediately all its industries for investments by ASEAN investors;
    2. accord immediately to ASEAN investors and their investments, in respect of all industries and measures affecting investment including but not limited to the admission, establishment, acquisition, expansion, management, operation and disposition of investments, treatment no less favourable than that it accords to its own like investors and investments ("national treatment").

2. Each Member State shall submit a Temporary Exclusion List and a Sensitive List, if any, within 6 months after the date of signing of this Agreement, of any industries or measures affecting investments (referred to in paragraph 1 above) with regard to which it is unable to open up or to accord national treatment to ASEAN investors. These lists shall form an annex to this Agreement. In the event that a Member State, for justifiable reasons, is unable to provide any list within the stipulated period, it may seek an extension from the AIA Council.

3. The Temporary Exclusion List shall be reviewed every 2 years and shall be progressively phased out by 2010 by all Member States except the Socialist Republic of Vietnam, the Lao People's Democratic Republic and the Union of Myanmar. The Socialist Republic of Vietnam shall progressively phase out the Temporary Exclusion List by 2013 and the Lao People's Democratic Republic and the Union of Myanmar shall progressively phase out their Temporary Exclusion Lists by 2015.

4. The Sensitive List shall be reviewed by 1 January 2003 and at such subsequent periodic intervals as may be decided by the AIA Council.

Article 8

Most Favoured Nation Treatment

1.   Subject to Articles 7 and 9 of this Agreement, each Member State shall accord immediately and unconditionally to investors and investments of another Member State, treatment no less favourable than that it accords to investors and investments of any other Member State with respect to all measures affecting investment including but not limited to the admission, establishment, acquisition, expansion, management, operation and disposition of investments.

2.   In relation to investments falling within the scope of this Agreement, any preferential treatment granted under any existing or future agreements or arrangements to which a Member State is a party shall be extended on the most favoured nation basis to all other Member States.

3.   The requirement in paragraph 2 shall not apply to existing agreements or arrangements notified by Member States to the AIA Council within 6 months after the date of signing of this Agreement.

4.   Nothing in paragraph 1 shall prevent any Member State from conferring special treatment or advantages to adjacent countries under growth triangles and other sub-regional arrangements between Member States.

Article 9

Wavier of Most Favoured Nation Treatment

1.   Where a Member State is temporarily not ready to make concessions under Articles 7 of this Agreement, and another Member State has made concessions under the said Article, then the first mentioned Member State shall waive its rights to such concessions. However, if a Member State which grants such concessions is willing to forego the waiver, then the first mentioned Member State can still enjoy these concessions.

2.   Having regard to the late entry into ASEAN of the Socialist Republic of Vietnam, the Lao People's Democratic Republic and

the Union of Myanmar, the provisions of paragraph 1 of this Article shall only apply to the Socialist Republic of Vietnam for a period of 3 years, and the Lao People's Democratic Republic and the Union of Myanmar for a period of 5 years from the date this Agreement comes into force.

Article 10

Modification of Schedules, Annexes and Action Plans

1. Any modification to Schedules I and II, and Action Plans thereof shall be subject to the approval of the Co-ordinating Committee on Investments (CCI) established under Article 16(4) of this Agreement.

2. Any modification to or withdrawal of any commitments in Schedule III and Action Plans thereof and the Annexes shall be subject to the consideration of the AIA Council in accordance with the provisions of the ASEAN Protocol on Notification Procedures.

Article 11

Transparency

1. Each Member State shall make available to the AIA Council through publication or any other means, all relevant measures, laws, regulations and administrative guidelines which pertain to, or affect, the operation of this Agreement. This shall also apply to international agreements pertaining to or affecting investment to which a Member State is also a signatory.

2. Each Member State shall promptly and at least annually inform the AIA Council of the introduction of any new or any changes to existing laws, regulations or administrative guidelines which significantly affect investments or its commitments under this Agreement.

3. Nothing in this Agreement shall require any Member State to provide confidential information, the disclosure of which would impede law enforcement, or otherwise be contrary to the public

interest, or which would prejudice legitimate commercial interests of particular enterprises, public or private.

Article 12

Other Agreements

1. Member States affirm their existing rights and obligations under the 1987 ASEAN Agreement for the Promotion and Protection of Investments and its 1996 Protocol. In the event that this Agreement provides for better or enhanced provisions over the said Agreement and its Protocol, then such provisions of this Agreement shall prevail.
2. This Agreement or any action taken under it shall not affect the rights and obligations of the Member States under existing agreements to which they are parties.
3. Nothing in this Agreement shall affect the rights of the Member States to enter into other agreements not contrary to the principles, objectives and terms of this Agreement.

Article 13

General Exceptions

Subject to the requirement that such measures are not applied in a manner which would constitute a means of arbitrary or unjustifiable discrimination between countries where like conditions prevail, or a disguised restriction on investment flows, nothing in this Agreement shall be construed to prevent the adoption or enforcement by any Member State of measures:

1. necessary to protect national security and public morals;
2. necessary to protect human, animal or plant life or health;
3. necessary to secure compliance with laws or regulations which are not inconsistent with the provisions of this Agreement including those relating to:

    1. the prevention of deceptive and fraudulent practices or to deal with the effects of a default on investment agreement.

2.   the protection of the privacy of individuals in relation to the processing and dissemination of personal data and the protection of confidentiality of individual records and accounts.

3.   safety.

4.   aimed at ensuring the equitable or effective imposition or collection of direct taxes in respect of investments or investors of Member States.

Article 14

Emergency Safeguard Measures

1.   If, as a result of the implementation of the liberalisation programme under this Agreement, a Member state suffers or is threatened with any serious injury and threat, the Member State may take emergency safeguard measures to the extent and for such period as may be necessary to prevent or to remedy such injury. The measures taken shall be provisional and without discrimination.

2.   Where emergency safeguard measures are taken pursuant to this Article, notice of such measure shall be given to the AIA Council within 14 days from the date such measures are taken.

3.   The AIA Council shall determine the definition of serious injury and threat of serious injury and the procedures of instituting emergency safeguards measures pursuant to this Article.

Article 15

Measures to Safegurd the Balance of Payments

1.   In the event of serious balance of payments and external financial difficulties or threat thereof, a Member State may adopt or maintain restrictions on investments on which it has undertaken specific commitments, including on payments or transfers for transactions related to such commitments. It is recognized that particular pressures on the balance of payments of a Member State in the process of economic development or

economic transition may necessitate the use of restrictions to ensure, inter alia, the maintenance of a level of financial reserves adequate for the implementation of its programme of economic development or economic transition.

2.   Where measures to safeguard balance of payments are taken pursuant to this Article notice of such measures shall be given to the AIA Council within 14 days from the date such measures are taken.

3.   The measures referred to in paragraph (1):

    1.   shall not discriminate among Member States;

    2.   shall be consistent with the Articles of Agreement of the International Monetary Fund;

    3.   shall avoid unnecessary damage to the commercial, economic and financial interests of any other Member State;

    4.   shall not exceed those necessary to deal with the circumstances described in paragraph 1; and

    5.   shall be temporary and be phased out progressively as the situation specified in paragraph 1 improves.

4.   The Member States adopting the balance of payments measures shall commence consultations with the AIA Council and other Member States within 90 days from the date of notification in order to review the balance of payment measures adopted by it.

5.   The AIA Council shall determine the rules applicable to the procedures under this Article.

Article 16

Institutional Arrangements

1.   The ASEAN Economic Ministers (AEM) shall establish an ASEAN Investment Area Council (in this Agreement referred to as "the AIA Council") comprising the Ministers responsible for investment and the Secretary-General of ASEAN. The ASEAN Heads of Investment Agencies shall participate in the AIA Council meetings.

2.   Notwithstanding Article 21 of this Agreement, the AIA Council shall be established upon the signing of this Agreement.

3.   The AIA Council shall supervise, co-ordinate and review the implementation of this Agreement and assist the AEM in all matters relating thereto.

4.   In the performance of its functions, the AIA Council shall establish a Co-ordinating Committee on Investment (CCI) comprizing senior officials responsible for investment and other senior officials from relevant government agencies.

5.   The Co-ordinating Committee on Investment shall report to the AIA Council through the Senior Economic Officials Meeting (SEOM).

6.   The ASEAN Secretariat shall be the secretariat to the AIA Council and the Co-ordinating Committee on Investment (CCI).

Article 17

Settlement of Disputes

1.   The Protocol on Dispute Settlement Mechanism for ASEAN shall apply in relation to any dispute arising from, or any differences between Member States concerning the interpretation or application of this Agreement or any arrangement arising therefrom.

2.   If necessary, a specific dispute settlement mechanism may be established for the purpose of this Agreement which shall form an integral part of this Agreement.

Article 18

Amendments

Any amendments to this Agreement shall be made by consensus and shall become effective upon the deposit of instruments of ratification or acceptance by all signatory governments with the Secretary-General of ASEAN.

Article 19

Supplementary Agreements or Arrangements

The Schedules, Action Plans, Annexes, and any other arrangements or agreements arising under this Agreement shall form an integral part of this Agreement.

Article 20

Accession of New Members

New members of ASEAN shall accede to this Agreement on terms and conditions agreed between them and signatories to this Agreement and by depositing the instrument of accession with the Secretary-General of ASEAN.

Article 21

Final Provisions

1.   This Agreement shall enter into force upon the deposit of instruments of ratification or acceptance by all signatory governments with the Secretary-General of ASEAN. The signatory governments undertake to deposit their instruments of ratification or acceptance within 6 months after the date of signing of this Agreement.

2.   This Agreement shall be deposited with the Secretary-General of ASEAN, who shall promptly furnish a certified copy thereof to each Member State.

IN WITNESS WHEREOF, the undersigned being duly authorised by their respective Governments, have signed this Framework Agreement on the ASEAN Investment Area.

Done at Manila, Philippines this 8th day of October 1998, in a single copy in the English language.

APPENDIX 11: PROTOCOL ON DISPUTE SETTLEMENT MECHANISM

The Governments of Brunei Darussalam, the Republic of Indonesia, Malaysia, the Republic of the Philippines, the Republic of Singapore, the Kingdom of Thailand and the Socialist Republic of Vietnam, Member States of the Association of South East Asian Nations (ASEAN);

RECALLING the Framework Agreement on Enhancing ASEAN Economic Cooperation signed in Singapore on 28 January 1992, as amended by the Protocol to Amend the Framework Agreement on Enhancing ASEAN Economic Cooperation signed in Bangkok on 15 December 1995 (the "Agreement");

RECOGNIZING the need to expand Article 9 of the Agreement to strengthen the mechanism for the settlement of disputes in the area of ASEAN economic cooperation;

Have Agreed as Follows:

Article 1

Coverage and Application

1.　　The rules and procedures of this Protocol shall apply to disputes brought pursuant to the consultation and dispute settlement provisions of the Agreement as well as the agreements listed in Appendix 1 and future ASEAN economic agreements (the "covered agreements").

2. The rules and procedures of this Protocol shall apply subject to such special or additional rules and procedures on dispute settlement contained in the covered agreements. To the extent that there is a difference between the rules and procedures of this Protocol and the special or additional rules and procedures in the covered agreements, the special or additional rules and procedures shall prevail.

3. The provisions of this Protocol are without prejudice to the rights of Member States to seek recourse to other fora for the settlement of disputes involving other Member States. A Member State involved in a dispute can resort to other fora at any stage before the Senior Economic Officials Meeting ("SEOM") has made a ruling on the panel report.

Article 2

Consultations

1. Member States shall accord adequate opportunity for consultations regarding any representations made by other Member States with respect to any matter affecting the implementation, interpretation or application of the Agreement or any covered agreement. Any differences shall, as far as possible, be settled amicably between the Member States.

2. Member States which consider that any benefit accruing to them directly or indirectly, under the Agreement or any covered agreement is being nullified or impaired, or that the attainment of any objective of the Agreement or any covered agreement is being impeded as a result of failure of another Member State to carry out its obligations under the Agreement or any covered agreement, or the existence of any other situation may, with a view to achieving satisfactory settlement of the matter, make representations or proposals to the other Member State concerned, which shall give due consideration to the representations or proposals made to it.

3. If a request for consultations is made, the Member State to which the request is made shall reply to the request within

ten (10) days after the date of its receipt and shall enter into consultations within a period of no more than thirty (30) days after the date of receipt of the request, with a view to reaching a mutually satisfactory solution.

Article 3

Good Offices, Conciliation or Mediation

1. Member States which are parties to a dispute may at any time agree to good offices, conciliation or mediation. They may begin at any time and be terminated at any time. Once procedures for good offices, conciliation or mediation are terminated, a complaining party may then proceed to raise the matter to SEOM.
2. If the parties to a dispute agree, procedures for good offices, conciliation or mediation may continue while the dispute proceeds.

Article 4

Senior Economic Officials Meeting

1. If the consultations fail to settle a dispute within sixty (60) days after the date of receipt of the request for consultations, the matter shall be raised to the SEOM.
2. The SEOM shall:
    a) establish a panel; or
    b) where applicable, raise the matter to the special body in charge of the special or additional rules and procedures for its consideration.
3. Notwithstanding Article 4 paragraph 2, if the SEOM considers it desirable to do so in a particular case, it may decide to deal with the dispute to achieve an amicable settlement without appointing a panel. This step shall be taken without any extension of the thirty (30)-day period in Article 5 paragraph 2.

Article 5

Establishment of Panel

1. The function of the panel is to make an objective assessment of the dispute before it, including an examination of the facts of the case and the applicability of and conformity with the sections of the Agreement or any covered agreement, and make such other findings as will assist the SEOM in making the rulings provided for under the Agreement or any covered agreement.

2. The SEOM shall establish a panel no later than thirty (30) days after the date on which the dispute has been raised to it.

3. The SEOM shall make the final determination of the size, composition and terms of reference of the panel.

Article 6

Function of the Panel

1. The panel shall, apart from the matters covered in Appendix 2, regulate its own procedures in relation to the rights of parties to be heard and its deliberations.

2. The panel shall submit its findings to the SEOM within sixty (60) days of its formation. In exceptional cases, the panel may take an additional ten (10) days to submit its findings to SEOM. Within this time period, the panel shall accord adequate opportunity to the parties to the dispute to review the report before submission.

3. The panel shall have the right to seek information and technical advice from any individual or body which it deems appropriate. A Member State should respond promptly and fully to any request by a panel for such information as the panel considers necessary and appropriate.

4. Panel deliberations shall be confidential. The reports of panels shall be drafted without the presence of the parties to the dispute in the light of the information provided and the statements made.

Article 7

Treatment of Panel Result

The SEOM shall consider the report of the panel in its deliberations and make a ruling on the dispute within thirty (30) days from the submission of the report by the panel. In exceptional cases, SEOM may take an additional ten (10) days to make a ruling on the dispute. SEOM representatives from Member States which are parties to a dispute can be present during the process of deliberation but shall not participate in the ruling of SEOM. SEOM shall make a ruling based on simple majority.

Article 8

Appeal

1. Member States, who are parties to the dispute, may appeal the ruling by the SEOM to the ASEAN Economic Ministers ("AEM") within thirty (30) days of the ruling.

2. The AEM shall make a decision within thirty (30) days of the appeal. In exceptional cases, AEM may take an additional ten (10) days to make a decision on the dispute. Economic Ministers from Member States which are parties to a dispute can be present during the process of deliberation but shall not participate in the decision of AEM. AEM shall make a decision based on simple majority. The decision of the AEM on the appeal shall be final and binding on all parties to the dispute.

3. Since prompt compliance with the rulings of the SEOM or decisions of the AEM is essential in order to ensure effective resolution of disputes, Member States who are parties to the dispute shall comply with the ruling or decision, as the case may be, within a reasonable time period. The reasonable period of time shall be a period of time mutually agreed to by the parties to the dispute but under no circumstances should it exceed thirty (30) days from the SEOM's ruling or in the event of an appeal thirty (30) days from the AEM's decision. The Member States

concerned shall provide the SEOM or the AEM, as the case may be, with a status report in writing of their progress in the implementation of the ruling or decision.

Article 9

Compensation and the Suspension of Concessions

1.　If the Member State concerned fails to bring the measure found to be inconsistent with the Agreement or any covered agreement into compliance therewith or otherwise comply with SEOM's rulings or AEM's decisions within the reasonable period of time, such Member State shall, if so requested, and no later than the expiry of the reasonable period of time, enter into negotiations with any party having invoked the dispute settlement procedures, with a view to developing mutually acceptable compensation. If no satisfactory compensation has been agreed within 20 (twenty) days after the date of expiry of the reasonable period of time, any party having invoked the dispute settlement procedures may request authorization from the AEM to suspend the application to the Member State concerned of concessions or other obligations under the Agreement or any covered agreements.

2.　However, neither compensation nor the suspension of concessions or other obligations is preferred to full implementation of a recommendation to bring a measure into conformity with the Agreement or any covered agreements.

Article 10

Maximum Time-Frame

Member States agree that the total period for the disposal of a dispute pursuant to Articles 2, 4, 5, 6, 7, 8 and 9 of this Protocol shall not exceed two hundred and ninety (290) days.

Article 11

Responsibilities of the Secretariat

1.   The ASEAN Secretariat shall have the responsibility of assisting the panels, especially on the historical and procedural aspects of the matters dealt with, and of providing secretarial and technical support.
2.   The ASEAN Secretariat shall have the responsibility of monitoring and maintaining under surveillance the implementation of the SEOM's ruling and AEM's decision as the case may be.
3.   The ASEAN Secretariat may offer good offices, conciliation or mediation with the view to assisting Members to settle a dispute.

Article 12

Final Provisions

1.   This Protocol shall be deposited with the Secretary-General of ASEAN who shall promptly furnish a certified copy thereof to each Member State.
2.   This Protocol shall enter into force upon the deposit of instruments of ratification or acceptance by all signatory governments with the Secretary-General of ASEAN.

IN WITNESS WHEREOF, the undersigned, being duly authorized thereto by their respective Governments, have signed the Protocol on Dispute Settlement Mechanism.

DONE at Manila, this 20th day of November 1996 in a single copy in the English Language.

Appendix 1

Covered Agreements

1.   Multilateral Agreement on Commercial Rights of Non-Scheduled Services among ASEAN, Manila, 13 March 1971.

2.	Agreement on ASEAN Preferential Trading Arrangements, Manila, 24 February 1977.

3.	Memorandum of Understanding on the ASEAN Swap Arrangements, Kuala Lumpur, 5 August 1977.

4.	Supplementary Agreement to the Memorandum of Understanding on the ASEAN Swap Arrangement, Washington D.C., 26 September 1978.

5.	Second Supplementary Agreement to the Memorandum of Understanding on the ASEAN Swap Arrangement, Denpasar, Bali, 9 September 1979.

6.	Agreement on the ASEAN Food Security Reserve, New York, 4 October 1979.

7.	Basic Agreement on ASEAN Industrial Projects, Kuala Lumpur, 6 March 1980.

8.	Supplementary Agreement of the Basic Agreement on ASEAN Industrial Projects ASEAN Urea Project (Indonesia), Kuala Lumpur, 6 March 1980.

9.	Supplementary Agreement of the Basic Agreement on ASEAN Industrial Projects ASEAN Urea Project (Malaysia), Kuala Lumpur, 6 March 1980.

10.	Amendments to the Memorandum of Understanding on the ASEAN Swap Arrangement Colombo, Sri Lanka, 16 January 1981.

11.	Basic Agreement on ASEAN Industrial Complementation, Manila, 18 June 1981.

12.	Third Supplementary Agreement to the Memorandum of Understanding on the ASEAN Swap Arrangement, Bangkok, 4 February 1982.

13.	ASEAN Ministerial Understanding on Plant Quarantine Ring, Kuala Lumpur, 8-9 October 1982.

14.	ASEAN Ministerial Understanding on the Standardization of Import and Quarantine Regulation on Animal and Animal Products, Kuala Lumpur, 8-9 October 1982.

15.	Protocol to Amend the Agreement on the ASEAN Food Security Reserve, Bangkok, 22 October 1982.

16.	ASEAN Customs Code of Conduct, Jakarta, 18 March 1983.

17.	ASEAN Ministerial Understanding on Fisheries Cooperation, Singapore, 20-22 October 1983.

18. Basic Agreement on ASEAN Industrial Joint Ventures, Jakarta, 7 November 1983.

19. ASEAN Ministerial Understanding on ASEAN Cooperation in Agricultural Cooperatives, Manila, 4-5 October 1984.

20. ASEAN Ministerial Understanding on Plant Pest Free Zone, Manila, 4-5 October 1984.

21. Agreement on ASEAN Energy Cooperation, Manila, 24 June 1986.

22. ASEAN Petroleum Security Agreement, Manila, 24 June 1986.

23. Agreement on the Preferential Shortlisting of ASEAN Contractors, Jakarta, 20 October 1986.

24. Supplementary Agreement to the Basic Agreement on ASEAN Industrial Joint Ventures, Singapore, 16 June 1987.

25. Fourth Supplementary Agreement to the Memorandum of Understanding on the ASEAN Swap Arrangement, Kathmandu, Nepal, 21 January 1987.

26. Protocol on Improvements on Extensions of Tariff Preferences under the ASEAN Preferential Trading Arrangement, Manila, 15 December 1987.

27. Memorandum of Understanding on Standstill and Rollback on Non-Tariff Barriers among ASEAN Countries, Manila, 15 December 1987.

28. Revised Basic Agreement on ASEAN Industrial Joint Ventures, Manila, 15 December 1987.

29. Agreement Among the Government of Brunei Darussalam, the Republic of Indonesia, Malaysia, the Republic of the Philippines, the Republic of Singapore, and the Kingdom of Thailand for the Promotion and Protection of Investments, Manila, 15 December 1987.

30. Protocol on Improvements on Extension of Tariff Preferences under the ASEAN Preferential Trading Arrangement, Manila, 15 December 1987.

31. Agreement on the Establishment of the ASEAN Tourism Information Centre, Kuala Lumpur, 26 September 1988.

32. Financial Regulations of the ASEAN Tourism Information Centre, Kuala Lumpur, 26 September 1988.

33. Memorandum of Understanding Brand-to-Brand Complementation on the Automotive Industry Under the Basic Agreement on

ASEAN Industrial Complementation (BAAIC), Pattaya, Thailand, 18 October 1988.

34. Protocol to Amend the Revised Basic Agreement on ASEAN Industrial Joint Ventures, 1 January 1991.

35. Supplementary Agreement to the Basic Agreement on ASEAN industrial Projects – ASEAN Potash Mining Projects (Thailand), Kuala Lumpur, 20 July 1991.

36. Agreement on the Common Effective Preferential Tariff Scheme for the ASEAN Free Trade Area, Singapore, 28 January 1992.

37. Second Protocol to Amend the Revised Basic Agreement on ASEAN Industrial Joint Ventures, Manila, 23 October 1992.

38. Ministerial Understanding on ASEAN Cooperation in Food, Agriculture and Forestry, Bandar Seri Begawan, 28-30 October 1993.

39. Memorandum of Understanding on ASEAN Cooperation and Joint Approaches in Agriculture and Forest Products Promotion Scheme, Langkawi, Malaysia, 1994.

40. Third Protocol to Amend the Revised Basic Agreement on ASEAN Industrial Joint Ventures, 2 March 1995.

41. Protocol to Amend the Agreement on the Common Effective Preferential Tariff (CEPT) Scheme for the ASEAN Free Trade Area (AFTA), Bangkok, 15 December 1995.

42. Protocol to Amend the Agreement on ASEAN Preferential Trading Arrangements, Bangkok, 15 December 1995.

43. ASEAN Framework Agreement on Services, Bangkok, 15 December 1995.

44. ASEAN Framework Agreement on Intellectual Property Cooperation, Bangkok, 15 December 1995.

45. Protocol Amending the Agreement on ASEAN Energy Cooperation, Bangkok, 15 December 1995.

46. Basic Agreement on ASEAN Industrial Cooperation, Singapore, 26 April 1996.

47. Protocol to Amend the Agreement Among the Government of Brunei Darussalam, the Republic of Indonesia, Malaysia, the Republic of the Philippines, the Republic of Singapore, and the Kingdom of Thailand for the Promotion and Protection of Investments, Jakarta, 12 September 1996.

Appendix 2

Working Procedures of the Panel

I. Composition of Panels

1. Panels shall be composed of well-qualified governmental and/or non-governmental individuals, including persons who have served on or presented a case to a panel, served in the Secretariat, taught or published on international trade law or policy, or served as a senior trade policy official of a Member State. In the nomination to the panels, preference shall be given to individuals who are nationals of ASEAN Member States.

2. Panel members should be selected with a view to ensuring the independence of the members, a sufficiently diverse background and a wide spectrum of experience.

3. Nationals of Member States whose governments are parties to the dispute shall not serve on a panel concerned with that dispute, unless the parties to the dispute agree otherwise.

4. To assist in the selection of panelists, the Secretariat shall maintain an indicative list of governmental and non-governmental individuals possessing the qualifications outlined in paragraph 1, from which panelists may be drawn as appropriate. Members may periodically suggest names of governmental and non-governmental individuals for inclusion on the indicative list, providing relevant information on their knowledge of international trade and of the sectors or subject matter of the covered agreements, and those names shall be added to the list upon approval by the SEOM. For each of the individuals on the list, the list shall indicate specific areas of experience or expertize of the individuals in the sectors or subject matter of the covered agreements.

5. Panels shall be composed of three panelists unless the parties to the dispute agree, within 10 days from the establishment of the panel, to a panel composed of five panelists. Members shall be informed promptly of the composition of the panel.

6.   The Secretariat shall propose nominations for the panel to the parties to the dispute. The parties to the dispute shall not oppose nominations except for compelling reasons.

7.   If there is no agreement on the panelists within 20 days after the date of the establishment of a panel, at the request of either party, the Secretary-General, in consultation with the SEOM Chairman, shall determine the composition of the panel by appointing the panelists whom the Secretary-General considers most appropriate in accordance with any relevant special or additional rules or procedures of the covered agreement or covered agreements which are at issue in the dispute, after consulting with the parties to the dispute. The SEOM Chairman shall inform the Members of the composition of the panel thus formed no later than 10 days after the date the Chairman receives such a request.

8.   Member States shall undertake, as a general rule, to permit their officials to serve as panelists.

9.   Panelists shall serve in their individual capacities and not as government representatives, nor as representatives of any organization. Member States shall therefore not give them instructions nor seek to influence them as individuals with regard to matters before a panel.

II. Panel Proceedings

1.   In its proceedings the panel shall follow the relevant provisions of this Protocol. In addition, the following working procedures shall apply.

2.   The panel shall meet in closed session. The parties to the dispute, and interested parties, shall be present at the meetings only when invited by the panel to appear before it.

3.   The deliberations of the panel and the documents submitted to it shall be kept confidential. Nothing in this Protocol shall preclude a party to a dispute from disclosing statements of its own positions to the public. Member States shall treat as confidential information submitted by another Member State to the panel which that Member State has designated as

confidential. Where a party to a dispute submits a confidential version of its written submissions to the panel, it shall also, upon request of a Member State, provide a non-confidential summary of the information contained in its submissions that could be disclosed to the public.

4. Before the first substantive meeting of the panel with the parties, the parties to the dispute shall transmit to the panel written submissions in which they present the facts of the case and their arguments.

5. At its first substantive meeting with the parties, the panel shall ask the party which has brought the complaint to present its case. Subsequently, and still at the same meeting, the party against which the complaint has been brought shall be asked to present its point of view.

6. Formal rebuttals shall be made at a second substantive meeting of the panel. The party complained against shall have the right to take the floor first to be followed by the complaining party. The parties shall submit, prior to that meeting, written rebuttals to the panel.

7. The panel may at any time put questions to the parties and ask them for explanations either in the course of a meeting with the parties or in writing.

8. The parties to the dispute shall make available to the panel a written version of their oral statements.

9. In the interest of full transparency, the presentations, rebuttals and statements referred to in paragraphs 5 to 9 shall be made in the presence of the parties. Moreover, each party's written submissions, including any comments on the descriptive part of the report and responses to questions put by the panel, shall be made available to the other party or parties.

10. Any additional procedures specific to the panel.

SELECT BIBLIOGRAPHY

Alburo, Florin A, "The ASEAN Summit and ASEAN Economic Co-operation", in Seiji Naya and Akira Takayama (eds), *Essays in Honour of Professor Shinichi Ichimura* (Singapore: ISEAS, and Honolulu: Resource Systems Institute, East-West Center, 1990), pp 299-306.

Anand, RP and PV-Quisumbing (eds), *ASEAN Identity, Development & Culture* (Manilla: UP Law Centre & EW Center Culture Learning Institute, 1981).

Anderson, Kym, "Is an Asian-Pacific Trade Bloc Next?" (1991) Vol.25 No 4 *JWT* pp 27-40.

APEC Website: <www.apecsec.org.sg>

APEC Secretariat, *Implementing the APEC Vision, Third Report of the Eminent Persons Group*, August 1995 (Singapore: APEC Secretariat, 1995).

APEC Secretariat, Economic Committee, *The Impact of Subregionalism in Apec* (Singapore: APEC Secretariat, 1997).

ASEANWEB, ASEAN Website: <www.aseansec.org>

ASEAN Institutes of Strategic and International Studies, *A Time for Initiative — Proposals for Consideration of the Fourth ASEAN Summit*, 4 June 1991.

ASEAN Secretariat, *Report of the ASEAN Eminent Persons Group (EPG) on Vision 2020* (Singapore: ASEAN Secretariat, November, 2000).

ASEAN Secretariat, *Strengthening the Mechanism of ASEAN, With Special Reference to the ASEAN Secretariat*, a report prepared for the Asean Standing Committee by a Panel under the Chairmanship of Tan Sri Ghazali Shafie, 1991.

ASEAN Secretariat, *ASEAN Economic Cooperation for the 1990s* (Philippines: Philippine Institute for Development Studies and ASEAN Secretariat, 1992), a report prepared for the ASEAN Standing Committee.

ASEAN Secretariat, *ASEAN — An Overview* (3rd ed) (Jakarta: ASEAN Secretariat, 1991).

ASEAN Secretariat, *Investing in ASEAN* (Jakarta: ASEAN Secretariat, 1991).

ASEAN Secretariat, *ASEAN Documents Series 1967–1988* (3rd ed) (Jakarta: ASEAN Secretariat, 1988).

ASEAN Secretariat, *ASEAN Documents Series 1988–1989* (Jakarta: ASEAN Secretariat, 1989).

ASEAN Secretariat, *ASEAN Documents Series, 1991–1992, Supplementary Edition* (Jakarta: ASEAN Secretariat, 1992).

ASEAN Secretariat, *ASEAN Update*, various issues (Jakarta: ASEAN Secretariat).

Broches, Aron, "Convention on the Settlement of Investment Disputes Between States and Nationals of Other States of 1965: Explanatory Notes and Survey of Its Application", in XVIII *Yearbook of Commercial Arbitration* (1993) at p 627.

Broinowski, Alan (ed), *ASEAN into the 1990s* (New York: St. Martin's Press, 1990).

Castro, Amado A, "Economic Cooperation and the Development of an ASEAN Culture", in Anand, RP and PV-Quisumbing (eds), *ASEAN Identity, Development & Culture* (Manilla: UP

Law Centre & EW Center Culture Learning Institute, 1981), pp 226–244.

Chalermpalanupap, Termsak, Special assistant to the Secretary-General of ASEAN, "The Need of a Legal Framework for ASEAN Integration", paper presented at the International Law Conference on ASEAN Legal Systems and Regional Integration, Asia-Europe Institute, University of Malaya, Kuala Lumpur, 3–4 September 2001.

Chee Peng Lim, "Asean co-operation in industry: Looking back and looking forward", in Sopiee, Noordin et al (eds), *ASEAN at the Crossroads* (Malaysia: Institute of Strategic and International Studies, 1987).

Chia Siow Yue (ed), *APEC — Challenges and Opportunities* (Singapore: ISEAS,1994).

Chinadaily, "China and Southeast Asia eye world's largest free-trade area", 2 November 2001, http:/www1.chinadaily.com.cn/news/ 2001-11-02/41900.html.

Chng Meng Kng, "ASEAN's Institutional Structure and Economic Co-operation" (1990) 6 *ASEAN Economic Bulletin*, pp 268–282.

Crouch, Harold, *Domestic Political Structures and Regional Economic Co-Operation* (Singapore: ISEAS, 1984).

Davidson, Paul J, *The Legal Framework for International Economic Relations: ASEAN and Canada* (Singapore: ISEAS, 1997).

Davidson, Paul J (ed), *Trading Arrangements in the Pacific Rim* (New York: Oceana Publications, 1995–), cited as *TAPR*.

Davidson, Paul J, "Regional Economic Zones in the Asia-Pacific: An Economic Law Perspective", in Toh Mun Heng and Linda Low (eds), *Regional Cooperation and Growth Triangles in ASEAN* (Singapore: Times Academic Press, 1993), pp 193–209.

Davidson, Paul J, "ASEAN Industrial Joint Ventures" (Ottawa: ASEAN Canada Business Council, 1989).

Davidson, Paul J, "The Canada/ASEAN Economic Cooperation Agreement" (1982) 24 *Mal LR* pp 372–388.

The Development Bank of Singapore Ltd., Economic Research Department, "The US-Canada Free Trade Agreement: Implications for Singapore", Singapore Briefing No 11, November 1989.

Dobson, Wendy, and Lee Tsao Yuan, "APEC — Co-operation amidst Diversity" (1994) 10 *ASEAN Economic Bulletin*, pp 231–244.

Drummond, Stuart, "Fifteen Years of ASEAN" (1982) Vol XX No 4 *Journal of Common Market Studies*, pp 301–319.

Drysdale, Peter, *International Economic Pluralism — Economic Policy in East Asia and the Pacific* (Sydney: Allen & Unwin Inc, 1988).

Economic and Social Commission for Asia and the Pacific, *Development Papers No 10: Foreign Investment, Trade and Economic Cooperation in the Asian and Pacific Region* (Bangkok: United Nations, 1973), ST/ESCAP/1006.

Elek, Andrew, "Trade Policy Options for the Asia-Pacific region in the 1990's: The Potential of Open regionalism" (1992) 82 *American Economic Review*, pp 74–78.

Emmerson, Donald K, "ASEAN as an International Regime" (1987) 41 *Jour. of Int'l Affairs,* pp 1–16.

English, H Edward, "An OECD of the Pacific? A Canadian Perspective", APRRC W/P-1 (Ottawa: Asian Pacific Research and Resource Centre, Carleton University, 1990).

Fernandez, Perfecto V, "Law and Culture in the ASEAN: Towards New Structures for Economic-Cultural Development", in Anand, RP and PV-Quisumbing (eds), *ASEAN Identity, Development & Culture* (Manilla: UP Law Centre & EW Center Culture Learning Institute, 1981), pp 319–331.

Flint, David, "Legal Aspects of Australian-ASEAN Commercial Co-Operation" (1980) 1 *Lawasia NS*, pp 155–172.

Garnaut, Ross, "ASEAN and the Regionalization and Globalization of World Trade" (1998) 14 *ASEAN Economic Bulletin*, pp 215–223.

Gautama, S, "Recognition and Enforcement of Foreign Judgements and Arbitral Awards in the ASEAN Region" (1990) 32 *Mal LR*, pp 171–188.

Halib, Mohammed and Tim Huxley, *An Introduction to Southeast Asian Studies* (Singapore: ISEAS, 1996).

Han Soo Kim and Ann Weston, "A North American Free Trade Agreement and East Asian Developing Countries" (1993) 9 *ASEAN Economic Bulletin*, pp 287–300.

Harris, Phil, *An Introduction to Law* (2nd ed) (London: Weidenfeld and Nicolson, 1984).

Hartono, Sunaryati, "Legal Development and the Promotion of Intra-ASEAN Trade and Investment" (1986) 1 *ASEAN Law and Society*, pp 31–41.

Harworth, Jennifer L, and Mark D Nguyen, "Law and Agreement in APEC", Document II.C.10 in, Davidson, Paul J (ed), *Trading Arrangements in the Pacific Rim* (Oceana Publications Inc.: New York, 1995).

Hass, *Basic Documents of Asian Regional Organisation* (Oceana Publications Inc.: New York, 1974), Vol IV.

Holloway, Nigel, "Development 1", *Far Eastern Economic Review*, 3 January 1991, p 34.

Imada, Pearl, and Seiji Naya (eds), *AFTA the Way Ahead* (Singapore: ISEAS, 1992).

Ingles, Jose D, "Problems and Progress in Regional Interaction: The Case of ASEAN", in Anand, RP and PV-Quisumbing (eds), *ASEAN Identity, Development & Culture* (Manilla: UP Law Centre & EW Center Culture Learning Institute, 1981), pp 217–225.

ISIS, *ASEAN, The Way Forward, The Report of the Group of Fourteen on ASEAN Economic Cooperation and Integration* (Kuala Lumpur: Institute of Strategic and International Studies (ISIS) Malaysia, 1987).

Jackson, John H, *The World Trading System — Law and Policy of International Economic Relations* (Cambridge/London: The MIT Press, 1989).

Jackson, John H, *The World Trading System — Law and Policy of International Economic Relations* (2nd ed), (Cambridge/London: The MIT Press, 1997).

Jap Kim Siong, "ASEAN: Recent Development in Trade Preferences and Comprehensive Double Taxation Agreements" (1978) 32 *Int'l Bureau of Fiscal Documentation*, pp 146–156.

Kohona, Palitha TB, *The Regulation of International Economic Relations Through Law* (Dordrecht: Martinus Nijhoff Publishers, 1985).

Kohona, Palitha TB, "Dispute Resolution Under the World Trade Organization: An Overview", in *Journal of World Trade* (1994) vol 28, no 2, pp 23–47.

Konan, Denise Eby, "The Need for Common Investment Measures within ASEAN" (1996) 12 *ASEAN Economic Bulletin*, pp 339–350.

Lacanlale, Agerico O, "Community Formation in ASEAN's External Relations", in Anand, RP and PV-Quisumbing (eds), *ASEAN Identity, Development & Culture* (Manilla: UP Law Centre & EW Center Culture Learning Institute, 1981), pp 378–409.

Lan Luh Luh, "Legal Aspects of the Proposed East Asian Economic Grouping", in *Problems and Prospects in International Business: Perspectives From Asia and the Pacific*, Conference Proceedings of the Academy of International Business, June 1992, pp 31–35.

Lee Tsao Yuan (ed), *Growth Triangle — The Johor-Singapore-Riau Experience* (Singapore: ISEAS, 1991).

Lipson, Charles, "Why are some international agreements informal?" (1991) 45 *International Organization*, pp 495–538.

Lloyd, Dennis, *The Idea of Law* (Middlesex: Penguin Books, 1964).

Lopez, Carolina Albero, and Jacint Soler Matutes, "Open Regionalism versus Discriminatory Trading Agreements: Institutional and Empirical Analysis" (1998) 14 *ASEAN Economic Bulletin*, pp 253–272.

Malanczuk, Peter, *Akehurst's Modern Introduction to International Law* (8th ed) (New York: Routledge, 2001).

Melchor, Jr, Alejandro, "A Perspective of the Emerging Asia-Pacific Region" (1981) 15 *Int'l Lawyer*, pp.131–138.

Meyanathan, Sahathavan and Haron, Ismail, "ASEAN trade cooperation: A survey of the issues", in Sopiee, Noordin et al (eds), *ASEAN at the Crossroads* (Malaysia: Institute of Strategic and International Studies, 1987).

Menon, Jayant, *Intra-Industry Trade and the ASEAN Free Trade Area*, Pacific Economic Papers, No 251, January 1996 (Canberra: Australia-Japan Research Centre, 1996).

Ministry of Trade and Industry, Malaysia, *Practical Guide to ASEAN Preferential Trading Agreement* (Malaysia: MITI, 1986).

Morrison, Charles E, "Progress and Prospects in Foreign Policy and Cooperation Among the ASEAN Countries", in Anand, RP and PV-Quisumbing (eds), *ASEAN Identity, Development & Culture* (Manila: UP Law Centre & EW Center Culture Learning Institute, 1981), pp 356-377.

Morrison, Charles E, "ASEAN: Forum, Caucus, and Community" (1997) 14 *ASEAN Economic Bulletin*, pp 150-158.

Muntarbhorn, Vitit, *The Challenge of Law — Legal Cooperation Among ASEAN Countries* (Bangkok: Institute of Security and International Studies, Chulalongkorn Univ., 1987).

Muntarbhorn, Vitit, "ASEAN Free Trade Area: Legal Implications and Beyond", paper presented to the Singapore Conferences on International Business Law, 9–11 September 1992.

Muntarbhorn, Vitit, "ASEAN and the Treaty-Making Process", in *ASEAN Economic Cooperation for the 1990s* (Philippines: Philippine Institute for Development Studies & the ASEAN Secretariat, 1992), pp 106-117.

Naya, Seiji and Michael G Plummer, "ASEAN Economic Co-operation in the New International Economic Environment" (1991) 7 *ASEAN Economic Bulletin*, pp 261–276.

Naya, Seiji and Michael G Plummer, "Economic Co-operation after 30 Years of ASEAN" (1997) 14 *ASEAN Economic Bulletin*, pp 117–126.

Oei, Anna, "A Comparative Analysis of Tax Incentives in ASEAN Countries" (1985) 27 *Mal LR*, pp 211–226 and 417–439.

Oorjitham, Santha, "ASEAN+3 = EAEC", Asiaweek.com, 15 March 2000, www.asiaweek.com/asiaweek/toc/2000/03/15

Page, Timothy I, "The North American Free Trade Agreement and its Implications for Canada's Relationship with the Countries of the Asia-Pacific", paper presented at the Fifth Trade Policy Forum, PECC, Kuala Lumpur, August 1991.

Pangestu, Mari, Hadi Soesastro and Mubariq Ahmad, "A New Look at Intra-ASEAN Economic Co-operation" (1992) 8 *ASEAN Economic Bulletin*, pp 333–352.

Parliament of the Commonwealth of Australia, *Australia and ASEAN — Report from the Standing committee on Foreign Affairs and Defence* (Canberra: Australian Government Publishing Service, 1980).

Paterson, Robert K, "The Economic Cooperation Agreement Between Canada and ASEAN: Charting a Foreign Investment Course in Southeast Asia" (1985) *UBC Law Rev*, pp 389-404.

Paterson, Robert K, and Martine MN Band (eds), *International Trade and Investment Law in Canada* (2nd ed) (Scarborough: Carswell, 1995).

Pelkmans, Jacques, "Institutional requirements of ASEAN with special reference to AFTA", in Pearl Imada and Seiji Naya (eds), *AFTA the Way Ahead* (Singapore: ISEAS, 1992), pp 99–133.

Petri, Peter A, "AFTA and the Global Track" (1997) 14 *ASEAN Economic Bulletin*, pp 190–201.

Philippine Institute for Development Studies, *ASEAN Economic Cooperation for the 1990s*, A Report Prepared for the ASEAN Standing Committee (Philippines: Philippine Institute for Development Studies and the ASEAN Secretariat, 1992).

[Philippines] Tariff Commission, *Philippine Tariff Concessions in the ASEAN Preferential Trading Arrangements* (Quezon City: Tariff Commission, 1986).

Pourian, Heydar, "The Role of Legal Risk in Country Risk Analysis", in Lacey, John R (ed), *The Law and Policy of International Business* (Lanham, Maryland: University Press of America, 1991), pp 189–204.

Quisumbing, Purification Valera, "Can ASEAN Forge a Viable Legal Regime for Regional Cooperation?" (1981) 56 *Philippine Law Journal*, pp 209–224. Also published as "Problems and Prospects of ASEAN Law: Towards a Framework for Regional Dispute Settlement'", in RP Anand, and PV-Quisumbing (eds), *ASEAN Identity, Development & Culture* (Manilla: UP Law Centre & EW Center Culture Learning Institute, 1981), pp 300–318.

Quisumbing, Purificacion V, and Benjamin B Domingo (eds), *EEC and ASEAN: Two Regional Community Experiences* (Manila: Foreign Service Institute and UP Law Center, 1983).

Quisumbing, Purification Valera, "An ASEAN Perspective on the Legal and Institutional Aspects of the Community Emerging Legal Framework of ASEAN", in Purificacion V Quisumbing and Benjamin B Domingo (eds), *EEC and ASEAN: Two Regional Community Experiences* (Manila: Foreign Service Institute and UP Law Center, 1983), pp 69–88.

Quisumbing, Purification Valera, "ASEAN Legal Cooperation: Quest and Challenge", in PV-Q, *Vital ASEAN Documents, 1967–1984*, *ASEAN Regional Law Series* Vol 1 (Manilla: Academy of ASEAN Law and Jurisprudence, 1985), pp 1–16.

Quisumbing, Purification Valera, and Elizabeth Aguiling-Pangalangan, *Vital ASEAN Documents, 1967-1984*, *ASEAN Regional Law Series* Vol 1 (Manilla: Academy of ASEAN Law and Jurisprudence, 1985).

Ramos, Fidel Valdez, Former President of the Republic of the Philippines, "The World to Come: ASEAN's Political and Economic Prospects in the New Century", Address to The

Economic Strategy Institute's (ESI) Global Forum 2000: "The World to Come-Value and Price of Globalization", Ronald Reagan International Trade Center, Washington DC, USA, 17 May 2000.

Reich, Arie, "From Diplomacy to Law: The Juridicization of International Trade Relations" (1996/97) 17 *Northwestern Journal of International Law & Business*, pp 775–849.

Rieger, Hans Christoph, and Tan Loong-Hoo, "Background Paper — Colloquium on ASEAN Economic Co-operation: The Tasks Ahead", in *ASEAN — The Tasks Ahead* (Singapore: ISEAS, 1987), pp 35–80.

Rieger, Hans Christoph, *ASEAN Economic Cooperation Handbook* (Singapore: ISEAS, 1991).

Rieger, Hans Christoph, "The Treaty of Rome and its Relevance for ASEAN" (1991) 8(2) *ASEAN Economic Bulletin*, pp 160-172.

Ryan, Mr Justice Kevin, "Multilateral Regulation of Trade and Investment in the Pacific Basin" (1986) 2(4) *International Review of Computers Technology and the Law*, pp 75-83.

Sandhu, KS, et al (eds), *The ASEAN Reader* (Singapore: ISEAS, 1992).

Santiago, Joseph Sedfrey S, "The ASEAN Free Trade Area (AFTA): Preliminary Legal Implications for the Philippines", paper presented at the 1992 ASEAN Law Association Conference, pp 179–201.

Santiago, Joseph Sedfrey S, "A Postscript to AFTA's False Start: The Loss of Sovereignty Issue" (1995) 12 *ASEAN Economic Bulletin*, pp 18–28.

Sathirathai, Surakiart, "The International Movement on Protection of Intellectual Property Rights and GATT: An Analysis of Thailand's Position" (1987) 29 *Mal LR*, pp 329–336.

Severino, Rodolfo C, Secretary-General of ASEAN, Asia Policy Lecture: "What ASEAN is and what it stands for", The Research Institute for Asia and the Pacific, University of Sydney, Australia, 22 October 1998.

Severino, Rodolfo C, Secretary-General of ASEAN, "Regional Economic Integration: The Challenges Ahead", Keynote Address at the Second Regional Workshop on "Beyond AFTA: Facing the Challenge of Closer Economic Integration", Bangkok, 2 October 2000.

Severino, Rodolofo C, Secretary-General of ASEAN, "Will ASEAN be Like the EU?", remarks at the European Policy Center, Brussels, 23 March 2001 (http://www.aseansec.org/secgen/sg_eu.htm).

Severino, Rodolfo C, Secretary-General of ASEAN, "The ASEAN Way and the Rule of Law", address at the International Law Conference on ASEAN Legal Systems and Regional Integration, Kuala Lumpur, 3 September 2001 (http://www.aseansec.org/newdata/asean_way.htm).

Shafie, Tan Sri Ghazali, et al, "Strengthening the Structure and Mechanism of ASEAN, with Special Reference to the ASEAN Secretariat", report prepared for the Asean Standing Committee, July 1991 (unpublished).

Shaun Seow and Phua Kok Kim, "Apec to focus on freer trade for region", *Straits Times*, 12 September 1992, at p 1.

Shenoy, George TL, "The Emergence of a Legal Framework for Economic Policy in ASEAN" (1987) 29 *Mal LR*, pp 116–130.

Shihata, Ibrahim FI, *Towards A Greater Depoliticization of Investment Disputes: The Roles of ICSID and MIGA* (Washington DC: International Commission for the Settlement of Investment Disputes, 1992).

[Singapore] Department of Trade, *ASEAN Preferential Tariffs* (Singapore: Department of Trade, 1981).

Singh, Dato' Ajit, "Implication of the Implementation of AFTA for the ASEAN Business Community", in *Citra Indonesia*, Vol 1/No 013 December 1995, p 24.

Singh, Dato' Ajit, "Towards One Southeast Asia" (1997) 14 *ASEAN Economic Bulletin*, pp 127–130.

Sinnadurai, Visu, *Multilateral Treaties between Asean Countries* (ASEAN Law Series) (Singapore: Butterworths, 1986).

Soesastro, Hadi, "The East Asian Economic Group (EAEG) Proposal and East Asian Concepts of the Pacific Basin" (Jakarta: Centre for Strategic and International Studies, February 1991).

Solidum, Estrella D, "The Role of Certain Sectors in Shaping and Articulating the ASEAN Way", in Anand, RP and PV-Quisumbing (eds), *ASEAN Identity, Development & Culture* (Manilla: UP Law Centre & EW Center Culture Learning Institute, 1981), pp 130–148.

Solidum, Estrella, "An ASEAN Perspective on the Decision-Making Process in the European Community", in Purificacion V Quisumbing and Benjamin B Domingo (eds), *EEC and ASEAN: Two Regional Community Experiences* (Manila: Foreign Service Institute and UP Law Center, 1983), pp 127–131.

Soliman, Josefina Nenita R, "A Primer — The Association of Southeast Asian Nations (ASEAN)" (1986) 1 *ASEAN Law and Society*, pp 109–123.

Sopiee, Noordin et al (eds), *ASEAN at the Crossroads* (Malaysia: Institute of Strategic and International Studies, 1987).

Sornarajah, M, "The New International Economic Order, Investment Treaties and Foreign Investment Laws in ASEAN" (1985) 27 *Mal LR*, pp 440–458.

Starke, JG, "The ASEAN Association as an entity of international law" (1983) 57 *Aust LJ*, pp 56–57.

Sucharitukul, Sompong, "ASEAN Partnership and Cooperation With Non-ASEAN Partners" [1991] *Singapore Journal of Legal Studies*, pp 562–594.

Sukrasep, Vinita, *ASEAN in International Relations* (Bangkok: Institute of Security and International Studies, 1989).

Surakiart Sathirathai, *Thailand and International Trade Law* (Bangkok: Graduate Institute of Business Administration, 1987).

Suthiphand Chirathivat, "ASEAN Economic Integration with the World through AFTA", Chapter 2, in Tan, Joseph (ed), *AFTA in the Changing International Economy* (Singapore: ISEAS, 1996).

Symonds, Peter, "ASEAN makes tentative moves toward an East Asian economic bloc", World Socialist Web Site, 30 November 2000, http:/www.wsws.org/articles/2000/nov2000/asea-n30_prn.shtml.

Tambunlertchai, Somsak, "ASEAN Research and Training Institute on Foreign Investment: A Proposal", Chapter 9 in *Economic and Social Commission for Asia and the Pacific, Development Papers No 10: Foreign Investment, Trade and Economic Cooperation in the Asian and Pacific Region* (Bangkok: United Nations), ST/ESCAP/1006, pp 235–240 and 246–255.

Tan, Gerald, "Intra-ASEAN Trade Liberalisation: An empirical analysis" (1982) 20 *Journal of Common Market Studies*, pp 321–331.

Tan, Gerald, "ASEAN Preferential Trading Arrangements — An Overview" (1987), in KS Sandhu, et al (eds), *The ASEAN Reader* (Singapore: ISEAS, 1992), pp 237–241.

Tan, Joseph (ed), *AFTA in the Changing International Economy* (Singapore: ISEAS, 1996).

Thambipillai, Pushpa and J Saravanamuttu, *ASEAN Negotiations — Two Insights* (Singapore: ISEAS, 1985).

Togashi, Janis Y and Pearl Imada, *The Legal Framework for Investment in ASEAN: Investment Regulations and Incentives*, Private Investment and Trade Opportunities Economic Brief No 8 (Hawaii: East-West Center, 1992).

Toh Mun Heng and Linda Low (eds), *Regional Cooperation and Growth Triangles in ASEAN* (Singapore: Times Academic Press, 1993).

Trebilcock, Michael J, and Robert Howse, *The Regulation of International Trade* (2nd ed) (London and New York: Routledge, 1999).

United Nations, *Economic Cooperation for ASEAN*, Report of a United Nations Study Team on ASEAN Economic Cooperation (United Nations, 1973).

US International Trade Commission, *East Asia: Regional Integration and Implications for the United States* (Washington: USITC Publication 2621, May 1993).

Vatikiotis, Michael, "Bet on Batam", *Far Eastern Economic Review*, 6 September 1990, at p 13.

Vatikiotis, Michael, "Search for a hinterland", *Far Eastern Economic Review*, 3 January 1991, pp 34–35.

White, George O, "From Snowplows to Siopao — Trying to Compete in a Global Marketplace: The ASEAN Free Trade Area" (2000) 8 *Tulsa Journal of Comparative & International Law*, pp 177–199.

Winslow, VS, "Fundamental Law in the ASEAN Nations: A Study in Diversity" (1986) 1 *ASEAN Law and Society*, pp 42–49.

Wong, Steven CM and Ahmad Ikram Haji Abdullah, *Sustaining Pacific Trade Dynamism — Exploring Policy Linkages*, selected papers from the Fifth PECC Trade Policy Forum, Kuala Lumpur, 19–21 August 1991 (Kuala Lumpur: Institute of Strategic and International Studies, 1992).

Yoonaidharma, Sudharma, "Thailand's Experience in International Trade Law and GATT" (1989) 31 *Mal LR*, pp 335–343.

Yuan, Jing-dong and Lorraine Eden, "Export Processing Zones in Asia: A Comparative Study" (1992) XXXII *Asian Survey*, pp 1026–1045.

INDEX